God's Own Ethics

God's Own Ethics

Norms of Divine Agency and the Argument from Evil

Mark C. Murphy

Great Clarendon Street, Oxford, OX2 6DP,
United Kingdom

Oxford University Press is a department of the University of Oxford.
It furthers the University's objective of excellence in research, scholarship,
and education by publishing worldwide. Oxford is a registered trade mark of
Oxford University Press in the UK and in certain other countries

First Edition published in 2017

Impression: 1

Published in the United States of America by Oxford University Press
198 Madison Avenue, New York, NY 10016, United States of America

British Library Cataloguing in Publication Data
Data available

Library of Congress Control Number: 2016960540

ISBN 978–0–19–879691–6

Printed and bound by
CPI Group (UK) Ltd, Croydon, CR0 4YY

For Jeanette

Contents

Acknowledgments

I owe great debts to philosophers who took time from the development of their own excellent work to read drafts of this manuscript and to offer comments and suggestions. Kevin Vallier, Heath White, and Scott Davison deserve my thanks on this score, as well as Anne Jeffrey, who not only read and commented carefully on chapter drafts while she was in the thick of her dissertation work, but also listened to me whine and complain about them.

A number of good philosophers offered criticisms on various portions of the argument. I thank Karl Adam, Julia Annas, Robert Audi, Bill Blattner, Tom Christiano, Terence Cuneo, Steve Davis, Michael DePaul, Trent Dougherty, Paul Draper, Michael Gorman, John Greco, Keith Hankins, Tobias Hoffmann, Chris Howard, Stephen Kershnar, Mark Lance, Brian Leftow, Alasdair MacIntyre, Christian Miller, David Owen, Adam Pelser, Ryan Preston-Roedder, Alex Pruss, Mike Rea, Travis Rieder, Connie Rosati, Danny Shahar, Jeff Speaks, Jim Sterba, Jada Twedt Strabbing, Mark Timmons, Patrick Todd, Chris Tucker, Peter van Inwagen, Matthias Vorwerk, Brandon Warmke, and Ray Yeo. I benefited also from the thorough comments of two anonymous readers at Oxford University Press. I am grateful also to Phil Dines, the copyeditor, for his great care and good sense in getting the manuscript in shape.

I presented some of this material to Georgetown graduate seminars on the problem of evil and on the explanation of reasons for action. The discussion in these seminars was tremendously helpful, and I thank the students in these seminars, especially Gabe Broughton, Jake Earl, Quentin Fisher, and Kelly Heuer, for their critical feedback. I also presented portions of the manuscript at the Challenges to Moral and Religious Belief conference at Purdue University, the Baylor–Georgetown–Notre Dame Philosophy of Religion conference, the Theistic Ethics Workshop, and colloquia at Arizona, Wake Forest, and Catholic University of America. I am grateful to the audience members at these events, who generously engaged with my arguments and offered useful criticisms.

I am grateful to the editors of the *Stanford Encyclopedia of Philosophy* for permission to use some of the material from my entry "Perfect Goodness." I thank also Oxford University Press for permission to use some of the material from "Toward God's Own Ethics" (*Challenges to Moral and Religious Belief*, ed. Michael Bergmann and Patrick Kain, 2014, pp. 154–71), and Palgrave Macmillan generously allowed my use of some of the text of "Intention, Foresight, and Success" (*Human Values: New Essays on Ethics and Natural Law*, ed. David S. Oderberg and Timothy Chappell, 2004, pp. 262–78). I thank the journal *Faith and Philosophy* for allowing use of a few paragraphs from my "Divine Command, Divine Will, and Moral Obligation" (15 (1998), pp. 3–27) and the journal *Quaestiones Disputatae* for allowing use of a few paragraphs from my "Suárez's 'Best Argument' and the Dependence of Morality on God" (5 (2014), pp. 30–42).

Since 2011 I have held the Robert L. McDevitt, K.S.G., K.C.H.S. and Catherine H. McDevitt L.C.H.S. Chair in Religious Philosophy at Georgetown University. Receiving this chair has been a great gift and I am keenly aware of the prudence and generosity of the McDevitts as I carry out my academic work. I hope that this book honors their memory.

One of the central themes of this book is that God, excellent in ways that unimaginably outstrip us, did not have to love us; this love was contingently, freely bestowed. Thus God's loving the likes of us calls not for praise but rather for thanks, and gratitude. The model for this divine love with which I am most familiar and of which I am most sharply aware is the love of my wife, Jeanette. Her excellences far surpass my own and she would have made no mistake by failing to take up with the likes of me. That she did is, indeed, one of the blessings for which I am most grateful. I dedicate this book to her.

M. C. M.
Herndon, Virginia

Introduction

0.1 God's Ethics and the Argument from Evil

This book is about God's ethics. By an agent's 'ethics' I mean, roughly, that agent's dispositions to treat various considerations as reasons, and as reasons of certain types. An agent's ethics fixes how various matters play a role in that agent's practical life, shaping and guiding that agent's deliberation and action.[1] When we say that Mother Teresa's ethics was an ethics of love, for example, what this means is that a loving agent wants things to go a certain way and wants to act a certain way, takes certain considerations as relevant or even overriding in deliberation, acts for certain reasons and does not act on others, and that Mother Teresa's agency was marked by those features. The aim of this book is to exhibit, in this sense of 'ethics,' *God's* ethics.

To announce this sort of investigation into divine agency sounds very pretentious. But whatever we think about the hubris involved in making claims about God's ethics, it is plain that there are large swaths of philosophy and theology in which views on this topic are not only affirmed but also wielded in making arguments about the very existence of a divine being. For no formulation of the argument from evil can get up and running without some premise involving God's ethics. Such arguments appeal to God's being very knowledgeable and very powerful, but they could not go anywhere without taking on board some premise concerning how God, were God to exist, would put that knowledge and power to use in deciding and acting. So we are told that God must be perfectly morally good, and *this* is what a perfectly morally good being would do; or God must be perfectly loving, and *this* is how a perfectly loving being would act. These are claims about God's ethics, that God's ethics are the ethics of a perfectly morally good being, or of a perfectly loving being. What's more, these claims must be interpreted sufficiently specifically to enable one to draw rather detailed conclusions about what God, were God to exist, would do or refrain from doing. So if it is pretentious to make claims about God's ethics, it is a pretension that is very well distributed in philosophy and theology, especially where the argument from evil is under discussion.

[1] One might complain that it is false or deeply misleading to speak of God's having any dispositions at all, perhaps on the basis that a disposition is a sort of potential, but there is nothing in God that is potential—God is pure actuality. Or one might complain that it is false or deeply misleading to think of divine agency as governed by deliberation—God exhibits no such complexity of inner life as deliberation entails. See 0.3 for a consideration of worries of this sort.

0.2 Conceptions of God

How even to begin a philosophical investigation of God's ethics? It is useful to start by articulating a *conception* of God, a formal account of what a being must be like to count as God. By making such a conception explicit, one might make available further evidence that will enable one to defend a view of what the ethics of such a being would have to be like. One might begin, as many formulations of the argument from evil begin, simply by saying that to be God is to be an omniscient, omnipotent, morally perfect being. But it makes sense to ask *why* the standard formulation of the problem of evil presents God as having these features. One answer is just that this is the traditional formulation. Another is that one might not care about whether there is a God unless God is taken to be omniscient, omnipotent, and morally perfect. But neither of these answers is particularly persuasive. Traditional formulations may be challenged. And surely the focus on the existence of an omniscient, omnipotent, morally perfect being but not on a being limited in one of these ways is not just the result of a brute preference but has a rationale that can be articulated.

The argument from evil as now standardly formulated appeals to God's moral goodness and omnipotence and omniscience as providing for us the basis for an account of what God is willing and able to do. But it is important that one way of responding to the problem of evil is to offer a reformulation or reinterpretation of the divine attributes that generate the problem—for example, a denial of God's omnipotence, or a clarification of what omnipotence involves[2]—and in order to help us to see what counts as legitimate modification of one's account of the divine and what counts as mere capitulation, it is useful to have on hand a formal account of what makes an attribute count as a divine attribute and what makes a certain interpretation of a divine attribute superior to other possible interpretations. In *The Problem of Evil*, for example, van Inwagen plumps for a view that he ascribes to Anselm: that to be God is to be the greatest possible being (2006, p. 32). It is because God is the greatest possible being that omnipotence, omniscience, and moral perfection are to be ascribed to God, for the greatest possible being would exhibit all of these features. And indeed van Inwagen appeals to this conception in offering a reinterpretation of omniscience, which on the traditional understanding entails that God knows the truth-values of propositions concerning future free actions of creatures: on van Inwagen's view, no being could know what agents will freely do, but as the inability to know this does not constitute an imperfection for any agent, that fact does not count against God's existence (van Inwagen 2006, pp. 80–3).

It is with an Anselmian conception of God that I will be primarily interested in this book, especially in Part I, though for reasons discussed in Chapter 1 (1.2–1.3), I would

[2] Plantinga's classic response to the argument from evil in *The Nature of Necessity*, for example, includes a clarification of the nature of omnipotence: it is false, argues Plantinga, that a being that is omnipotent is able to bring about the obtaining of any logically possible state of affairs (Plantinga 1974, pp. 180–4).

characterize this 'Anselmian being' as *absolutely perfect* rather than *the greatest possible*. But there are a few alternative conceptions that it is important to acknowledge and distinguish from this conception. One of these is that to be God is to be worthy of complete worship (Hartshorne 1966, pp. 25–6; Pike 1970, pp. 149–60; Geach 1977, p. 56; Rachels 1971, p. 325). Sometimes included within worship-worthiness are other features that bear on our proper relationship to the divine: that God is properly the supreme object of loyalty, devotion, alliance, obedience, and so forth (R. Adams 1999, pp. 177–98). But I want to distinguish this conception—the *God-as-supremely-worthy-object-of-allegiance* conception—from the *God-as-supremely-worthy-of-worship* conception, which strikes me as importantly different. (I argue for this in more detail in Chapter 7; see 7.1–7.3.)

These distinctions between conceptions of God would be irrelevant to the question at hand—what is God's own ethics—if these descriptions were mutually entailing. But I doubt this. It may well be that complete worship cannot be given to a being conceived as less than perfect—how can one worship God as fully as possible while thinking "but you could have been better" or "there could have been a being greater than you"? (See also, for remarks along similar lines, Leftow 2012, p. 11.) It seems not obviously true, though, that *being perfect* entails *being supremely worthy of allegiance*. (I will present an extended argument against this entailment that depends on the outcome of the investigation of the early chapters; see 7.2–7.3.) We should begin at least by allowing that it is an open question whether these descriptions, which are not obviously mutually entailing, are indeed mutually entailing.

In this book I give the Anselmian conception, the conception of God as absolutely perfect, pride of place. This is not merely because Anselmianism is a fruitful way of providing an account of the divine attributes (Morris 1987a, Rogers 2000, Leftow 2011). The main reason is that the Anselmian conception of God is more metaphysically fundamental than the other conceptions: even if God's worship-worthiness and allegiance-worthiness play a more central role in the lives of theists than God's perfection, or are in some other way more salient, God's worship-worthiness and allegiance-worthiness asymmetrically depend on God's perfection, so that God's perfection is more explanatorily basic than these other features of God. I defend this view later (Chapter 7).

I have characterized the target of the investigation as God's ethics—that is, the ways in which various considerations are treated by God as reasons for action. And I have taken the conception of God with which we will begin to be that of God as an Anselmian, that is, an absolutely perfect, being. The question of what is the ethics of an Anselmian being occupies Part I of this book. After defending a certain account of the ethics of an Anselmian being, I will turn to other conceptions of God, acknowledging that the conclusions reached in Part I raise troubling questions for our conception of God as supremely worthy of worship and allegiance. Working out solutions to these problems is the main task of Part II.

0.3 Two Initial Objections

One sort of objection to which the views defended in this book are subject is simply to the particular conclusions reached and the arguments used to defend them. But there is another sort of objection, one against the very investigation that I am carrying out. This way of speaking about God as an agent, as an absolutely perfect being, as someone who can and perhaps should prevent earthly evils, seems to presuppose that God is just one being among others, even if a particularly special one. And that is an error that is condemned not only by those who reject 'ontotheology' but also by the high medieval tradition that held that in speaking of God we best follow the *via negativa* and the *via analogiae*. But the theses that this book aims to support indeed include positive theses about what an absolutely perfect being is and does. And so one might think that I have misconceived how we can sensibly think and speak of the divine, and in a way that vitiates this entire enterprise.

First, a merely defensive maneuver. This book is about God's ethics generally, not specifically about the problem of evil. But insofar as I am aiming to say something about the problem of evil, it can be no objection to my responses to the argument from evil that I use the same way of speaking of God that those who wield that argument employ. They employ talk of God as being 'a morally perfect being,' 'an omnibenevolent agent,' and the like. So this is not a line of argument that those who press the argument from evil, at least in its standard formulations, can wield against me.

Second, many writers in philosophical theology are unmoved by the charges of ontotheology, and indeed take the idea that we should not suppose that God is a being to be tantamount to atheism (van Inwagen 2006, pp. 18–19). Whatever exists is a being, these writers would say, and so if God is not a being, then God does not exist; and that is atheism. I confess that I find it baffling that one would respond to the charges of ontotheology in a way that commits one to the view that Thomas Aquinas was really an atheist; for Aquinas himself would not say that, properly speaking, we should say that God is *a* being.[3] But this book is not about that fight. Those who are perfectly happy with the flatfooted use of 'an absolutely perfect being' and the like will, for the most part,[4] find nothing to worry about.

Third, I accept in fundamentals the views that we speak most literally of God when we deny things of God and that in ascribing positive features to God, we are speaking analogically if we are speaking truly. But though many of the conclusions that I draw about God are negative—for example, I deny certain claims about God's being necessarily morally good (3.3–3.7)—I do not justify these denials by appeal to the *via negativa*. While the fact that we speak most literally of God when we deny that certain concepts are appropriately applied to God is itself a very informative truth about the

[3] For recent discussions that could be pressed into the service of views like Aquinas's against arguments like van Inwagen's, see (among other pieces of McDaniel's) McDaniel 2009, as well as Jacobs 2015.

[4] Though they may find their views in tension with the appeals that I make to the ideas of *goodness in itself* and *goodness by participation*; see section 4.4.

relationship between our thoughts and God, the particular denials themselves are typically not very informative, for each one of those denials is made true by the same fact: that our concepts are inadequate to the divine nature. But the appeal to the way of analogy allows, in my view, the assertion and denial of claims about God that are informative. Aquinas's doctrine of analogy holds that these features that are perfections when ascribed to humans are primarily realized in God, in such a way that goes beyond, is superior to, what our limited human concepts are able to capture (Aquinas, *Summa Contra Gentiles* I, §§30–5). So while defenders of the *via negativa* rightly note that we should deny of God that God has these perfections, inasmuch as our concepts are inadequate to the divine reality, we may affirm of God that God has those features inasmuch as God must exhibit them in a super-eminent way. Although that is the cash value of the conclusions that we draw about God, the reasoning that we go through in order to reach the conclusions about God that must be understood in this analogical way looks like ordinary reasoning.

Placed in the 'theology room,'[5] I assert that God is not really a being, but being itself; God is not a good being, but goodness itself; and so forth. Yet when I go through the reasonings about God in this book, I will speak of God as a being, as a good being, as an agent, and so forth. In doing so I am not denying that God's being a being must be understood in line with the doctrine of analogous predication. And, further, when I do so I am not speaking and reasoning any differently than paradigmatic adherents of the doctrine of analogy, including Aquinas, speak and reason.[6]

0.4 The Argument to Come

This book contains two Parts, each of which is preceded by a synopsis of the argument of that Part, and it would waste words to repeat those summaries here. But I can describe briefly here the overall argument of the book, which is organized by the three conceptions of God—God as absolutely perfect being, God as that being supremely worthy of worship, and God as that being supremely worthy of allegiance (0.2). Part I argues that the ethics of an absolutely perfect being is not the ethics now typically ascribed to that being, a familiar ethics of promoting, and preventing setbacks to, creaturely well-being. Thus the argument from evil, which assumes this familiar ethics, is ineffective at calling into question the existence of God when God is conceived simply as an absolutely perfect being. Part II argues that the conclusions of Part I have very different implications for God conceived in the other two ways. While this revised understanding of the ethics of an absolutely perfect being gives us no reason to doubt that an absolutely perfect being is necessarily worthy of worship, it does call into question whether such a being is necessarily supremely worthy of allegiance. Part II argues

[5] For a characterization of "the ontology room," see van Inwagen 2014b, p. 1.

[6] For a more detailed and edifyingly historically informed response to the charge of ontotheology, as well as an unyielding rejection of its well-foundedness, see M. Adams 2014.

that the absolutely perfect being is indeed not necessarily worthy of supreme allegiance, but can be contingently so, and that the evils of this world do not call into question the existence of an absolutely perfect being who is actually, albeit contingently, worthy of our full allegiance. Given the most defensible account of God's ethics, the argument from evil must fail against God conceived in any of these ways.

PART I

The Ethics of an Anselmian Being

Part I aims to provide an account of the ethics of an 'Anselmian,' that is, an absolutely perfect, being. The ethics of an Anselmian being is neither an ethics of maximal love nor an ethics of perfect moral goodness. Although these main conclusions of Part I are negative, Part I also includes a positive account of the ways in which the Anselmian being has reasons to promote and respect the good of creatures, and applies that account to the argument from evil understood as an argument against the existence of an absolutely perfect being.

Chapter 1 provides a more detailed account of the idea of an absolutely perfect being and the methodology by which one draws conclusions about such a being. Chapter 2 argues that the motivation that we can properly ascribe to an Anselmian being in virtue of that being's being loving does not go beyond that which we can properly ascribe to an Anselmian being in virtue of that being's being morally good. In Chapter 3, I argue that we have strong reasons to doubt that an Anselmian being is morally good in the familiar sense or in anything approximating that familiar sense. The force of these chapters in tandem is to massively unsettle commonly expressed convictions about the ethics of an Anselmian being. Chapters 4 and 5 are positive. They aim to defend, somewhat tentatively, a partial conception of the ethics of an Anselmian being. In Chapter 6 I consider how this conception of the Anselmian being's ethics should transform our understanding of the problem of evil.

1

Anselmianism about God

1.1 'An Anselmian Being'

This first part of the book asks what we should think about God's ethics, given only the conception of God as absolutely perfect being. For an absolutely perfect being I will use the term 'the Anselmian being' or 'an Anselmian being.' I will be asking whether an Anselmian being does this, or an Anselmian being does that, or whether an Anselmian being has a certain feature, or not. Expressions of the form 'An Anselmian being does X' do not mean, in this context, *There exists a being that qualifies as the Anselmian being, and that being does X*. I am, rather, using the expression 'an Anselmian being' as a generic, in the same way that I might talk about what features 'a lion' exhibits when I say that a lion has four feet or that it is not true that a lion has a particular breeding season. The reason for emphasizing this is that I will sometimes say that it is false that an Anselmian being is X even though I in fact believe that God, the actual, existing, real God, who qualifies as the Anselmian being, is indeed X. What makes these consistent is that, because I am using 'an Anselmian being' as a generic, it is false that an Anselmian being is X, even though the actual perfect being is X, if the actual perfect being is not X *in virtue of* being the absolutely perfect being.

To illustrate: God spoke to Moses from a burning bush, and God is absolutely perfect, but it is false simply to say *an absolutely perfect being speaks from burning bushes*. The reason is that, though God is an absolutely perfect being who spoke from a burning bush, God's having spoken from a burning bush is not entailed by God's being an absolutely perfect being. We can draw *some* inferences about what an absolutely perfect being is or does from the bare fact of God's being certain ways or having done certain things; these are inferences that the absolutely perfect being *possibly* is those ways or *possibly* does those things. Compare: if we take 'a lion' or 'the lion' generically, we cannot conclude from *Elsa is a lion* and *Elsa is yellow* that the lion is yellow. But we can conclude that the lion is possibly yellow. Similarly, from *God spoke from a burning bush* and *God is an absolutely perfect being* it does not follow that the generic expression *the absolutely perfect being speaks from burning bushes* is true, but only that *the absolutely perfect being possibly speaks from burning bushes* is true.

I belabor this point in order to emphasize that it can never be an adequate criticism of any claims about the falsity of certain ascriptions of features to the Anselmian being that God does in fact exhibit those features. Suppose I were to, say, deny that an

Anselmian being is loving. One might retort: "But God loves us, and God is an absolutely perfect being. And you, Murphy, believe both of those claims. So how can you deny that the Anselmian being is loving?" The answer is, of course, that if I deny that God's being loving is an entailment of God's being absolutely perfect, then I can affirm both that it is true that God is loving and that it is not true that an Anselmian being is loving, just as I can affirm that it is true that God spoke from a burning bush while denying that an Anselmian being speaks from burning bushes. As God actually exhibits features that it is not true that an Anselmian being has[1]—imagine what one would be committing oneself to by claiming that God does not have any feature that it is not true that the Anselmian being has—one cannot argue simply from God's exhibiting some feature to the Anselmian being's exhibiting that feature.

1.2 Reasoning about the Anselmian Being: The Distributive Assumption Defended

This book is going to make use of the understanding of God as Anselmian being to argue for certain theses about what God's ethics amounts to. But the particular conclusions that one reaches about God's ethics, and the confidence that one can place in those conclusions, by relying upon God's being an Anselmian being will differ depending on what sorts of reasoning about the divine perfection one takes to be appropriate. The traditional[2] way of reasoning about what it is to exhibit maximal greatness is to proceed intuitively, by considering what properties we take, on reflection, to count as unqualified good-making properties, features that unqualifiedly make a being better for having them. (These are what Scotus calls "pure perfections" (*Ordinatio* 1.3.1, in *Philosophical Writings*, p. 24).) It would be deeply ambiguous to say simply that it is better for the being to have them than not, for that leaves unanswered the sort of goodness at issue. The claim is not that having these features is just good, *tout court*, or that it improves the world that this being exhibits them, or that it improves the well-being of the being that has them. Rather, the thesis is that *the being* is better for having them; the value at stake is thus, unsurprisingly, the sort of value that Sumner calls "perfectionist" value (Sumner 1996, pp. 23–4).

There are various constraints on properties that are candidates to be counted as unqualified good-making properties within an Anselmian conception—for example, that their presence cannot presuppose the presence of imperfections in the being that exhibits them,[3] and that the good-making property in question must have an intrinsic

[1] If one wishes to hold that an absolutely perfect being is only contingently X, one should frame one's thesis as holding (in part) that it is false that an Anselmian being is X, not as holding that an Anselmian being is not X. To say that an Anselmian being is not X is to say that any being who qualifies as the Anselmian being would not be X, and so necessarily any Anselmian being is not X.

[2] This is Anselm's own way of proceeding in the *Proslogion*.

[3] So Adams notes that God's perfection does not include cuteness, as cuteness seems to entail weakness, or smallness, something of that sort (R. Adams 1999, p. 31).

maximum (Mann 1975, p. 151; Murphy 2002a, pp. 60–1). But once these various formal constraints are met, the notion that some feature is a perfection is to be defended largely as a matter of what seems to be the case on reflection.

The first stage of the traditional Anselmian method for working out the features exhibited by God is the identification of unqualified good-making properties; the second is the explicitation of what those properties are and of what would constitute the intrinsic maximum for the valuable realization of each of those properties. So, for example, once *powerfulness* is identified as an unqualified good-making property, and omnipotence its intrinsic maximum, the task becomes to explain more fully what omnipotence amounts to. Is it *being able to do anything*? *Being able to do anything within the limits of the logically possible*? Or is it to be characterized in some way alternative to the 'can do anything within a certain range' construction?[4] In this stage, one has to secure both the internal consistency of the alleged perfection and the coherence of that alleged perfection with other affirmed perfections. So we care not only about freeing omnipotence from (e.g.) the Paradox of the Stone; we also care about explaining why omnipotence, however characterized, is compatible with God's not even possibly doing something malicious, which impossibility is (we may suppose) part of God's perfect goodness.

The two stages of the ascription and working out of the divine perfections are even more closely connected than this rough description lets on, for it is not enough to come up with an account of a given divine perfection that is suitably hemmed in so that it does not conflict with itself or with other divine perfections. One has to show that the property so characterized can not only be coherently ascribed to a being along with the other divine perfections; it must also be shown that the property so characterized is at the intrinsic maximum of value for exhibiting that feature. On the traditional understanding of the Anselmian God, one cannot simply truncate a perfection by characterizing it in a way that it does not generate conflict; one must do so in a way that explains *why* the truncation does not involve yielding any value but is only a clarification of how a being might reach maximal metaphysically possible greatness along that dimension. For example, on the traditional view, it is perfectly fine to say that the fact that God does not exhibit a level of power that is intrinsically impossible to realize does not count as making God less than perfect; it is *not* fine to say that God exhibits less than maximal power simply in order to make sure that it fits with other divine perfections. For the latter would sacrifice some of the value of powerfulness, giving it up for the purpose of securing some other perfection. The traditional way assumes that for any good-making feature some realization of which counts as a divine perfection, it is impossible to realize *that* good-making feature more valuably than it is realized in the absolutely perfect being. It must be impossible for the absolutely perfect being to be worse than any other being along *any* dimension of perfection.

[4] See, for example, Geach 1977, pp. 3–39, and Pearce and Pruss 2012.

We may call this the *distributive assumption*: God exhibits the maximal level of the divine perfections, understood distributively—for *each* unqualified good-making property that God exhibits, God exhibits *that property* to the intrinsic maximum of its value. If powerfulness is a good-making feature, then it is impossible for a being to exhibit powerfulness more valuably than God does. If knowledge is a good-making feature, then it is impossible for a being to exhibit knowledge more valuably than God does. And so forth.

The distributive assumption is controversial, but it should not be confused with an even more controversial assumption, that of *atomism* about the value of each of these perfections. An atomist would hold that for each perfection, what constitutes the intrinsic maximum of the value of that perfection is independent of that perfection's relation to other divine perfections. Consider, for example, the thesis (the plausibility of which I am not commenting on) that having the power to do evil is not itself valuable, and does not improve the perfection of the being who has it, even with respect to the perfection of powerfulness itself, because the value of moral goodness renders the power to do evil entirely worthless. This thesis is not compatible with the atomism, for it holds that the value of moral goodness contributes to the fixing of the value of power. But this thesis is entirely compatible with the distributive assumption, which says only that the Anselmian being has each perfection to the intrinsic maximum of that perfection's value. It is, after all, obviously compatible with the distributive assumption that the intrinsic maximum of the value of power is at a point that does not include the power to do evil.

But one might note that the perfect being theologian who is traditional in this way is always held hostage by the possibility that it could turn out that the only way to render the divine perfections compatible with one another would be to fix one of them at less than its intrinsic maximum. Watching traditional perfect being theologians juggle all of those divine perfections can give one the sense that even if one does not know which ball is going to get dropped, one of them definitely is; given a variety of genuinely distinct divine perfections, the odds that all of them can be realized at their maxima seem, to many, slim.[5]

This concern is what most gives force, I think, to Yujin Nagasawa's suggestion that Anselmians about God refrain from endorsing the distributive assumption (Nagasawa 2008). Nagasawa points out that if one formulates the Anselmian idea in terms of "the best possible combination of power, knowledge, and goodness," or perhaps, we might say, more generically as "the most perfect possible being," such a formulation does not commit one to any particular view on the level of value realized for each perfection, but only in the total package, so to speak, of great-making features. The traditional method that I have endorsed identifies A, B, and C as great-making

[5] For an expression of this worry, see Diller 1999, p. 237. How serious a problem this is depends on how rich one takes the set of divine perfections to be. One might think that, so long as one holds to a relatively sparse view of what the pure perfections are, the worries about conflict are not all that pressing.

properties and then takes on the task of showing that a being can exhibit A, B, and C *each* to its most valuable point; this is what I labeled the distributive assumption. The revisionist Anselmian, by contrast, jettisons that task and instead suggests that we ask what the most valuable possible realization of A, B, and C *all together* is. There is no presumption that this will result in A, B, and C *each* being realized to its most valuable point in the most perfect possible being. Thus the task that the revisionist sets for him- or herself is less demanding and so easier to fulfill than that set by the more traditional view. If it is pointed out to the revisionist that on his or her current account of divine perfection, there is a great-making feature that might be exhibited more fully and valuably, the revisionist can point out simply that while this may be true, the result would necessarily be a loss of value overall, a decrease in the total package of value realized. If it is pointed out to the revisionist that his or her account of the divine perfections generates a conflict between distinct divine perfections, the revisionist can happily concede the conflict and ratchet down the level of value that the most perfect possible being realizes.

I do not think that the defender of the distributive assumption should challenge the thesis that it is necessary and sufficient for being God that a being exhibit a total package of perfections that is maximally valuable. Given this agreement, Nagasawa can note that his view is logically weaker than an Anselmianism that endorses the distributive assumption; his suggestion is that the key idea of Anselmianism does not entail the distributive assumption, and as the distributive assumption can give headaches to the Anselmian, the Anselmian has good reason not to commit to it. And in practice there may be little reason for a fight between Anselmians who accept the distributive assumption and those who do not. On the assumption that, if there is an account of the Anselmian being that satisfies the distributive assumption and otherwise passes muster, then it will indeed realize the greatest total package of value—this is a plausible, but not entirely trivial assumption, given the organicity of value—one who does not accept the distributive assumption can simply note that he or she has a fallback view that does not make perfect being theology hostage to the divine perfections all playing together so nicely.

But I think that Anselmians about God should affirm the distributive assumption; when one focuses on what God would have to be like were the distributive assumption not satisfied, we can see that an embrace of maximal greatness understood non-distributively is not safe harbor for the Anselmian. I want to press two distinct worries for the revisionist Anselmian: one about the explanation of the Anselmian being's perfection, the other about the value of the package of features exhibited by the Anselmian being.

First, on explanation. Suppose one accepts Nagasawa's revisionist view and comes to settle on a particular combination of perfections to ascribe to the Anselmian being, and the degrees to which these are realized are fixed by what would, in combination with the other good-making properties, bear the greatest overall package of value; and stipulate that these features do not satisfy the distributive assumption. But now there is a pressing question to ask this revisionist Anselmian: *Why* is it that the Anselmian being has all of these great-making features in the particular combination of levels at which their value in combination is maximized?

The answer "it's trivial—that's what makes that being the Anselmian being" is merely a jokey muddling of the *de re*/*de dicto* distinction. Of course construed *de dicto*, it is silly to ask why troglodytes live in caves, but construed *de re*—why do *these* people, *these* troglodytes—live in caves, the question is perfectly meaningful. And this is what we may ask about God here.

This question, posed to the revisionary Anselmian, seems impossible to answer. If all of the properties are realized in the precise combination and to the precise degree that greatness of that being is maximized, what could explain that convergence? That it is posited to be a *de re* necessity does not seem to me to be sufficient to cast aside the mystery; when some combination of facts obtaining looks a marvelous coincidence, adding that the presence of that combination is necessary increases rather than decreases the mystery.

And there are obstacles to thinking that any explanation could be forthcoming. Surely nothing wholly distinct from God could be the explanation: there is no being who tinkers with God to ensure that its good-making properties are combined at the right degrees to realize the maximal level of value. Surely not each good-making property, or its instantiation, individually can do such explanatory work: for what needs explanation is the *coordination* of the ways that these features are exhibited in God. And surely not God, who *ex hypothesi* has these good-making features to the requisite degrees: for such a being's existence is not logically prior to its having the features to the requisite degrees.

Perhaps the revisionist will retort simply that such problems also arise for the traditional Anselmian, who accepts the distributive assumption. But it is just false that this particular challenge must be met by one who accepts the distributive assumption, for there is no *coordination* of the levels of the perfections that is required by one who defends that sort of Anselmianism: each perfection is exhibited to its intrinsic maximum.[6] And, taking a point from Swinburne (though not the use to which he puts it), one who accepts the distributive assumption needs no explanation how it could be limited in the value of particular perfections, for none of these are so limited (Swinburne 2004, pp. 96–7).

So while Nagasawa's view is, strictly speaking, logically weaker than traditional Anselmianism and thus could not be less likely than it to be true, we have reason to think that the option that Nagasawa's view wants to leave as a live option—that God could be maximally great without satisfying the distributive assumption—is not really

[6] Here is a worry, though. Does allowing the possibility that atomism about the perfections is false undermine this reply by reintroducing the need for coordination among the great-making properties? Perhaps so. I am far from convinced that atomism is an implausible thesis, so I would not be all that worried about taking it on.

a live option for the Anselmian. So Anselmian theists should endorse the distributive assumption.

Second, about value. Consider a traditional Anselmian view that accepts the distributive assumption. Suppose—which must be supposed, in order for the revisionist view to be distinct from the traditional view—that there really are multiple divine perfections. Now, the traditional view does not require any very controversial view about the relative value of the various divine perfections. All that it requires is a *dominance* principle: if there is a being that is better than any other possible being with respect to *every* great-making feature, then that being is the greatest possible being.[7]

The revisionist view has a bigger problem with value. For, allowing that the distributive assumption may be false, it may be possible for the greatest possible being to be worse than some other possible being with respect to some great-making feature. What the revisionist thus requires is the view that one can *trade off* great-making features against each other. But unless there is a uniquely best trade-off, then the revisionist Anselmian is in trouble. For there are three possibilities: that at the top of the scale of greatness, (1) there is either a uniquely greatest being, (2) there are multiple equally good possible beings, or (3) there are multiple incommensurably good possible beings. If either the second or third option is the truth, then that would be trouble for the revisionist Anselmian. For it would not be entailed by a being's meeting the revisionist Anselmian's criterion for greatness that it exhibits any one of these particular combinations of good-making features. It would thus require explanation why any being that meets the revisionist Anselmian's criterion for greatness exhibits that particular combination. And thus there would be something logically prior to the Anselmian being's existing that would explain its existence. For otherwise one could not explain why one of these chart-topping combinations of perfections is realized rather than some other.

There is a further serious problem if the third option is true. When two things are incommensurably good in some domain of value, then it is rational to prefer the first over the second, or the second over the first, with respect to that domain of value. This is part of what distinguishes the equally from the incommensurably good; when two options are equally good, there is no reason to prefer one to the other, but when two options are incommensurably good, there is a reason to prefer one to the other, and a reason to prefer the other to the one. If, then, two possible beings at the top of the greatness chart are incommensurably good, then it could be rational to prefer either to the other. This entails that it could be rational to prefer that some other array of great-making features be realized rather than the array that the actual Anselmian being

[7] One might say: Well, abstracta are necessary existents. So the Anselmian being is not greater than every other being with respect to every perfection, as necessary existence is a perfection, and the Anselmian being is not greater than abstracta along that dimension. First, I think the perfection in question is existence, and I deny that the way that the Anselmian being exists is no better than the way that abstracta exist; the Anselmian being exists in itself, the abstract only through the activity of the Anselmian being. For those who would deny this (e.g. van Inwagen 2009), one could get by with a weaker dominance principle: if one being is better than every other possible being along some dimension and no worse than any other possible being along any dimension, then it is the greatest possible being.

exhibits, even when one's preference is restricted to the range of perfectionist value. One should not, in reflecting on the greatness of the Anselmian being, be able to acknowledge its greatness correctly while fully rationally wishing that it were different in some fundamental way.

One might think that this objection to the revisionist view is not very pressing, for it is a real problem only if we do not think that the greatness scale is single-peaked. If there really is a uniquely best package of features that a being might exhibit, then the revisionist has little to be concerned about from this objection. But even aside from the intuitive point that it seems very dubious that there is a uniquely best trade-off of, say, knowledge, power, and goodness, I think that the very reasons for thinking that there are *multiple* distinct, irreducible perfections suggest that the value of those perfections will not admit of a unique trade-off scale. And so these problems about value constitute a further reason for thinking that the traditional Anselmian is right to hold fast to the distributive assumption.

1.3 Reasoning about the Anselmian Being: The Absolute Greatness Assumption Defended

In addition to this distributive assumption, there is an additional assumption made by the traditional understanding of Anselmian methodology that is much harder to make precise. The assumption is that the perfections exhibited by God are *sufficiently valuable*. This is embarrassingly vague. But start with a crucial point made by Jeff Speaks against any Anselmianism that characterizes God simply as the best possible being: if it turned out that Michael Jordan is the greatest possible being—if developments in our understanding of good-making properties and the modality with which these properties are exhibited led us to the view that Jordan is as good as a being could get—we should not conclude that Michael Jordan is God (Speaks forthcoming). We should conclude, rather, that there is no God, at least no God as conceived by the Anselmian. So we must hold that to qualify as God it is not enough to be the best being possible. A being must also be sufficiently great.

An implication of this way of thinking about Anselmian perfection is that the question of how valuable the exhibiting of some feature is is to some extent independent of the size of the range with respect to which it can possibly be exhibited. We should not think that, in considering how valuably some good-making feature can be realized, it is a matter of indifference what the size of the metaphysical possibility space for exhibiting that feature is, so long as the greatest possible being fills it up. Take powerfulness, for example. Suppose that we consider our rough-and-ready understanding of the range of power that a being might exhibit. The upper limit of this range is what God has to have. Substantively, our rough-and-ready understanding takes the exhibiting of power to this upper limit to include a lot of really impressive abilities, including the ability to bring matter into existence *ex nihilo*. But suppose that our rough-and-ready understanding is terribly flawed. We are, instead, in massive error about the range of powers that a being can exhibit. As a matter of fact, necessarily, all matter exists *a se* and necessarily, with the exception of one particle, which exists contingently. Of course, we must now suppose that God, having the limit of all power, is able to bring that particle into existence *ex nihilo*, though God would not be able to bring into existence or destroy any other matter. The point here is that God, in the former scenario, has a good deal more of a valuable capacity than God has in the latter scenario, even though under both understandings God would have power to the metaphysically possible limit of having power.

The moral I draw is that on the traditional conception, it is not enough for a being to be absolutely perfect that that being has the good-making properties to their metaphysically necessary limits, where it is a matter of indifference what those limits are.[8] For being perfect in that way is entirely relative to the size of the modal space for the realization of those good-making features, and if that modal space is cramped, then even a being who exhibits the good-making features to their necessary limits may be not very impressive after all. One might retort: What more could one ask than the realization of good-making features to their modal limit? Well, one could reasonably ask for no more. But the concept of God is not the concept of that being of which one could reasonably ask no more. It is the concept of a being that is, absolutely speaking, great. And so I endorse a second tenet of traditional Anselmianism, which I will call the *absolute greatness* assumption. I offered above a tepid formulation of it: the metaphysical limit of the good-making properties permits a being who exhibits those properties to that limit to be sufficiently great, absolutely speaking.

What counts as adequate greatness is of course the question. One might be satisfied either just leaving this adequacy condition vague or supplementing Anselmianism with an account that describes adequacy in non-Anselmian terms, e.g., adequacy being defined in relation to worship-worthiness.[9] But it seems plain to me that the latter move is explicitly a giving up on Anselmianism. If what matters is worship-worthiness, then that is the master concept that is driving the account of the divine nature, not Anselmianism. And it seems also pretty plain that, whether we leave the boundary

[8] The revisionist Anselmian view defended by Nagasawa gives up the absolute greatness requirement, and allows in principle the toning down of the good-making properties to any point required to achieve coherence. But it seems plain that the possibility of God's existence depends on the cooperation of the absolute range of the possible; if the greatness allowed by the range of the metaphysically possible is not sufficiently great, then there is no God. This is Speaks's Michael Jordan objection. But the revisionist view as stated does not accommodate this truth. I think, then, that even if the revisionist does not accept my defense of the distributive assumption, the revisionist should supplement his or her view by adding some version of the absolute greatness assumption. So we may tinker with the formulation of the distinct divine perfections for the sake of achieving coherence, with the understanding that if the outcome is not sufficiently impressive, the being so characterized will not count as an Anselmian being. This reduces some of the allure of the revisionist conception, which is built on the indefinite revisability of our understanding of the divine perfections. But it would still not bear the full weight of the commitments borne by the traditional formulation, which makes not only the absolute greatness assumption but the distributive assumption.

[9] As Hoffman and Rosenkrantz (2002, pp. 15–16) explicitly do; see also Rogers 2000, p. 2.

vague or not, the appeal to *adequate* or *sufficient* greatness suggests that we are appealing to some sort of relational notion of goodness to do the work: to say that God must be great enough to be supremely worthy of worship or of allegiance or of obedience is to characterize the divine nature in relation to creaturely nature. For, after all, God is worthy of worship and allegiance and loyalty *by creatures*, not by God. (God is worthy of God's love, but not God's worship; see section 7.1 for further discussion.) And it seems to me not only anathema for the Anselmian, but a mistake in terms of theism generally, to take God's fundamental nature to be defined relationally, especially when it seems possible that God might have never created.[10]

It might seem that the rejection of the supplementing of Anselmianism with alternative methods to specify what would count as 'sufficient' or 'adequate' greatness for a being to count as God dooms Anselmianism to arbitrariness or incompleteness. No: it just means that the Anselmianism should think that there is no nonarbitrary stopping point for the notion of sufficient greatness other than absolute perfection. For if sufficient greatness will have to be characterized in terms of relational value, but no such relational value can be relied upon in the divine case, then we must take absolute perfection to be the standard for divinity.

And after all, once one allows that one can make value judgments about the realization of good-making properties that float free of which of these realizations is metaphysically possible, then there must be room to hold that absolute perfection involves an unsurpassable realization of value for each good-making property, and not simply unsurpassable realization of that value within the range given by metaphysical possibility. Does that mean that the Anselmian being need not be logically coherent? Of course not. What it means is that it is a commitment of traditional Anselmianism as I understand it that, though the greatest value realizable by way of some perfection is not defined in relation to the limits of metaphysical possibility, nevertheless all such are within the limits of metaphysical possibility. In other words, for any good-making property, there is some greatest realization of that property, and in all such cases, it is possible for God to realize it. God is not 'held back' in value by the limits of metaphysical possibility.

Here is a metaphor. Suppose that a monarch asked for the absolutely shiniest coat. We might wonder whether to take this demand as a relatively modest demand for a coat exhibiting the highest level of shininess that the tailors can possibly realize—they are, within the limits set by technology and the laws of nature, to produce a coat with the highest shininess level. To understand the monarch's demand this way is to understand it such that it is guaranteed to be possible to comply with the demand, for the demand is interpreted so as to ensure that the object of the demand can be made. But we might understand the demand in a way that does not make such an assumption. We

[10] Well, what if one takes God necessarily to create? I still think that is a problem. The theist should think that the necessity of creation, were it such, would be due to facts about God's perfection. This is, for example, the view taken in Kretzmann 1991.

can understand absolute shininess *absolutely*: that there is such a thing as *being shiny* and that this admits of degrees; that shininess involves reflecting the light that falls upon it; and absolute shininess would be, say, reflecting all such light, without loss. We can thus ask, independently of whether this coat can in fact be made, whether our technology allows it, whether the laws of physics allow it, whether metaphysical necessity allows it, what would count as meeting this demand: it is to peg out the shininess meter. On this reading, there is no guarantee that the monarch's demand can be met. We may (do) have to simply answer that the demand does not fit within the range of the possible.

The working out of a detailed traditional version of Anselmianism is not my aim in this book. (For much more complete attempts, see Morris 1987a and Rogers 2000.) My aim here has just been to give some reason to hold that the traditional conception, understood in terms of the distributive and absolute greatness assumptions, is the most promising form for Anselmianism to take. The adoption of such a view has implications—some obvious, some less obvious—for how one employs Anselmianism to draw conclusions about the Anselmian being; I consider some of these in the following section.

1.4 Key Anselmian Theses

It is worth making explicit here various Anselmian theses upon which I will rely in Part I.

The first is that, obviously, for any feature God might exhibit, whether necessarily or contingently, God's exhibiting that feature must be compatible with God's being absolutely perfect. For God's being necessarily perfect entails the impossibility of God's having any imperfection-entailing feature.

The second is that there are no features that God necessarily exhibits that are not perfections or logical implications of perfections. This is perhaps less obvious. There may be alternative routes to this thesis that take as their starting points particular uncontroversial divine perfections or combinations of divine perfections. But more directly one can appeal simply to the idea that a being all of whose necessary features are perfections is better than a being whose necessary features include features that are not perfections. To include in God's necessary array of features those that are not perfections or explained by perfections is to make God less *purely* perfect—and a being who is less purely perfect is not as great as a being who is more purely perfect. So there are no *brute* necessary truths about God's nature; all such truths are made true by God's perfection.

The third is that for any divine perfection, that perfection must have an intrinsic maximum.[11] We should be careful here. It is not necessary that for any feature P some

[11] It is clear that this way of putting the intrinsic maximum thesis depends on the adoption of the distributive assumption of the traditional view. The revisionist has to hold an alternative formulation, on which the *combination* of good-making features has an intrinsic maximum.

realization of which is a divine perfection there is a maximum at which P can be exhibited and the divine perfection is constituted by God's exhibiting P at that maximum. Rather, the requirement that a divine perfection have an intrinsic maximum means that for each divine perfection there is an extent beyond which it cannot be realized *in a more valuable way*. As far as this constraint is concerned,[12] it is okay for P to be indefinitely increasable if, beyond some degree, having P does not make a being who has P to a greater degree better than a being who has P to a lesser degree. Even if P has a highest possible degree, it is okay for God to fail to realize P to that degree, if realizing it to some other degree is no worse than exhibiting it to the highest degree. What is crucial is that for any good-making property, there is a way of exhibiting that property that is unsurpassable in value.

The fourth and fifth claims are methodological rather than metaphysical. The fourth is just a reminder that the sort of value that the Anselmian being exhibits is nonrelational (1.2). We are therefore not to ascribe some feature to the Anselmian being simply because it is in some way better *for us* that the Anselmian being have it, or that it is better *from our particular point of view*, or better *for some human purpose*. To hold that the value of the Anselmian being's perfection is human-centered in this way would be nearly as silly as to say that the Anselmian being's perfection is kudzu-vine-centered-value or amoeba-centered-value. And so we are never to treat as a sufficient objection to an account of divine perfection simply that we could not obey a being like *that*, or be loyal to a being like *that*. Appeal to such premises all on their own would be decisive only if perfection were conceived anthropocentrically, and anthropocentric value is relational value. Of course, premises like these could be *part* of an argument against a certain conception of divine perfection, but it is not *itself* disqualifying of a conception of divine perfection that humans might appropriately fail to have some particular positive response to it.[13] Because Anselmian perfection is *nonrelational* goodness,[14] it is no objection, all by itself, to a certain conception of God's perfection that it does not exhibit some form of relational goodness, and it is no defense, all by itself, of a certain conception of God's perfection that it does exhibit some form of relational goodness.

[12] As noted above (1.2), one might press explanatory questions about why, if there are multiple ways of realizing some divine perfection, the Anselmian being realizes a particular one of them. But that is a distinct issue. My point here is that the absolute perfection of the Anselmian being entails that, for each divine perfection, there must be an unsurpassable level of value that can be reached with respect to that perfection.

[13] Call 'awwww-someness' the worthiness that some very small cute animals exhibit in virtue of which the appropriate response by humans is their saying 'awwww...' in these animals' presence. Puppies are, no doubt, awwww-some. But the Anselmian being is not awwww-some, and indeed the Anselmian being's awesomeness precludes its being awwww-some. But that some beings are worthy of a positive response by humans that the Anselmian being is not worthy of is not a problem with Anselmianism about God, or the basis of a proof that there could be no Anselmian being. Awwww-someness is not a pure perfection.

[14] That Anselmian perfection is nonrelational goodness is a different claim than that it is goodness of something nonrelational. Now, there are very good reasons to think that Anselmian perfections cannot be constituted by anything that is not the Anselmian being or an aspect of the Anselmian being. But that is not the point being made here, which is that the Anselmian being's being good is not the Anselmian being's being good *for us*, *to us*, or anything like that.

The fifth is the most contentious: if we take as a given the metaphysical possibility of an Anselmian being, then in characterizing the perfections of the Anselmian being, we should conceive them as 'pressing outward.' That is, there is rational pressure toward characterizing the Anselmian perfections in a substantively more expansive way. If one simply held that the Anselmian being exhibits features to their metaphysically possible limit, then there would be such pressure only when we are dealing with what we already accept to be possible for a being to exhibit, and it would be trivial that the Anselmian being would have to exhibit those features to the limit of their value. The absolute greatness assumption—especially in conjunction with my gloss on it—supports a stronger methodological point. It is that, if we are taking the coherence of the Anselmian conception of God for granted, we should think that if we have some reason to think that an Anselmian being would be greater for having some feature to some degree, then that is itself a reason—not conclusive, of course, but a reason—to think that it *is* possible for a being to exhibit that feature. And it would therefore count as a reason—again, obviously not conclusive, but a reason—to judge the Anselmian being to exhibit that feature.

Some recent formulations of Anselmianism treat God's perfection as simply filling up whatever value space is left open by the given structures of modality. But if a being's being great enough to be God depends on those structures' being permissive enough for God to exhibit value to an absolutely high degree, then these standard formulations cannot be right. If it looks like God would be greater if God were to (e.g.) know the truth-values of counterfactuals of freedom, then that is reason to think that God knows counterfactuals of freedom. If we have some reason to doubt that counterfactuals of freedom have truth-values, then we have a philosophical problem of the most standard sort: reasons for and against belief in some philosophical proposition. The point is that on the Anselmian view, the metaphysical theses do not take priority.[15]

[15] This piece of methodology will be put to work in Chapter 4, where I argue for a certain conception of divine ethics on the basis of what expands most fully the Anselmian being's *sovereignty*.

2

Is the Anselmian Being Loving?

2.1 Love and Moral Goodness

As I noted in the Introduction (0.1), formulations of the argument from evil must include a premise that informs us about God's motivations—a premise that tells us what God would want to do with all of that power and knowledge. Overwhelmingly, contemporary formulations of that argument have filled this need by relying on the claim that God is perfectly morally good. But it is worth noting that there are other premises that defenders of the argument from evil could rely upon, premises that might seem even more likely to secure the conclusion of the argument from evil than the premise that God is morally perfect. For even if somehow we could give an account of how the fact that the world contains evils that it seems that an omnipotent, omniscient, perfectly morally good being would eliminate does not count decisively, or even much at all, against theism, it is hard to see how one who surveys the world could think that it is a creation of, and under the governance of, a *perfectly loving* being. Since theists often do take *being loving*, even *being supremely loving*, or even *being love* to be features of God, this sort of challenge to theism is worth taking seriously. Recall that our task in these early chapters, though, is not precisely to ask whether and to what extent *God* is loving, but to ask whether *the Anselmian being* is loving (1.1). Is it, then, a necessary truth that any being who qualifies as an Anselmian being must be loving?

My aim in this chapter is not to defend a simple denial that the Anselmian being is loving. My thesis is slightly more complex than that. It concerns the limit to which we should ascribe *being loving* to the Anselmian being: it is that in whatever sense it is true that the Anselmian being is loving, the sense in which it is loving does not go beyond that which is appropriate to ascribe to it simply in virtue of its having to be morally perfect. If the Anselmian being must perfectly satisfy the norms of moral goodness, and perfect satisfaction of the norms of moral goodness itself entails that the being who satisfies those norms is in some way, to some extent, or even supremely, loving, that is fine; I have no interest in this chapter in taking issue with the line of reasoning that as the Anselmian being is perfectly morally good, and perfect moral goodness involves being loving to a certain extent, then the Anselmian being must be loving to that extent. What I want to deny here is that there is any sense in which the Anselmian being is necessarily loving that *goes beyond* that captured by the Anselmian being's having to be perfectly morally good.[1]

What conditions would have to be met for an Anselmian being to be loving in a way that goes beyond that given by the Anselmian being's being morally good? First, this further sense in which the Anselmian being is loving must be a divine perfection, or an implication of a divine perfection. Such is a requirement of the Anselmian view with which we are working (1.4). Second, this sense in which the Anselmian being is loving must entail there are some actions to which one must be motivated in virtue of being loving in that sense to which one need not be motivated simply in virtue of being completely perfectly morally good. My claim, then, is that no conception of *being loving* satisfies both of these desiderata. The only sense in which the Anselmian being must be loving is the sense in which the Anselmian being must be morally good.

2.2 Moral Goodness

There are multiple plausible and incompatible ways to conceive of moral goodness—here, and in what follows, I have in mind that moral goodness that is a feature of agents[2]—and one cannot remain entirely neutral between them in presenting arguments concerning the extent to which moral goodness is to be ascribed to the Anselmian being. It is helpful, though, that some conceptions of moral goodness would pretty obviously be the wrong sort of conception by which to assess *divine* moral perfection. Even if it were plausible to think of moral goodness as, say, adherence to some set of norms that equally vulnerable agents would agree to in order to further their own ends—that is, something like the view forwarded by Gauthier (1986)—this would be a very unpromising conception of moral goodness to ascribe to the absolutely perfect being. (If this is not obvious, an argument to this effect can be found in 3.3.)

I suggest that we think of moral goodness as *appropriate responsiveness to value,* or to particular sorts of value; to be morally good is for one's agency—one's desires, one's deliberation, one's action—to be fittingly responsive to values of the sorts that are at stake in morality.[3] If one is a utilitarian about morality, presumably this is because the

[1] I aim to rule out, then, two related theses: first, that the ethics of an Anselmian being is an ethics of love that goes beyond an ethics of perfect moral goodness, and second, that one can appeal to the Anselmian being's perfect love in a formulation of the argument from evil against the existence of an Anselmian being that has some force independent of and in addition to a formulation of the argument from evil that appeals to the Anselmian being's perfect moral goodness alone.

[2] We sometimes speak of the moral goodness of states of affairs—its being morally good that suffering is eased, for example. But I have in mind moral goodness that is ascribed to agents, not states of affairs.

[3] The view of moral goodness described here is, as formulated, incompatible with a buck-passing account of value of the sort defended by Scanlon (1998, pp. 95–100), for it treats value as explanatorily prior to the appropriateness of the responses to that value, while the buck-passing account reverses this explanatory priority. While I reject the buck-passing account, I do not think that my main line of argument

utilitarian norm expresses that agents are to maximize overall well-being, for the relevant value at stake is the agent-neutral value of well-being, and the fitting response to well-being is to promote it. Or, if one is a Kantian, the norm not to treat persons as mere means but rather as ends-in-themselves expresses that the appropriate response to the value of persons as subsistent ends is to respect that value. And so forth (Murphy 2001, pp. 162–71).

To be a norm of moral goodness is (in part) to be a norm such that there can be no way to properly respond to the relevant values other than in the way specified by the norm. Moral norms are *mandatory* norms, and they have their mandatory character from the fact that the way that they specify for agents to act in light of the relevant values is not simply one eligible option but the only eligible option in the relevant circumstances.[4]

I want to add two more conditions to the bare-bones view of moral goodness that I have just described, one less controversial, one more controversial. Sometimes there are attempts to characterize the domain of the moral wholly in terms that concern the formal features of the moral, rather than its content. To say that the moral concerns appropriate responsiveness to value of a certain type is one such partial attempt. Sometimes a further appeal is made to some impartiality constraint (for example, Milo 1995) or to some reason-givingness condition (Smith 1994, p. 184) (more on this below in this section), or the like. But I want to add a plausible but not uncontroversial substantive constraint on the notion of moral goodness that is in use in this book. The sort of moral goodness that I have in mind is what I will call 'familiar welfare-oriented' moral goodness. On this conception of moral goodness, while it may be possible that there are differences among kinds of agents (humans, God, angels, Martians) in terms of the relevant criteria of moral goodness for those agents, one constant is that the welfare of rational and perhaps sentient beings generally is one of the values to which morally good agency positively responds. An agent is morally good in this familiar sense only if that being treats setbacks to the well-being of rational and other sentient beings as to-be-prevented and so fails to prevent them only when there are other values that bear on the choice that make it appropriate to fail to act for the sake of well-being on that occasion.[5] If the Anselmian being exhibits familiar welfare-oriented moral

depends on the explanatory priority here going one way rather than the other. Since the central arguments upon which I rely concern the Anselmian being's reasons for action, and the buck-passer's account of value analyzes value in terms of reasons, it would make my argument rather simpler to formulate if I could assume the truth of the buck-passing conception.

[4] This is compatible with some moral norms being *pro tanto*. They mandate action in the circumstances that there are not stronger reasons to the contrary.

[5] This is very rough and clearly not correct as it stands. Some of the considerations that might allow someone not to treat setbacks to well-being as reasons in favor of an action might not themselves be reasons to perform an incompatible action but instead other sorts of conditions that affect the weight that reasons properly have in deliberation. (For example, what Raz calls "exclusionary permissions" are not reasons against performing the action in question but considerations that permit one not to give some fact weight in deliberation that otherwise might have such weight (Raz 1999 [1975], pp. 89–91). If there are such exclusionary permissions, then one who exhibits familiar welfare-oriented moral goodness might fail

goodness, then that being's ethics is an ethics of preventing setbacks to well-being unless there exist considerations that make it appropriate, or not inappropriate, not to prevent such setbacks—perhaps that there is some greater good at stake, perhaps that preventing it would result in a worse evil, and so forth.[6]

Why place such a constraint on the conception of moral goodness in play, when it is admitted that this is not a universally-agreed-upon view? Two reasons. First, I am not interested in making any trouble for the idea that there is some purely formal sense in which the Anselmian being is morally good, whereas I want to call into question (in Chapter 3) certain substantive, though very widely accepted, views about the moral goodness of the Anselmian being. Second, it is this familiar welfare-oriented sense of moral goodness that those considering the argument from evil have in mind when they appeal to God's moral goodness as a way of getting to what God's ethics is. Indeed, it has been thought of as simply *cheating* to allow too much variance from our ordinary understanding of human morality in thinking through questions of divine ethics. As Mill writes,

> If in ascribing goodness to God I do not mean what I mean by goodness; if I do not mean the goodness of which I have some knowledge, but an incomprehensible attribute of an incomprehensible substance, which for aught I know may be a totally different quality from that which I love and venerate...what do I mean in calling it goodness?...To say that God's goodness may be different in kind from man's goodness, what is it but saying, with a slight change of phraseology, that God may possibly be not good? (Mill 1964 [1865], pp. 42–3)

Moral goodness is appropriate responsiveness to morally relevant value, whatever that is, though we take for granted that included within that morally relevant value is the well-being of rational and perhaps sentient beings generally. The second, more controversial thing that I want to say about the moral goodness that is plausibly ascribed to the Anselmian being is that the sort of appropriateness of the response to value is *rational* appropriateness, simply acting in response to these values in a way that those values give reason to respond to them. To respond appropriately to morally relevant value is to do what there is good reason[7] to do as a response to those values.

to take a setback to well-being as to-be-prevented even in absence of any reasons to the contrary.) As my focus in this book is on the reasons given by the well-being of creatures and not on the conditions that modify the reason-giving force of that well-being, there is no point in pursuing the question of the best formulation here.

[6] In formulating the view I want to remain neutral about what reasons are reasons of the right sort for failing to prevent setbacks to well-being. What is important here is the common ground, that if God fails to prevent setbacks to well-being, it is only on account of some good reason that God had.

[7] Throughout this book, I use 'reasons' in this normative, not motivational, sense. A reason, in this normative sense, is a fact that renders action choiceworthy in some way. I do not assume that a reason in this sense is something that is actually known to the agent for whom it is a reason, nor do I assume that a reason in this sense is something that actually motivates the agent for whom it is a reason. Surely there is some way in which, to be a normative reason for an agent, that reason must be knowable and possibly motivating. But exactly what sort of cognitive accessibility and motivating power something must have to be a reason for an agent is not something on which I will take a precise stand. As we are dealing primarily with God here, whose cognitive access is without bound and who suffers from no motivational failures, the pressure to provide a fuller account is minimal.

There is one general and one specific set of considerations in favor of this view of how to understand the moral goodness that is to be ascribed to God. The general consideration is just plausibility of a certain sort of internalism about morality, that which Michael Smith labels "rationalism" (Smith 1994, p. 62), though it would need to hold in a somewhat strengthened form to provide support for this conception of moral goodness. The rationalist thesis as Smith formulates it asserts no more than that an act's being morally right for an agent to perform entails the agent's having a good reason to perform it (Gert 2008). The strengthened rationalist thesis asserts that an action's being the morally best action for an agent to perform entails that it is the action that the agent has most reason to perform. What is being supposed here is that rationality, with respect to morality, is very demanding: moral requirements just are rational requirements, so that a failure to act morally is a failure to act fully rationally.

There are various arguments for this view, and I will do no more than sketch a few of them here. One concerns the relationship between moral norms, blame, and reasons. The violation of moral norms is something for which agents are typically properly blamed; but if such agents had adequate reason for violating those norms, it is hard to see why such blame is appropriate. ("I know you had perfectly adequate reasons to do that, but...how dare you?" The question answers itself. You dared because you had good enough reason to dare.)[8] This tie between the appropriateness of blame for an agent's failing to act a certain way and the presence of decisive reasons for the agent to act that way is extremely plausible, has both a grounding in our intuitions about cases and a theoretically satisfying rationale, and is something that moral theorists of opposing metaethical stances seem keen to accommodate. So given that the violation of moral norms is something for which agents, in the absence of rational incapacitation, are rightly blamed, it must be the case that agents, in the absence of rational incapacitation, have decisive reasons to act in accordance with those norms.

Another such argument for strengthened moral rationalism is built on the appropriateness of characterizing moral norms as *demands*. In nondefective demands, one has decisive reason to do what is demanded of one (Murphy 2002a, pp. 24–7). ("I demand that you do this, though you have adequate reason not to" is a misfire.) But in standard cases of demands, the existence conditions of the demand (that is, what makes it true that a demand was issued) are distinct from the nondefectiveness conditions of the demand (that is, what makes it true that the demand is in no way deficient as a demand). Thus, defective demands are possible, for those who give the demands can be confused or insincere about whether the presuppositions of the demand are fulfilled. But there is no such room with moral demands, for moral demands are characterized as demands just in virtue of their being like nondefective demands, with the

[8] The presupposition that there be some reason to comply with a norm that one is properly blamed for is what creates the tension with motivational internalism that Williams struggles with in Williams 1995b; that the relevant reasons must be decisive if we are to make sense of blame is also argued for in Darwall 2006, p. 98 and Sobel 2007, pp. 164–5.

result that there is no gap between their existence and nondefectiveness conditions. So if one is subject to a moral demand, it is a demand in accordance with which one has decisive reason to act.

I take the strengthened rationalist thesis to be a truth of metaethics. But if one is unconvinced by the case for a strengthened rationalist thesis as a general truth about moral rightness, one may be more moved by the idea that even if there are some plausible conceptions of moral goodness that do not require the strengthened rationalist or even the rationalist thesis to be true, it is implausible to ascribe any conception of moral goodness *to the Anselmian being* that does not take there to be this tight connection between moral goodness and reasons for action.

I formulate the argument for this thesis in terms of divine freedom and divine rationality. Standard Anselmianism holds, and any formulation of the argument from evil presupposes, that the Anselmian being is a *rational* agent. We must think of the Anselmian being as exhibiting perfect practical rationality, as being practically flawless. And so any specification of moral goodness as a divine perfection must fit with perfect rationality as a divine perfection.

Standard Anselmianism also holds, and any formulation of the problem of evil presupposes, that the Anselmian being is a *free* agent. What this freedom amounts to is controversial, but it includes at least the following: the Anselmian being's acting on that being's practical judgments is not constrained by compulsions or habits, but only—and 'constrained' is probably the wrong word here—by that being's own assessment of what is worth doing and not worth doing. (See also Swinburne 1993, p. 148.) It is crucial to the perfection of divine freedom—whether this is just one aspect of the Anselmian being's perfect agency or is a distinct perfection is not really important for this purpose—that the Anselmian being is not *made* to act one way or another. Paradigmatically, this precludes some other agent making it to be the case that the Anselmian being acts one way rather than another. But it does not seem to me that the threat to the divine freedom can be restricted simply to what is in a straightforward sense *external* to the Anselmian being. Just as we think that a human agent is unfree not only if his or her agency is constrained by an external force but also if his or her agency is limited by internal drives or compulsions, it seems to me that if the Anselmian being's agency is limited by other than that being's assessment of the reasons to act one way or another, then the Anselmian being is not exhibiting the perfection of freedom.

If one is perfectly rational and perfectly free, then if necessarily one ϕs, then necessarily one has decisive reason to ϕ. Note that the necessities are *within* the conditional. The claim is not that, necessarily, a perfectly rational, perfectly free agent acts only on decisive reasons. After all, there may be underdetermination by reasons of what is to be done, and a perfectly rational being might in those cases exhibit discretionary choice. But we can say that if a rational, free being *necessarily does* act a certain way, the only explanation for that would be that the good reasons possessed by this agent decisively count in favor of performing that action.[9] If one is a perfectly rational and perfectly free agent, then one's action is guided solely by the reasons that one has, and so any necessity that attaches to acting a certain way must come from the reasons that are guiding one. And the only way that reasons can guide one necessarily in such a case is if those reasons are decisive.[10]

For an Anselmian being to exhibit familiar welfare-oriented moral goodness would be for that being necessarily to prevent setbacks to well-being unless that being had reasons of the right sort for not doing so. The Anselmian being could exhibit familiar welfare-oriented moral goodness, though, only if that being's exhibiting it is compatible with divine rationality and divine freedom. It follows that the Anselmian being exhibits familiar welfare-oriented moral goodness only if the well-being of humans and other sentient animals gives that being decisive reasons to prevent setbacks to it, at least in the absence of reasons of the right sort to the contrary.[11] The same must also be true of any of the other, as-yet-unspecified morally relevant values at stake in agency.

So aside from general metaethical arguments for the sort of strengthened rationalist thesis that would entail that the values at stake in moral goodness must be reason-giving for anyone in a particularly strict way, we have grounds to hold that any conception of moral goodness to be ascribed to the Anselmian being must satisfy this reason-givingness constraint.

We will return to this conception of moral goodness again in Chapter 3 (3.6), dealing with some objections to the arguments just offered and the plausibility of the

[9] Of course there are puzzles about the compatibility of freedom and perfect rationality, puzzles of the sort explored by Rowe (2005). Nothing here constitutes a contribution to that discussion; I am simply assuming that any difficulties regarding the tension between them can be resolved.

[10] 'Perfect freedom,' as understood here, involves not being necessitated either by exterior forces or by interior compulsions to act one way rather than another. It does not require that in every choice situation it is possible for the perfectly free agent to act otherwise. If a perfectly free agent is also perfectly rational, then when the reasons decisively favor one course of action, it is not possible that that agent do anything other than what the reasons decisively favor.

[11] Why think that it is the well-being of creatures that must give reasons to the Anselmian being to promote it? Why not think that the fact *it is morally required of the Anselmian being to promote the well-being of creatures* is the relevant reason? One basis for denying this is would be if Dancy were right, and *its being morally required* is never a good reason to do something. Dancy holds that to say that an action is morally required is to say (roughly, and not exhaustively) that, taking into account all the relevant reasons for and against performing that action, the reasons weigh in favor of performing it. If the being required were itself a reason, then such judgments would have to be false, for they would not have taken into account all relevant reasons. So Dancy concludes:

> That an action is...right is no reason to do it. It is the features that make an action...right that are the reasons for doing it, and to say that it is...right is merely to express a judgment about the way in which other considerations go to determine how we should act (Dancy 2004, p. 16).

I reject Dancy's argument, holding that *its being morally required* can be a Razian protected reason that is distinct from and can substitute for the reasons on which it is based. But even if Dancy is wrong, all we need is a premise of his argument—that any reasons of moral requiredness would have to be based on more fundamental reasons for the action at stake—to see that we should not appeal to *its being morally required* to promote the well-being of creatures as the reason for the Anselmian being to act in accordance with familiar welfare-oriented moral goodness. There would have to be reasons more basic than reasons of moral requiredness, say reasons of well-being, that make it true that there are reasons of moral requiredness to act in accordance with familiar welfare-oriented moral goodness.

conception generally. But the foregoing will suffice for the argument of the present chapter. I now turn to the argument that the extent to which the Anselmian being is loving does not go beyond the extent to which the Anselmian being is morally good in the sense just described.

2.3 Necessary Love Does Not Go beyond Necessary Moral Goodness

The value that is at stake in moral goodness and the value that is at stake in love[12] are one and the same, or, at least, the value that is at stake in love is *included* in the value at stake in moral goodness. The Anselmian being is supposed to love *persons*, at least, on the standard view, and of course the value of persons is going to be included in the value relevant to moral goodness to which God is perfectly responsive. So any divine response that is rationally necessitated simply by the value that is at stake in the response of love will already be included in the response that is rationally necessitated by the value that is at stake in the response of moral goodness. For *being loving* both to be a divine perfection and to motivate in a way that moral goodness does not, then, it must be the case that it is a divine perfection to be motivated in particular ways toward some value—say, that of created persons—in a manner that goes beyond that rationally necessitated by that value.

There are two possibilities. (1) Even if the value of created persons does not rationally necessitate the Anselmian being's having a certain response to it, nevertheless that being is motivated to act in a particular way that goes beyond what is rationally necessitated, and that being's having that motivation is or is entailed by a divine perfection. (2) Even if the Anselmian being is rationally necessitated to respond in a certain way to the value of created persons, that necessitation may be *consequent* on that being's having love for those persons, and that love is itself a divine perfection.[13]

(1) Put to the side whether *being loving* can plausibly be independently characterized as a divine perfection. (I will return to this issue in sections 2.4 and 2.5.) As I noted previously (2.2) in considering the sort of moral goodness that may suitably be ascribed to the Anselmian being, it is a bad idea to ascribe to the Anselmian being some necessary pattern of action that is such that that being does not have decisive reason to act in accordance with that pattern. It is incompatible with ascribing the appropriate freedom to the absolutely perfect being also to hold that that being must act a certain way in spite of the fact that that being would have perfectly adequate reason to act a contrary way.

[12] By 'love' here I mean the sort of love being ascribed to the Anselmian being and which is supposed to make trouble for the existence of God due to the existence of evil.

[13] Nygren's extraordinarily influential account of divine Agape is ambiguous with respect to whether it affirms the first or the second of these possibilities. I think Nygren has the resources to affirm the second, given his view that Agape creates value (Nygren 1969 [1938], p. 30).

(2) Here is an alternative view. One might avoid the conclusion that the Anselmian being's agency is limited by something other than good reasons by holding that the Anselmian being does indeed have decisive reasons to act in particular loving ways—so there is no threat to the divine freedom from that being's being unable to act in ways that that being has entirely adequate reasons to act. These reasons are, however, the *result* of the Anselmian being's loving created persons, where the necessity of the Anselmian being's loving created persons[14] is established otherwise than through an appeal to that being's rational agency.

Put to the side, again, whether *being loving* can plausibly be independently characterized as a divine perfection. I have very strong doubts about the conception of the reason-givingness of love suggested in this view. I admit that this may sound like a very foolish objection. It is extremely commonsensical to say that one has good, that is, normative reasons to do something for someone because one loves him or her. But I think that this commonsensical thing to say is very misleading about reasons and their source.[15]

I want to proceed so far as possible independently of a commitment to a certain view or views of love. So consider various classes of view. One might understand what is going on in loving someone to be simply treating prospects to further their well-being, or their projects, or whatever, as reasons of a certain kind, and perhaps to treat opportunities for greater unity with that someone as reasons as well. On this view it is constitutive of love to treat these as reasons, perhaps as decisive reasons. But this is not a view on which being loving *explains* one's having decisive reasons to go along. When we say that one *treats* certain reasons as decisive, what we mean is that, regardless of whether these reasons are in fact decisive at ruling out some option or ruling in some other, the agent allows some consideration to play that role in his or her deliberation. So if all that we mean when we say that the Anselmian being loves created persons is that the Anselmian being allows the well-being of created persons to guide that being's agency in certain ways, it does not follow from this that the well-being of created persons gives the Anselmian being decisive reasons to act one way rather than another. So it is really a variant on the previous view, in which one treats certain considerations as overriding, even if they in fact are not. Since we are now considering views on which the value of created persons *does* give the Anselmian being such reasons, this possibility is not really relevant to our present discussion.

There is another view of love that one might think of as primarily cognitivist—as involving having a certain knowledge of the beloved, or taking certain stances toward him or her wrapped up with cognitivist notions—say, *attending to*, something like that.

[14] This necessity is hypothetical, that is, necessarily, if there are created persons, then the Anselmian being loves them. At this point I take for granted that one can appeal to the view that the Anselmian being will be loving while not insisting that the Anselmian being must create at all, much less create persons.

[15] It goes without saying that love can be a source of *motivating* reasons. Love is supposed to be a motivating state. But it is false that to be a motivating reason is to be or entails the existence of a corresponding normative reason.

But knowledge does not give rise to new reasons; it *reveals* them. Velleman's view (1999) is something like this; it takes love to be a state in which the value of another qua rational nature is revealed to one. That this does not give new reasons but reveals them is implicitly endorsed by Velleman when he acknowledges that, *really*, one has no more reason to save one's beloved from death than one has reason to save the perfect stranger from death (Velleman 1999, p. 373). And so love, thus understood, does not explain reasons in the right way.

Suppose that instead we view love in terms of a certain sort of desire, or disposition to desire, or otherwise conative matter. We now seem to have gotten around to a view of love in which it could be the source of new reasons. Now I am suspicious generally about the capacity of desire-like states to generate reasons for action (see Quinn 1993b and Murphy 2001, pp. 72–6), but I do not want my objections to turn on these suspicions.[16] So let us take a modest approach and allow that even if some desire-like states are themselves reason-giving, not all of them are.

Is *love* understood in this way going to be reason-giving? It is tempting to imagine a parent with his or her child, and think about the way that the child's well-being gives the parent reasons for action that go beyond the reasons given by the child simply qua helpless fellow human, and think that these reasons are somehow due to the love that the parent has for the child. But this seems to me to be a mistake: what is relevant here is centrally not the *love* that the parent has for the child—as if the parent might lose those reasons just by ceasing to love the child—but the *relationship* in which the parent stands to the child, that is, *being the child's parent* (or caretaker, or guardian, or whatever). (See Kolodny 2003; also Pruss 2012a, p. 16.) Indeed, it is the relationship itself that partly explains and justifies the parent's loving the child. Parents are typically bad parents if they do not love their children, and if their failure to love is due to something that they could have done differently—perhaps they fostered a love of a lifestyle incompatible with caring well for their children, and so came to resent them—we would blame the parents for their failure to love.[17] When we detach these relationship features from the fact of love, it seems to me that we have very little basis for thinking of the fact of love as reason-giving in the right way, that is, that it involves the value of the beloved necessitating a certain sort of agential response.

Now, one might respond to these worries by suggesting that perhaps we should not appeal to love as the key move. Rather, we should say that the Anselmian being necessarily stands in a certain relationship to creatures, and it is that relationship which gives that being reason to treat them in a certain way, and it is that relationship which

[16] As noted above (n. 13), Nygren assumes that love can be value-conferring in a very straightforward way, and I think that is an unfortunate commitment of his position.

[17] While I accept in essentials Kolodny's relational view of love and its reasons, I would rather not conceive of the relationship itself as necessarily valuable but rather as value-conferring without having to be thought of as itself valuable. It seems implausible to me that we must treat the relationships themselves as valuable to have an account of how the persons connected in those relationships give each other reasons for action. The relationship may be in the *background*, not even a constituent part of the reasons in question, though part of their explanation. Cf. Schroeder 2007a, pp. 23–40.

explains why the Anselmian being must adopt the right sort of loving stance with respect to created persons. One might object here that we have not seen yet good reason to think that the Anselmian being necessarily creates, and so it may not be true that the Anselmian being necessarily stands in any relation to creatures. But that does not make trouble for the proposal I am currently considering. The proposal is just that, *given* the existence of created persons, the Anselmian being necessarily loves them, and the reason that the Anselmian being loves them is some relationship in which, if there are any creatures, that being necessarily stands in that relation to those creatures. In order to falsify the thesis that I proposed for consideration at the beginning of the chapter—that the Anselmian being's being loving entails that this being responds to created persons in a way that goes beyond that which is entailed by the Anselmian being's being morally good—it must also be the case that the actions thus called for are not part of what moral goodness requires of the Anselmian being.

So there are two conditions that this proposal must satisfy in order to make trouble for the thesis of this chapter: first, that there is some relationship in which the Anselmian being necessarily stands with respect to creatures that gives that being necessitating reasons to love them; and second, that the love required by these reasons nevertheless does not turn out to be morally required. I want to begin by commenting briefly on the second of these conditions. I am not sure by what criterion it can be plausibly denied that the state of affairs described in this proposal is one in which the Anselmian being is morally bound to love creatures. For it looks as if there are beings of a valuable kind, creatures of the Anselmian being, who in virtue of a normatively relevant relationship give the Anselmian being reasons to act in ways that involve protection, promotion, etc. of those creatures' well-being. Just as parents' failure to love their children and friends' failure to love their friends are, among other things, moral failures, it looks as if the failure to love here would be a moral failure as well. But I am not going to insist on this point. For one thing, I am not so interested in making this argument depend on some controversial demarcation of the domain of the moral. But more importantly, I will in Chapter 3 be denying that standard moral norms apply to the Anselmian being (3.3–3.7), so even if I were to offer convincing reasons that this account of the way in which the Anselmian being must love creatures does not threaten the officially formulated thesis of this chapter, I would not avoid any of the work to come.

So I turn to the first point. Whatever relationship to which one appeals to explain why the Anselmian being necessarily loves creatures, it has to be a relationship that the Anselmian being necessarily has with creatures. (Here again I do not mean to say that necessarily there must be creatures, but that necessarily, if there are creatures, then the Anselmian being is related to them in that way.) But there seems to be only one relation that the Anselmian being necessarily stands in with respect to creatures that might fit the bill: *being the creator of*.

So this is the question: Is *being the creator of* a special relationship that accounts for not only *a* reason to love, acting on which would require actions beyond what the value of the creatures necessitates, but a *requiring* reason, one that an agent would need good reason not to act upon?[18] This strikes me as very hard to see. What we have here is, as so far characterized, merely a *causal* relationship. It is not a *social* relationship. And it is not a relationship of *equals*. (It is thus in that way entirely unlike the relationship of parents to children, all of whom are equals in virtue of their common humanity.) And it does not seem to me that in analogous cases with which we are familiar, we take there to be such reasons present. Suppose I am an artist, and produce a work of art, which we will stipulate to be the bearer of a certain value, and requiring a response from others on account of that value. Is the fact that I am the artist who brought it into existence a reason that requires a further response, beyond that which the work of art itself calls for? This seems false to me: it seems that we recognize a variety of sorts of responses from makers of works of art to those works, from treating them with special attention to treating them as no more or no less important than works produced by other artists to treating them as less important.[19] Suppose an artist must save a work from a burning museum. One can tell stories about relationships between artists and their work that would make saving one's own art over an objectively more impressive piece come out as an obviously reasonable, perhaps even mandatory response; one can tell a story in which what calls the shots is simply the value of the works at stake; one can tell a story in which preserving a less valuable piece over one's own more valuable piece looks reasonable, even perhaps a mandatory response. These seem to be the product of contingent histories that the artist might have with the work, and perhaps other contingent features of the artist. But it does not look like we have reason to think that the causal relationship as such is enough to generate, *as a matter of necessity*, the relevant reasons to love the artwork in ways that go beyond what the value of the artwork requires.

One might insist that there is a disanalogy between artwork and persons that vitiates my point here. After all, there is a burgeoning literature (see, for example, DeGrazia 2012) that revolves around the issue of what is (misleadingly)[20] labeled the requirements that parents are under in virtue of 'creating' children. One might think that, surely, I would need to engage with such arguments in order to dismiss the idea that simply in virtue of standing in a creator–creature relationship to human beings, the Anselmian being would be rationally necessitated to love them. But note that the characteristic way in which arguments in this literature are framed is by formulating the requirements that parents have to act in certain welfare-promoting ways toward their children as implications of some broader moral principles, for which the act of bringing those children into existence is merely a triggering condition. So it seems plain that no such arguments, even if successful in the parent–child context, could be successful in establishing that the Anselmian being has reasons to act for the well-being of

[18] I will argue in Chapter 3 (3.4), following Gert (2004), that this is an important distinction: not every good reason is a requiring reason.

[19] One might think that one has an exclusionary permission to treat one's own artwork with *less* solicitude than that created by others.

[20] For what is misleading about that label, see Aquinas, *Summa Theologiae* Ia 45, 5.

humans unless the Anselmian being is subject to those moral norms that provided the basis for the explanation of those requirements.[21] As the question we are asking here is whether the Anselmian being is loving in some way that goes beyond what is entailed by the moral norms on which the Anselmian being must act, then, the possibility that there are moral principles that explain why the Anselmian being treats creatures in particular ways does nothing to support answering that question in the affirmative.

2.4 Against *Being Loving* as an Anselmian Perfection: The Supreme Degree Formulation

I have argued so far against a number of ways of holding that the Anselmian being has a necessary love for rational and other sentient creatures that makes necessary that being's acting for the sake of those creatures in a way that goes beyond what moral goodness would require. I rejected as implausible what we might call 'reasons-prior' accounts of the Anselmian being's necessary love for creatures, that is, views on which the Anselmian being's loving rational and other sentient creatures in this morality-surpassing way is due either to the value of those creatures or to the value of those creatures in light of some privileged relationship between creator and creatures. I also rejected what we might call 'reasons-posterior' views, on which the Anselmian being's reason to act in these ways is explanatorily posterior to the Anselmian being's being perfectly loving, and what we might call 'no reasons' views, on which the Anselmian being necessarily acts in loving ways, while lacking reason to do so, on account of the Anselmian being's being perfectly loving.

In this section and section 2.5, I want to raise further difficulties for the 'reasons-posterior' and 'no reasons' views. My main target is the 'reasons-posterior' account, though the worries that I raise extend to the 'no reasons' view as well. One might be unimpressed by my particular worries about reasons-posterior accounts of divine love, holding that my scruples about the reason-giving force of orectic states like love are a thin basis for calling into question the notion that the Anselmian being acts in gratuitously loving ways toward creatures, and holding that perhaps one can *just see* that God's being creator of finite persons makes necessary God's having reasons to love them that go beyond what their bare, nonrelational value would require.[22] So it would be useful if I could raise an independent line of criticism against any such reasons-posterior view. I thus raise the following independent line of criticism: it is very implausible from the point of view of Anselmianism to hold that, on the reasons-posterior or no-reasons view of divine love, *being loving* is a divine perfection. It is easy to see how it would count as an aspect of a divine perfection on the reasons-prior view; it

[21] In Chapter 3 I deny that the Anselmian being is under such moral requirements.

[22] Recall, though, that there are two independent sources of worry about this position: one is about the reason-giving force of desires and desire-like states generally, the other about whether, even given the reason-giving force of such states, reasons of love could be plausibly so grounded.

would be an aspect of the Anselmian being's perfect rational agency, on which the Anselmian being is fittingly responsive to all reasons. But whether it could so count on the reasons-posterior or no-reasons view is another matter altogether.

Consider the property *being loving*. Surely that property is not, all by itself, an Anselmian perfection. For being loving comes in degrees, and when a property comes in degrees, it is not just exhibiting that property—that is, having it to some degree or other—that counts as an Anselmian perfection. Rather, the good-making property must be present to the intrinsic maximum of its value (1.4). Perhaps the intrinsic maximum is realized by exhibiting that property to the *fullest* degree—if that property is something like more-is-better—or perhaps by exhibiting it to the *appropriate* degree—if that property exhibits an optimal level, or something like that. I will call the former a 'supreme degree' way of realizing a great-making property, and the latter an 'optimal level' way of realizing a great-making property. (I stipulate that when a great-making property counts as a divine perfection by virtue of being realized at the optimal level, this is not due to its being realized in the supreme degree.) In either case, an alleged perfection that consists in the exhibiting of that property has the right sort of *intrinsic maximum*, a point beyond which one cannot more valuably realize that property, either because the property cannot be realized more fully, or if it can be realized more fully, its realization would not be more valuable.

It is a nonnegotiable feature of Anselmianism that Anselmian perfections have intrinsic maxima (1.4). If they do not, then for any putatively absolutely perfect being, it will always be true that that putatively absolutely perfect being is surpassable. So it is a decisive objection to any putative Anselmian perfection that it does not exhibit an intrinsic maximum.

So, does *being loving* have an intrinsic maximum of either sort—of the supreme degree or optimal level sort? Begin with the supreme degree formulation. On this way of conceiving it, being loving involves being motivated to act in the most loving way, or perhaps a most loving way. We need some way of characterizing that most loving way of being motivated. Taking a clue from the fact that love is typically characterized in terms of its aiming at the good of the beloved and unity with the beloved (Stump 2010, p. 91)—the lover wants both that the beloved be well-off, and that the lover and the beloved be together—we should characterize the intrinsic maximum of love in terms of aiming at these objectives with respect to the beloved. Supposing, then, the existence of some object, one might say that one loves that object to the fullest degree possible if one wills the most complete possible good of that object and wills the most complete possible unity with that object.

I begin by noting that this just seems a very implausible conception of what being absolutely perfect in love is like. If the objects of love are all those beings that have a good, then being maximally loving in this sense would require that, for every plant and animal, God must will its maximal good and God's maximal unity with that object. With every blade of grass, with every dung beetle, with every earthworm, with every honey badger, with every human, with every angel. This is *not* the view that for every such being God necessarily wills the good of and unity with that being in a way that is *fitting* given the relationship between God and creature; that view would be a version of the optimal level conception. Rather, it is the view that God must want the *maximum* good of and as *complete* unity as possible with every being that has a good and with which some sort of unity is possible. I submit that this does not look at all like the way we ordinarily think of a person being perfect in love: to be perfect in love is characteristically conceived in terms of appropriateness, so that one's love is appropriate to the relationship.[23] And it does not seem to me that matters are fundamentally different if we alter the class of objects that the perfection of love is supposed to concern: whether we include only sentient beings, or only rational beings. For not only is it unobvious why the perfection of love would concern only how one responds to sentient or even rational beings,[24] it also seems that our ordinary conception of being excellently loving involves appropriateness conditions, so that the extent to which one is motivated toward the good of another and seeks union with that other is fitting to the relationship between them.

So one worry is that taking the perfection of love in the supreme degree sense is at odds with our ordinary conception of what being excellently loving consists in. Suppose we put that worry to the side, and again take for granted for the moment some set of objects that are potential objects of love. Being maximally loving with respect to those objects would mean that, for each of those objects, one wills the most complete possible good of those objects and the most complete possible unity with those objects. But if there is no such thing as the most complete possible good of any of those objects—if, for one of those beings, for any good realized for it, it is possible for its good to be realized to a greater degree—then there will be no such thing as willing the most good for that being. And if there is no such thing as the most complete possible unity with any of those objects—if, for one of those beings, for any unity realized between the lover and it, it is possible for there to be greater unity—then there will be no such thing as willing the most unity for that being. In that case, love, understood in the supreme degree sense, will fail to have an intrinsic maximum. And nothing counts as a divine perfection that lacks an intrinsic maximum (1.4).

I do not have a decisive argument here, as much will depend on one's substantive views on the nature of well-being and the extent to which God and creatures can be unified. The following strikes me as a persuasive view, though, based on a survey of the

[23] This is beautifully discussed in Pruss 2012a (pp. 44–6) where he argues that while everyone is bound to love everyone, the form of the required love varies with the relationship. Pruss's view thus has no need of the idea that there is such a thing as an intrinsic maximum of love (though some remarks of Pruss's suggest that he does think that there is such an intrinsic maximum). See also Stump's discussion of these "offices of love" (2010, p. 98).

[24] Note that one cannot say that there is simply something about rational creatures that makes them *due* such love. That would return us to something more like an account of moral goodness. So long as there is a being that has a good, and unity in some nontrivial sense is possible with that being, it is unclear why it is not the sort of being that is a relevant object of love for a being who is perfectly loving in the supreme degree sense.

accounts of human well-being taken seriously by philosophers who work on the nature of that sort of value. It seems that on any plausible conception of well-being—hedonistic, desire-fulfillment, objective list (Parfit 1984, pp. 493–502 and Murphy 2001, pp. 46–100)—the extent to which one is well-off does not have an intrinsic maximum. The balance of pleasure over pain, having desires fulfilled, the realization of objective goods like knowledge, aesthetic experience, friendship, and so forth—all of these seem to me to be indefinitely increasable, and in ways that improve the subject's well-being overall. And while I cannot say much about what unity with God consists in for created rational beings like us, the following also seems like a plausible conjecture: given the infinite ontological gap between God and creatures, it is hard to believe that there is some degree of unity with God attainable by a creature such that there is no increase in the unity with God that God can make possible for that creature: one can be made closer to God in some respect while being made more distant from God in none, and so greater unity with God will always be possible. So it seems to me that when one attempts to characterize being loving in the supreme degree way with respect to some set of creatures—say, the actual ones—there is no such thing as God's having a maximal love toward those creatures.[25]

So the first worry is that *being loving* in the supreme degree sense is not how we ordinarily think of the perfection of love, and the second worry is that *being loving* in this sense does not admit of an intrinsic maximum. Note that, as stated, these worries *assume* some set of creatures. And one might suggest that the perfection *being loving* is going to be realized only with respect to some actually existing beings. But note that this is a counterintuitive idea, on standard theism. After all, if the idea is that the Anselmian being created *out of love*, and there were no beings other than the Anselmian being yet, the Anselmian being was not responding out of love *for them*; the love was anticipatory, creating because by creating that being would bring into existence creatures of whom it would be true that they benefited by being created and sustained by divine action. Nor could we, on this view alone, appeal to the perfection of love to explain why the Anselmian being created some particular sort of creatures rather than others. (And it is not as if we think this way only in the divine case. We think of love as partially explaining why some people who are in a position to have large families have large families, why they have children rather than tend to already-existing huge numbers of goldfish, etc.)

But if this is true, then there are surely even graver reasons to deny that being loving has a maximal level. For there could always be more beings that could be created by the Anselmian being; and the Anselmian being's anticipatory love could motivate that being to bring those creatures into existence. So whatever disposition the Anselmian

[25] Might God have a maximal love but that maximal love not be manifested in anything like maximal motivation to the good of and unity with creatures? One possibility, considered and rejected below, is that this maximal motivation is self-effacing. But one might refrain from offering any particular theory of why maximal love need not result in maximal loving motivation. This possibility I also consider and reject below at the end of this section.

being has to bring good to creatures, to confer existence to them that will be a benefit, it could always be greater. So, again, we should deny that being loving has a fullest degree that could be realized.

Now, one might make the following general objection. This argument looks very much like arguments that hold that, since there is no best possible world, then an omniscient, omnipotent being's creative act can always be surpassed, and so there cannot be a greatest possible being (Rowe 1993, Wielenberg 2004). My view is that such arguments are failures (Murphy 2013). So why doesn't my argument concerning the lack of an intrinsic maximum of lovingness here fail, and in just the way that the no-best-world argument fails? My response is that there is a crucial difference between *being rational* and *being loving*; there are features of rationality that undermine the force of the argument from no-best-world, but these features are not shared by love.

To see these differences takes some showing. One first has to look in some detail at the structure of the no-best-world argument and why it fails. Say that the Anselmian being 'actualizes a world' when some maximal state of affairs obtains as a result of that being's choosing to create or choosing to refrain from creating. (Whether the Anselmian being actualizes a world is, on this definition, not an open question; it actualizes some world, and the only questions are whether they will include items other than itself and if so, which ones.) Suppose that there is an infinite number of possible worlds each of which is within the Anselmian being's power to actualize. For each of these worlds, there is another that is better from a moral perspective, i.e. for each world, one who takes the moral point of view will prefer some other world's being actual to its being actual. Since a possible world is a maximal state of affairs, the Anselmian being cannot actualize more than one of these. So whichever world the Anselmian being actualizes, it will be true that it could have actualized a morally better one. One might think that it is clear that an action of actualizing a world that is better from a moral point of view is morally better than an action of actualizing a world that is worse from a moral point of view. It follows that in a 'no-best-world' scenario, there is no agency that the Anselmian being could exhibit that is unsurpassable. Since the Anselmian being is perfectly good only if its agency is unsurpassable, necessarily, the Anselmian being is not perfectly good.

The argument, then, is this:

(1) Necessarily, the Anselmian being actualizes some world
(2) Necessarily, for each actualizable world W_1, there is an actualizable world W_2 such that from the moral point of view W_2 is preferable to W_1
(3) Necessarily, for whatever world that the Anselmian being actualizes, there is a morally better world that the Anselmian being does not actualize yet could have (from (2))
(4) Necessarily, for whatever world that the Anselmian being actualizes, its act of actualizing that world is not as morally good as some other act that it does not perform but could have (from (3))

(5) Necessarily, for whatever world that the Anselmian being actualizes, its agency is not as morally good as it could have been (from (4))
(6) Necessarily, the Anselmian being's agency is not perfectly good (from (1), (5))

In my view, the main sticking point in this argument[26] is the move from (3) to (4). It does not follow from the fact that any *world* actualized by God is morally surpassable that any *act of actualizing a world* is morally surpassable. It is easy to be tempted by the following line of thought. If we think of an action as a state of affairs to be evaluated in terms of moral goodness in the same way that any other state of affairs is to be evaluated, then there is a pretty straightforward argument for the view that any act of actualizing a world will be surpassable. For if one prefers from a moral point of view the obtaining of possible world W_2 to the obtaining of possible world W_1, then it seems very plausible that one would, from the moral point of view, prefer the Anselmian being's actualizing W_2 to the Anselmian being's actualizing W_1.

This line of thought requires the assumption that the standard of moral goodness that applies to actions, in virtue of which a being's agency counts as morally good, is the same as the standard that applies to states of affairs generally. But this is not true. While the standard of moral goodness applying to states of affairs is third-personal in character—one considers various items, and asks what one would prefer from a particular perspective, the moral point of view—the standard of moral goodness applying to actions is first-personal in character, more closely tied to quality of the agent's deliberation in deciding what to do. We can put things in a slightly different way. We can consider an agent's action as simply an event in the world, and evaluate whether we prefer the agent's having performed it to the agent's having performed some other action. Or we can consider an agent's action as the outcome of deliberation, as a decision of what the agent is to do as a result of considering the various *reasons* in play. Even though, considered as an event, the Anselmian being's actualizing a world is necessarily surpassable, considered as an action, as a choice to carry out a plan, the Anselmian being's actualizing that world is unsurpassable.

If we think that the evaluation of worlds is distinct from the evaluation of actions, then there is room to resist the move from (3) to (4). One might object that this resistance is bound to come to nothing. A world is a maximal state of affairs; everything that is morally relevant, and thus can give an Anselmian being reason to choose to actualize one world over another, is included in its value. So it of course follows that, from the deliberative perspective, the Anselmian being must have more reason to realize a world with more value, and given the no-best-world scenario, it will follow that the Anselmian being never does what it has most reason to do, and thus the Anselmian being's action is never supremely morally good. But again, there is plenty of room for resistance. It does not follow from the fact that all of the value to be realized in the Anselmian being's acting is included in the world actualized that these are the only

[26] Taking for granted, that is, the understanding of the Anselmian being as required to act by the goods and evils in the various worlds that that being might create. I call this view into question in Chapter 3.

reasons that bear on the Anselmian being's choice. For there may be, in addition to these first-order reasons, second-order reasons (Raz 1999 [1975], p. 39). A second-order reason is a reason to act for, or not to act for, a reason; and that there are such reasons makes a difference in assessing actions in terms of their moral worth.

Engage in a bit of picture-thinking. Suppose we imagine the Anselmian being trying to choose which world to actualize in a no-best-world scenario. We imagine the Anselmian being trying to do so on the basis of first-order reasons of the value of various worlds that might be actualized. But the Anselmian being of course would know that this would be to no avail. That being cannot treat the fact that one world realizes more value than another world as a difference-making consideration, for if it were, that would render it unable to make any choice. The fact that relying on some consideration would undermine the possibility of reaching a decision is itself a consideration relevant to deliberation; if one has good reason to reach a decision, and relying on some consideration precludes one from reaching a decision, that very fact constitutes a reason relevant to one's deliberation. It is a second-order reason, a reason of the sort that Joseph Raz calls an "exclusionary" reason, a reason that directs one not to treat a first-order reason as relevant in one's deliberation (Raz 1999 [1975], p. 39).

If this account is right, then the reasons relevant to the Anselmian being's decision about which world to actualize are not exhausted by the first-order reasons constituted by the value of the worlds actualized; these reasons also include second-order reasons, reasons that direct the Anselmian being not to make the choice by comparing worlds' first-order value. The Anselmian being's decision to actualize a world might then be morally unsurpassable, in that it correctly responds to the reasons relevant to the choice in precisely the way that those reasons call for, even if the world that is thereby created is surpassable (Howard-Snyder and Howard-Snyder 1994, Langtry 2008, pp. 74–8). How does the Anselmian being decide which world, then, to actualize? By freely ruling out some set of worlds, say, on the basis of some nonarbitrary reason that would not rule out actualizing any world; if not, or such decision-making does not take the Anselmian being to a single world, then the Anselman being might just *pick*, in Ullman-Margalit and Morgenbesser's sense (Ullman-Margalit and Morgenbesser 1977).

The key bit of this response to the no-best-world argument is that the fact that relying on first-order reasons to reach a decision is doomed to lead to inaction explains the existence of second-order reasons, reasons that direct one to disregard some of those first-order reasons in deciding what to do. Practical reasoning can be, in a way, self-effacing: the force of some set of reasons can, together with the circumstances of action in which one finds oneself, direct one to disregard some of those very reasons in deliberation, in fixing what one is to do. In disregarding those reasons, one counts as in no way less rational, for it is reason itself that directs one to disregard those reasons.

Now suppose that one were to attempt to make the same sort of rejoinder to the argument that *being loving* in the supreme degree sense is not a divine perfection because it lacks an intrinsic maximum. The argument, recall, is this: For whatever loving response the Anselmian being has to creation, there is a more loving response that it could have had instead. Thus, the Anselmian being is never as loving as that being could be. If, with respect to being loving, more is better, then it follows that there is no such thing as a supremely loving being; the Anselmian being thus could not have *being loving* among its perfections, for no matter what level of love it exhibited, it would be a surpassable level.

Suppose, then, that one offers a rejoinder to this argument analogous to that which was offered to the no-best-world argument. Engage, the objector might suggest, in a bit of picture-thinking. Suppose we imagine the Anselmian being trying to select the most loving agency that it could exhibit. We imagine the Anselmian being trying to do so on the basis of first-order considerations concerning how loving these various forms of agency are. But the Anselmian being of course would know that this would be to no avail. That being cannot treat the fact that one sort of agency is more loving than another as a difference-making consideration, for if it were, that would render it unable to settle on some form of agency. The fact that relying on some consideration would undermine the possibility of selecting some agency-package is itself a consideration relevant to being loving; if being loving requires one to select some agency-package, and relying on considerations of love to do so precludes one from selecting some agency-package, that very fact constitutes a reason relevant to one's selection.

But this response fails, and so fails to call into question my argument that there is no intrinsic maximum of love and thus it cannot be a divine perfection. For what the response shows is that one who has good reasons, based on love, to select on the basis of considerations other than love does not do anything contrary to reason. *It does not show that the response thereby selected is not surpassable from the point of view of love.* It is crucial that the objection to the no-best-world argument is carried out entirely in the coin of *reasons*. This objection to the no-intrinsic-maximum argument similarly uses the coin of reasons, but this undermines that objection. Because it appeals to reasons not to realize ever greater good for the beloved or unite oneself ever closer to the beloved, the most that it can show is that a rational lover might rationally do something less than supremely loving; it does not show that by acting rationally out of love, what one does will inevitably turn out to be supremely loving.

The fact that reason tells you to disregard a reason can make you rational in disregarding it. The fact that a reason of love tells you to disregard a reason of love can make you rational in disregarding it, but it does not make you loving in so disregarding it. In both cases, your agency may be impeccable, but it does not follow that your agency is as loving as it can possibly be, even in the latter case.

A final worry. One might respond to these sorts of worries by claiming that I have too closely identified God's being perfect in love with God's being motivated in certain ways. If God might have a maximal love, without that maximal love's being manifested in anything like motivation toward the maximal good of and unity with creatures, then we could protect the compatibility of the affirmation of God's being perfectly loving in the supreme degree sense with the denial of there being an intrinsic maximum of the motivation toward the good of, and unity with, creatures. One possibility, just considered and rejected, is that this maximal motivation is self-effacing. But one might simply rest on the abstract formulation of the objection, without offering a particular account of why the presence of a supreme degree of love in the Anselmian being might not be manifested in a supreme degree of loving motivation.

I am not sure how to think about this proposal. Every divine perfection must have an intrinsic maximum; what, then, is *this* sort of divine love, and what constitutes *its* intrinsic maximum? It would be easy to state what it is by relating it to a set of dispositions, that is, dispositions to be motivated in certain ways. But this leads back to the problem. So, a first challenge: anyone who wishes to make such an appeal must be able to say what this allegedly more basic love is, and how we are to understand its intrinsic maximum. But there is a second challenge, as well. If we manage to satisfy the first challenge and characterize divine love in a way that does not render it susceptible to this sort of objection from no intrinsic maximum, we must go on to explain why it is that, nevertheless, a being who is loving in that sense necessarily is motivated in some ways that go beyond those ways that it is motivated in virtue of being perfectly morally good. Since the whole point of this alternative view is to emphasize the gap between divine love and the motivations that issue from it, it seems that this challenge cannot be met.

2.5 Against *Being Loving* as an Anselmian Perfection: The Optimal Level Formulation

These arguments against the supreme degree formulation of *being loving* as a divine perfection may lead one simply to acknowledge that this is a misguided way to characterize that perfection. We should not think of the perfection of being loving by thinking of paradigmatically loving acts or dispositions and then turning up the volume to the maximum, for thus conceived, there is no maximum lovingness, and so *being loving* would not be a divine perfection. Perhaps the better way to think of it is in terms of *optimality*—that there is an optimal level of love that God exhibits, for God loves the right objects in the right way and to the right degree.

There may be, I allow, something like a lower bound of being loving that any agent must exhibit who is not defective in some way. It is this: in whatever way that lovable beings' value gives reasons to love them, a nondefective agent must respond to those reasons by loving each of those lovable beings in that way. But thus understood, there is no motivational distance between the perfection of moral goodness, understood richly as full rational responsiveness to the relevant value (2.2), and the perfection of love.

Of course, that is only one optimal level view. Perhaps there is a higher level of responsiveness that is appropriate such that one who fails to have that response, even if possibly otherwise rational, nevertheless counts as not appropriately loving. I am doubtful that there is any. It would have to require enough of the absolutely perfect being to ensure that that being is necessarily motivated by the considerations of created persons' well-being, and in the right way. But since this is an optimality-not-supreme-degree view, the idea is not that the absolutely perfect being realizes the *most* possible love. I am not sure what could set the features of optimal love that goes beyond the reasons given by the objects of love yet that falls short of fullness or completeness.

Another way to see this point is to consider the idea of "offices of love," as employed under this description by Stump (2010) and in effect by Pruss (2012a). An office of love is a "particular kind of relationship between persons that shapes the sort of sharing and closeness suitable in that relationship and thus circumscribes the kind of union appropriate to desire in love" (Stump 2010, pp. 97–8); we can add that it also shapes the sort of benevolence that is appropriate. The sense of what is "appropriate" here concerns not only what is permitted, but also what is fitting or even required in virtue of the relationship. Now, this is one way to spell out an optimal level account of an intrinsic maximum of lovingness: it is to say that in whatever offices of love one finds oneself, one loves in a way that completely satisfies the conditions of that office. Thus, we need not have some abstract notion of being maximally loving to the supreme degree; we can just ask whether the more finely characterized offices of love are fulfilled.

But in order to employ this strategy here, we would need an account of what are the offices of love in which the Anselmian being necessarily stands with respect to us. As we noted above (2.3), the only relationship that the Anselmian being necessarily stands in with respect to creatures is *being the creator of*, and we have no sense how this would fix an office of love with respect to the Anselmian being's love for us, at least not in any sense that goes beyond what the norms of morality require. So I cannot see how an appeal to an optimal level account of the intrinsic maximum of the Anselmian being's being loving can satisfy the desiderata set out at the beginning of this chapter: that it both necessarily holds of the Anselmian being and motivates the Anselmian being in a way that goes beyond what the moral goodness of the Anselmian being would entail.

2.6 Is Love as Divine Perfection Divinely Revealed?

I have denied that the Anselmian being is loving in any sense that goes beyond the love entailed by that being's moral goodness. In the face of this view, it would be natural for theists of certain sorts to offer the following objection. "I believe that God is an absolutely perfect being," these objectors might begin, "but I do not believe that we discover which features are perfections through philosophical reflection and argument alone. We find these revealed in Scripture, and perhaps sacred tradition, as well. And what Scripture and sacred tradition reveal is that God is love (1 John 4:8). It's plain as day. And as there is nothing in God that is not perfection, we must hold that God's being loving is part of divine perfection, and thus that the Anselmian being is necessarily loving."

Put to the side here the possibility that the sense in which God is love is not distinguishable from the sense in which God is perfectly morally good.[27] The first point is that, as noted above (1.1), the fact that God actually exhibits some feature does not show that the Anselmian being has it, only that the Anselmian being possibly has it. That some triangle is isosceles does not show to be true *the triangle is isosceles*, though it does entail *the triangle is possibly isosceles*. Ditto with God and the Anselmian being. That there is an actual being who qualifies as the Anselmian being and is in some way loving does not show that the Anselmian being is loving in that way; it shows only that the Anselmian being is possibly loving in that way. And that is a thesis I of course accept.

Now it might of course be retorted that this revelation of divine love does not say merely that God is in fact loving; it presents God's being loving as a central, salient feature of God (Pruss 2012a, p. 3). The thrust of the objection, then, is that what is treated as a central, salient feature of God must belong to the divine essence, which is perfection. But even apart from the fact that I am dubious that what Scripture is giving here is a metaphysics lesson, I deny the view that what is treated in Scripture and sacred tradition as a central, salient feature of God must belong to the divine essence. A comparison: what is more central to Scripture than the idea of God as the *creator*—the ultimate source of everything else? But in the very same tradition in which God's status as creator is treated as absolutely central, it is also affirmed that God did not have to create, that God creates only contingently. From our point of view as creatures, God's being creator looms large (!), though it is not necessary that God creates. Similarly, from our point of view as creatures beloved of God, God's being loving may similarly loom large, even if it is not necessary that God is loving. It thus seems implausible to me to hold that just because some feature is prominently displayed in Scripture as a central, salient feature of God, that feature must be a necessary feature of God and hence a divine perfection.[28]

[27] As I will argue in Chapter 3, the Anselmian being is not morally good. So it would not do for me simply to rest on the qualification of this chapter, that God's love does not go beyond any sense in which God is morally good.

[28] It is important to note that a reading of the identification of God with love that has been central to Christian thought is just that God is a Trinity of persons, necessarily mutually loving (see Geach 1977, p. 124). This mutual love *is* maximal, in that these Persons are fully lovable and their good complete, so that their love must consist in appreciating and endorsing each other's complete goodness. But this does not, without further premises, entail anything about the Trinity's relation of love to creatures.

3

Is the Anselmian Being Morally Good?

3.1 Love and Moral Goodness, Again

In Chapter 2, I argued that the only senses in which *being loving* can be ascribed to the Anselmian being are those entailed by the Anselmian being's being morally good. For all that I have said so far, perhaps the Anselmian being is indeed perfectly morally good, and that being's exhibiting perfect moral goodness entails that that being is extraordinarily loving; perhaps not. That is of no matter to the thesis that I was trying to establish. What I was trying to establish is that, insofar as the Anselmian being is loving, its being loving is captured by its moral goodness, and its moral goodness explains its being loving. The Anselmian being stands in some loving relation to creatures insofar as the value of those creatures gives the Anselmian being reasons to stand in that relation; and since moral goodness just is responding to this sort of value in the way that such value gives reasons to respond to it, it follows that it is the moral goodness of the Anselmian being that accounts for whatever love the Anselmian being has for creatures.

This tight connection between divine love and divine moral goodness has a positive and a negative side for the defender of the view that the Anselmian being is loving. The defender of that view can appeal to the consensus notion that the Anselmian being is perfectly morally good, along with the consensus understanding of the relevant moral goodness as the familiar welfare-oriented sort. This appeal would yield the result that the Anselmian being's love extends very strongly to the promotion of the well-being of all rational, and even all sentient, creatures, and perhaps also to the bringing into existence of such beings as well, at least when their lives will be good for them. But it also has a downside. Everything turns on the Anselmian being's being perfectly morally good. Any doubts about the Anselmian being's being morally good can be taken up as objections to the Anselmian being's being loving.

There are grounds to doubt that the Anselmian being is morally good, taking as given that to be morally good is to be understood in the familiar welfare-oriented sense and that moral goodness, at least in the divine case, is characterized by the strong rationalist constraint that some action's being morally necessary for the Anselmian being entails that action's being rationally necessary for that being (2.2). The basis for this doubt is that it is unclear whether the well-being of rational and other sentient beings must give the Anselmian being reasons for action at all, and if so, whether they are reasons to perform the relevant type of actions, and if so, whether they are reasons of the right sort. Even if human moral goodness is goodness of the strongly rationalist, familiar welfare-oriented sort, it is unclear whether the Anselmian being is morally good at all, or whether its moral goodness is of the familiar welfare-oriented sort. But, given the argument of the previous chapters, the only hope for God's being necessarily loving is that the relevant values give the Anselmian being the right sorts of reasons for action. If the denial that the relevant values give the Anselmian being the right sorts of reasons for action is a basis for the denial that the Anselmian being is morally good, it is also to that extent a basis for the denial that the Anselmian being is loving.

3.2 Some Kantian-Style Objections

I begin with two objections to the proposal that the Anselmian being is not subject to norms of familiar welfare-oriented moral goodness.

First, one might wonder whether the notion that the Anselmian being is not subject to the norms of familiar welfare-oriented moral goodness is even a coherent position, at least given the assumption—which I do accept—that we human beings are subject, even necessarily subject, to those norms. One might say that for a norm to be a *moral* norm, it must be *universal*. For a norm to be universal is for it to apply to *every rational being*, or perhaps every rational being capable of acting on it. If, then, I concede that we human beings are subject to norms that direct us to promote creaturely well-being, and I allow that these norms are moral norms, then I am committed in virtue of the universality of the moral to holding that the Anselmian being is subject to these norms as well. And if we take morality to be essentially decisively reason-giving, as I argued in 2.2 that it is, then the Anselmian being has decisive reasons to act in accordance with those norms. Given the Anselmian being's perfect rationality, it will then follow that, necessarily, the Anselmian being acts in accordance with the norms of familiar welfare-oriented moral goodness.

My response here is to deny the thesis that universality, thus construed, is a conceptual requirement on the moral. This thesis is a controversial Kantian commitment on how we are to understand the jurisdiction of moral norms, not a thin, relatively neutral constraint on theorizing about the moral. I concede that the moral requires *some sort* of universality—perhaps all human beings, perhaps all embodied rational creatures, perhaps all rational creatures. But it is unclear why the moral requires the maximally strong conception of universality that Kant ascribes to it. In the absence of good reason to think that the moral must be thus construed, we should not move without further substantive argument from the claim that we are subject to some moral norms to the view that the Anselmian being is subject to those norms as well.[1]

[1] If one is committed to the view that the concept of the moral simply *must* involve this commitment to extraordinarily strong universality—a strange commitment, since nothing in our ordinary practical

One might try to reframe this argument in terms of conceptual constraints on *being a reason* rather than in terms of conceptual constraints on *being a moral norm*. This is the basis for a second Kantian, or at least quasi-Kantian,[2] objection. Suppose that one accepts that all *humans* have the reasons presupposed by familiar welfare-oriented moral goodness. But reasons bind rational agents generally. It is of course possible for there to be reasons that bind some proper subset of rational beings, one might concede, but only in virtue of reasons that all rational beings share. So while it may be true that I have a reason to teach students at Georgetown that you do not have, I have this reason in virtue of a reason that we both share (a reason to keep one's agreements) plus a circumstance that I am in that you are not (I have agreed to teach Georgetown students, while you haven't).[3]

If, then, we humans have reasons to act in accordance with welfare-oriented moral goodness, either (a) the Anselmian being similarly has such reasons or (b) we have those reasons due to some reason that we and the Anselmian being share, yet some circumstance gives us humans reasons to act in accordance with welfare-oriented moral goodness yet does not give the Anselmian being those reasons. If (a), then the Anselmian being does have the reasons that familiar welfare-oriented moral goodness presupposes. If (b), then to avoid the conclusion that the Anselmian being has those reasons, we need to account for the difference. (This difference cannot be explained in terms of the reasons that the Anselmian being has for not acting on those reasons, as the rider concerning reasons to the contrary is already included in the formulation of what familiar welfare-oriented moral goodness requires; see 2.2.) Given how normatively basic the reason to look after others' well-being seems to many to be,[4] one might find this an unpromising possibility. So one might think that this conception of reasons and reasons explanation, along with the truth that humans have the reasons presupposed by familiar welfare-oriented moral goodness, yields the result that the Anselmian being must have these reasons as well.

thought seems to require such strong universality to make sense of it—I am happy to have my arguments to come treated as an error theory, that there could not be any such thing as moral norms, for moral norms must be reason-giving and there are no norms sufficiently substantive to be moral norms that are reason-giving universally, in that strong sense of 'universally.' (We may also note here that major accounts of moral norms—Hobbesian, Humean, Aristotelian—would so obviously fail to satisfy this universality constraint construed strongly that they could be refuted as accounts of the moral just by noting their failure to characterize rational constraints on some possible type of rational being. More on these views below in 3.3.)

[2] I say at least quasi-Kantian because it is unclear whether this way of thinking really fits with the spirit of Kant's thoughts about reasons. Some recent commentators on Kant's practical philosophy (for example, Hill 1973 and Hampton 1998, pp. 125–66) have argued that the reasons that do not seem to be shared, on Kant's view—those arising from contingent desires, and which provide the content for hypothetical imperatives—must arise from a shared reason that agents have, a reason to take the effective means to one's ends. But this is a controversial position. For an argument that this is not the most defensible view either philosophically or as an interpretation of Kant's account of practical reason, see Schroeder 2005.

[3] Schroeder calls this way of thinking about reasons and their explanation the "Standard Model"; see his 2007a, p. 43.

[4] The basicality of welfare reasons is not, of course, a standard Kantian position. But I think that this way of thinking about reasons has some purchase far outside the Kantian fold.

I reject this conception of reasons and the ideal of explanation with respect to them that comes along with it. The notion that all differences between agents' reasons must be rooted in some common reasons that they all have is a substantive, very controversial position, not a truism about reasons and rationality. Here, in brief, is why I reject it. The view treats as privileged the fact that some reasons are shared by all agents; only such reasons are appropriate starting points for explanations of non-shared reasons. But when a reason is shared by all rational beings, that itself calls for explanation—why is it that some consideration gives a reason to all rational beings? In order to carry out this explanatory task, one would have to say what it is about that consideration, and what it is about the nature of reasons and rational beings, such that all rational agents have this consideration as a reason to act. But once one sees that this is the explanatory task that one has to carry out with respect even to putatively universally shared reasons, it is unclear why one could not go directly to that sort of explanation for reasons that are *not* shared by all rational beings. (This is, abstractly, the strategy that Schroeder uses in his 2007a.) One could, that is, appeal directly to clarification of the consideration at stake, the elucidation of what reasons are, and the nature of the rational beings who have that reason to explain the non-shared reasons, without having to subsume them under a reason had by all rational beings. And it is not as if the explanation of reasons that proceeds in this direct way is just an abstract possibility; there are accounts of reasons that do not share this Kantian presupposition—Humean[5] and Aristotelian[6] views, for example.

I concede that if one is wedded to this Kantian-style thought about reasons—that any reasons that are not shared by all rational beings exist in virtue of reasons that are shared by all rational beings—one may be left cold by what follows in this chapter. But it would be very strange if one controversial and only lightly defended view of the nature of reasons were taken for granted in the discussion of the Anselmian being's ethics. And once we allow other ways of thinking about reasons and their explanation, there is room to raise considerations that make clear why one might doubt that the Anselmian being exhibits familiar welfare-oriented moral goodness.

3.3 Logical Gaps between Well-Being and Reasons

Why might one doubt that the well-being of humans and other sentient beings must give reasons to all rational agents, including the Anselmian being, to prevent setbacks to it? The first thing to note is that there are logical gaps between facts about what is fundamentally good or bad for someone and facts about what there is reason to do. It is bad for me to be burned; that it is bad for me to be burned does not logically entail,

[5] For example, Schroeder 2007a; I discuss this sort of view in more detail in 3.3.

[6] For example, MacIntyre 1999, Foot 2001, Thompson 2004a, and Thompson 2007; I discuss this sort of view in more detail in 3.3.

though, that everyone has a reason to prevent my being burned.[7] So, if we consider propositions of the following sorts,

(1) X is fundamentally good (bad) for A
(2) X is a reason for anyone to promote (prevent) X,

it is clear that there is a gap between (1) and (2). I am not claiming, yet, that it is not metaphysically necessary that should a proposition of the form (1) hold true, then corresponding propositions of the form (2) hold true. I am noting only that these are not analytic truths, and if these are metaphysically necessary without being analytic truths, then some explanation of that necessity should be available.

But here is an important point. Philosophers have acknowledged the need to provide explanations here, and have tried to provide them. But these explanations have typically proceeded on the basis of considerations that are *specific to human beings*—to explaining why some *human being's* potentially being made worse off gives *other human beings* reasons to do something about it. Hobbesian theories, Humean theories, Aristotelian theories, and even Kantian theories[8] exhibit these features, and so are clearly unhelpful in showing that we and the Anselmian being are under a common morality. Indeed, the truth of any of these theories of the source of moral norms should incline one to deny that we and the Anselmian being are under such a morality. I consider these in turn.

Hobbesianisms, classical and contemporary. Hobbesian theories of moral norms are built on subjectivist theories of the good, instrumentalist accounts of rational action, and the fact of the mutual vulnerability of the agents bound by these norms. Even granting the instrumentalism about reason, the correctness of such a view should lead us to deny that we and the Anselmian being are under a common morality. Hobbes himself built his view on the presence of a common desire, the desire to avoid one's own violent death (Murphy 2000), and of course such an account would be inapplicable to an Anselmian being. Contemporary Hobbesians, like Gauthier, tend to want to avoid such a substantive psychological assumption, but must nevertheless build some substantial assumptions about the relevant agents' desires (e.g. non-tuism) into the theory to get it to yield determinate results (Gauthier 1986, p. 87). But we do not have at hand anything that would enable us to predict the desires of an Anselmian being,

[7] "Hold on," one might say. "Suppose that one defends a buck-passing conception of value, with the result that *being good for someone*—being a variety of value—is to be analyzed in terms of giving reasons. Doesn't it follow that there is no such gap?" First, it does not follow, for the reasons in terms of which well-being is to be characterized might not be reasons to promote it. Second, even if well-being is analyzed in terms of reasons, it may not be analyzed in terms of reasons that are reasons for all, rather than reasons for some subset of rational beings—say, the agent him- or herself, or some agents specially related to the welfare subject. And third, it seems to me that buck-passing accounts are at their least plausible when dealing with well-being as a form of value. I think that the concept of well-being applies univocally to humans and other animals, and it seems very implausible that the well-being of other animals is well-captured by reasons to respond to the features that constitute that well-being. (See also Kraut 2007, p. 74.)

[8] That is: all of the *plausible* versions of Kantianism, those that do not take the moral norms in question to be explained purely formally but in terms of some appeal to the value of rational agents.

especially if a conception of desire on which no desires are rationally required is assumed.[9] And of course the background of mutual vulnerability is totally inappropriate in the context of the Anselmian being. If Hobbesianism were the truth about the source of moral norms, then we would have reason strongly to doubt that we and the Anselmian being are under a common morality.

Humeanisms, classical and contemporary. The classical Humean—that is, Hume's—account of the source of moral norms holds that it is in virtue of our possession of a common sentiment—"sympathy" or "humanity"[10]—that we are under a common set of moral norms. Because we humans are built so as to care about our fellow human beings quite generally, we endorse a variety of norms that forbid the causing of harm to our fellows, as well as a variety of norms the general honoring of which has good results for our fellow human beings. Needless to say, even if it were true that our common human nature involves an emotional responsiveness of the sort that Hume describes, that would of itself be no use for thinking that the Anselmian being is subject to the norms to which we are subject. For no classical Humean could claim that it is a necessary feature of rational beings that they have passions of that sort. 'Tis as little contrary to reason, to lack sympathy, as to have it. And without a showing that the Anselmian being exhibits this rationally optional set of passions, the classical Humean view would give no reason to suppose that we and the Anselmian being are under a common set of moral norms.

Like the contemporary Hobbesian who tries to give an account of moral norms that does not rely on the positing of a universal, overriding fear of violent death, a contemporary Humean might try to get by without trying to explain the common set of moral norms in terms of the content of a contingent passion. Mark Schroeder, for example, argues for a Humeanism that is conservative about morality by endorsing a very permissive view of the reasons that an agent has along with a very restrictive account of how those reasons are properly accorded weight in deliberation. His basic idea is that it is very easy to show that one has *a* reason to act in accordance with moral norms, standardly conceived: if there is *any* desire one has such that one's acting in accordance with some moral norm helps to satisfy it, no matter how trivially, then one has a reason to act in accordance with that moral norm.[11] We expect such reasons to be weighty in the moral case, and Schroeder carves out space for this by making the weight of reasons not a direct function simply of how strong one's desire is and how much the action

[9] Perhaps God has some fixed desires that are not rationally required—say, desires characteristic of love? I argued that we cannot ascribe such to God in 2.3.

[10] It is an open question, disputed among Hume interpreters, whether these are different labels for one emotional propensity. No matter for my purposes: what matters is that each is the label for a substantively described emotional propensity that is contingent for rational beings and explains why we humans are under norms of morality.

[11] This follows from Schroeder's account of what it is to be a reason ("For *R* to be a reason for *X* to do *A* is for there to be some *p* such that *X* has a desire whose object is *p*, and the truth of *R* is part of what explains why *X*'s doing *A* promotes *p*"; see Schroeder 2007a, p. 59) and his account of *promoting* as increasing the likelihood of some outcome, relative to a baseline of doing nothing (Schroeder 2007a, p. 113).

serves that desire, but rather a function of whether the reasons of the sort relevant to deliberation direct one to place weight on those reasons in deliberation. But the reasons of the sort relevant to deliberation, reasons of the right kind, are, on Schroeder's view, all of the agent-neutral reasons.[12] So one might think that Schroeder's Humeanism, by appealing to a formal account of the nature of reasons and weighting rather than a substantive account of the content of a human passion, makes room for us and the Anselmian being to be under a common set of moral norms.

But I think Schroeder's account does not help to explain why we and the Anselmian being would be bound by a common set of moral norms. There are worries to raise here both about the notion that the Anselmian being has any reasons at all to act in ways required by familiar welfare-oriented moral goodness and about the notion that, given those reasons, these reasons would be particularly weighty.

The first thing to note is the programmatic character of Schroeder's defense of the view that all agents have reasons to act in accordance with familiar moral norms in virtue of the fact that acting on those norms promotes the satisfaction of any arbitrary desire. Schroeder offers an analogy to belief: he argues that for any proposition p, one has a reason to believe p if and only if p is true, and this reason can be explained by any desire whatsoever: whatever desire one has, it increases the likelihood of satisfying that desire if one has a true belief rather than a false one. (This surely can't be true of any arbitrary belief/desire pair. But it may be true for the vast run of them.) That one's beliefs form a web makes plausible the notion that even a proposition the truth of which seems distant from a given desire's satisfaction is relevant to the promotion of that desire's satisfaction (Schroeder 2007a, pp. 113–15).

The analogy to the familiar norms of morality and the reasons to promote them is very weak, though, and it is made much weaker by the fact that the agent with which we are concerned here is the Anselmian being. The 'web of actions' that would be the analog to the web of beliefs on which Schroeder relies is woven together not, as the web of belief is, by logical and evidential relations, but primarily by causal relations: acting in certain ways has predictable effects, given the causal structure of the world. That the connections are causal rather than logical/evidential is enough to make it less plausible that simply being an agent will be enough to make it the case that one has reasons to act in accordance with familiar welfare-governed morality. Even if successful, though, such an account of the ubiquity of such reasons would presuppose the circumstances of human life, that the normal causal connections hold between performance of the relevant actions and the bringing about of some, any, object of desire. But we do not have a basis to think that it must be true that the *Anselmian being's* failing to act in accordance with such norms *in any way* lowers the probability of its realizing the objects of any of its desires. This would be so only if the Anselmian being were limited

[12] By "agent-neutral reason" Schroeder means simply the reasons that are shared by all (where 'all' is fixed by context). He thus means something different by "agent-neutral" than, say, Nagel (1970) means by it. On Schroeder's terminology, the reason that everyone has to keep his or her promises is an agent-neutral reason; on Nagel's, that reason is not agent-neutral but agent-relative.

in power, such that its action would be constrained by the causal connections that hold in the ordinary course of nature. But that is not the Anselmian being's situation. The idea that failing to act in accordance with the norms of familiar welfare-governed morality must lower the probability of the Anselmian being's getting something that that being wants—and for *any* desire-set that the Anselmian being might have—is very hard to believe.

One can challenge the application of Schroeder's account of the ubiquity of reasons to act in accordance with commonsense morality to all possible rational beings—for the Anselmian being is one such being—without challenging that account as applied to the case of finite rational beings. But with respect to the issue of weighting it seems best to attack the basic account itself rather than its application to the special case of the Anselmian being. Schroeder identifies *deliberation* with the placing of weight on reasons to act (Schroeder 2007a, p. 129)—that is, making oneself more likely to act on those reasons. He identifies *correctness in deliberation* with placing that weight in the way that the reasons of the right sort require. And he identifies *reasons of the right sort*, with respect to any activity, to be the reasons that all those taking part in that activity share in virtue of taking part in that activity (Schroeder 2007a, p. 135). Thus correctness in deliberation involves placing weight on reasons in the way dictated by the reasons that all deliberators qua deliberators share. And since the class of all deliberators is the class of all agents, it is agent-neutral reasons—reasons that all agents share—that are the relevant reasons that determine what correct deliberation consists in (Schroeder 2007a, p. 142). So agent-neutral reasons are privileged, giving support to the view that they will be the reasons upon which a relatively large weight is placed in correct deliberation.

There are many points at which to take issue with this account, and it would not be productive to try to catalogue them here. (For persuasive critical responses, see Enoch 2011 and (especially) Rieder 2016.) I focus on one serious problem: that the move to agent-neutral reasons as privileged in deliberation is unjustified. First, even if it is true that the class of all agents and the class of all deliberators is coextensive—I doubt that this is true—it will not be true that the reasons that all agents have and the reasons that arise for deliberators qua deliberators are the same reasons. The only reasons that would be entitled to play the relevant role in Schroeder's account would be those reasons that all agents have *in virtue of engaging the activity of deliberation itself.* And nothing, even in Schroeder's programmatic and promissory account of the agent-neutral reasons to act in accordance with morality, suggests that these are reasons that arise in virtue of the activity of deliberation (that is, placing weight on reasons) itself. So Schroeder, by his own lights, casts the net too wide, claiming that all agent-neutral reasons will have a privileged place in weighting reasons, whereas no more than a proper subset of such reasons could be relevant.

Second, one can raise a worry about the privileging of agent-neutral reasons from the other direction. Schroeder's proposal for what constitutes reasons of the right kind draws upon the criteria for correctness in particular social practices, such as chess.

One can see why reasons of the right sort here would have to be shared, given that reasons in the context of such a practice are for the sake of setting standards to which the participants in the practice can hold each other. It is far from clear to me that deliberation is relevantly similar to chess here. The intrinsically social and shared character of games that ensures that correctness of chess moves is based on shared reasons is not present in the activity of deliberation, and so it seems to me that it is illegitimate to insist that the right kind of reasons that fix correctness in deliberation must be shared reasons. But the sharedness of such reasons is Schroeder's only way to guarantee that the allegedly ubiquitous moral reasons are reasons accorded a high level of weight.

From a different angle: when we attempt to explain correctness in terms of reasons, one of the central desiderata is that we protect the notion of *the correct* from the notion of *ought*—for we lose our grip on the idea that correctness is practice-specific if we allow all of the reasons that go into making for a true ought-statement to influence what goes into making a certain move within a practice correct. But it is crucial to the justifiability of offering such protection that the reasons in question are not treated as irrelevant: though some reasons for making a certain chess move—for example, that it would embarrass one's chess teacher, who needs embarrassing—do not count in favor of that move's being correct, they do count in favor of its being the move one ought to make, given the circumstances. Now consider how this is not possible when it comes to Schroeder's account of deliberation. Once he rules out some reasons as irrelevant to the proper placing of weight within the practice of deliberation, those reasons cannot have any place in determining what one ought to do: by being treated as irrelevant to correct deliberation, they also become irrelevant to what one ought to do.

When correctness is defined in terms of a proper subset of reasons, then questions of the following sort will be open, and properly so: Yes, I know that this is the correct chess move, but is it the move I ought to make here? Yes, I know that this is the correct way to sauté the onions for this recipe, but ought I to do it that way here? But it seems to me the same sort of question should now arise on Schroeder's view about ought and the outcome of correct deliberation: Yes, I know that this is the action that correct deliberation endorses, but is it what I ought to do here? This question should make sense, given that only a proper subset of reasons—agent-neutral ones—count as relevant for the purposes of determining how weight should be placed on reasons. Yet Schroeder's view *identifies* what one ought to do with what one would place most weight on in correct deliberation, so that the answer to the question must be Yes. So Schroeder's account of the reasons relevant to placing weight is defective in two directions: even by his own lights, the class of agent-neutral reasons is too broad to be the class of reasons that are of the right sort to determine weight; and the class of agent-neutral reasons is too narrow, so long as Schroeder identifies what one ought to do with what one has weightiest reason to do, where weight is defined in terms of correctness of deliberation. I do not think, then, either that Schroeder gives us reason to think that the Anselmian being must have the reasons that are relevant to welfare-oriented moral goodness or that Schroeder provides an adequate account of how those reasons, even if the Anselmian being had them, would have the requisite weight.

I do not think that the inability of Hume's and Schroeder's accounts to provide a basis for ascribing a familiar welfare-oriented moral goodness to God is due to features of their views that make those views eccentric qua Humean. It is pretty plain that once one denies that lacking some basic desire that is oriented toward the good of creatures must count as a defect in rational beings, it will be difficult to show that the Anselmian being's perfection entails that being's having an ethics of familiar welfare-oriented moral goodness. It thus seems to me that Humean accounts, classic or contemporary, give no explanation for, and indeed give us a strong basis to doubt, that we and the Anselmian being have similar reasons to act in accordance with familiar welfare-oriented moral goodness.

Aristotelianisms, classical and contemporary. What distinguishes an Aristotelian account of reasons and rational agency is that what constitutes such reasons and agency is fixed by the kind to which the agent belongs. Just as the goods and proper pursuit of those goods by dogs, or dolphins, or badgers are determined by the respective kinds to which those animals belong, the goods and proper pursuit of the goods of human life are determined by the kind to which we belong. Even if there is some abstract form of rationality by which we could assess beings of a very different kind from us as rational, in some sense, the Aristotelian holds that this form of rationality would not be sufficient to set the substantive norms that constitute morality.[13] This is Aristotle's view: Aristotle rejects the notion that "the gods," who do not share our kind, would share our virtues, and indeed says that any praise that "concerns actions appears trivial and unworthy of the gods" (*Nicomachean Ethics* 1178b16–18; for discussion see Nussbaum 1995, pp. 95–8). It is a view shared by Aquinas, whose natural law position, though departing from Aristotle's ethics in a number of respects, also affirms this close explanatory connection between the kind to which the human belongs and the norms of the natural law that bind the human. Contemporary followers of Aristotle and Aquinas, such as MacIntyre (1999), Foot (2001), and Thompson (2007), endorse this kind-rationality explanatory connection as well.

Of course, if this view is true, then we should not expect a rational being not of the human kind to be subject to the same moral norms to which we humans are subject. As Thompson writes, this sort of Aristotelianism "breaks with the received Kantian and Humean conceptions of practical rationality, each of which appears to claim possession of a table of principles of sound practical reasoning that would apply indifferently to humans, twin earthers and Martians alike" (Thompson 2004b, p. 61). Thompson's remark concerns rational animals not of our species. But the point will surely hold a fortiori of non-embodied rational beings like angels, and even more strongly of the

[13] Aristotelian views do not just provide modules—say, objectivist, perfectionist theories of well-being—that are then plugged into a generic account of rationality. As Thompson notes, there may be kinds of being whose rationality is properly characterized in Hobbesian terms, but for us there is justice.

Anselmian being, who is characteristically described as not belonging to a kind at all. If our preferred explanation of the binding power of moral norms upon us is of the Aristotelian sort, then we have reason to be very dubious of the notion that we and the Anselmian being are under a common morality.[14]

Kantianisms, classical and contemporary. As suggested above (3.2), there is a strain of Kantianism that does not take the explanation of moral norms to make any reference to features specific to our kind—we should say either that it is a conceptual truth that any basic reasons must apply to all rational beings, or perhaps that, though not a conceptual truth, the holding of norms of morality that apply to all rational beings is an upshot of formal truths about rationality that apply to all beings properly characterized as 'rational.' I reject such views as simply in error: it is not a conceptual truth that reasons exhibit such a structure, and it is not true that formal truths about rationality (for example, alleged requirements of universalization) are sufficient to generate the moral norms that we are under, much less that all rational beings must be under. (And since Kant took the categorical imperative to be synthetic rather than analytic, it is hard to see how such a formalistic view would even be faithful to Kant's own insights.)

But there is an important strand of Kant's thought that bypasses some of the grandiose claims that Kant occasionally seems to make on behalf of formal requirements on reason and defends instead a conception of morality and its shared reasons grounded in an account of how each agent must view him- or herself and other agents as being alike in their fundamental reason-giving force. There are different ways of specifying this strategy, but the basic idea is to move from the agent's commitment to seeing him- or herself to be valuable to a commitment to seeing other rational agents as valuable also. This move is made by way of an *equality* or *consistency* or *anti-arbitrariness* premise. The claim is that the particular way that one must value oneself as a rational agent commits one to seeing other rational agents as *equally valuable*, or that it commits one, *as a matter of consistency*, to treating other rational agents as valuable also, or that it would be *arbitrary* to value oneself in this way while failing to value other rational agents in that way also. For there are no plausible relevant differences that would justify treating oneself as valuable in that way while failing to treat others as valuable in that way. So Nagel, for example, argues that the rational requirement of altruism arises not from some formal constraints of rationality as such but from those constraints conjoined with a certain self-conception: that one is simply "one person among others" (Nagel 1970, p. 88). Kantian contractualist views emphasize the character of moral norms arising from the status of moral agents as not only free, but equal (Rawls 1971, Scanlon 1998, Darwall 2006). And recently neo-Kantian accounts more closely hewing to Kant's own account have invoked this sort of anti-arbitrariness condition (Markovits 2014).

[14] This point is emphasized in Davies's account of Aquinas on the problem of evil; see Davies 2011, p. 72. Since not only Aquinas's natural law view, but natural law accounts of practical reasonableness generally, tend to be Aristotelian (Murphy 2002b), they will inherit this inability to show, or even suggest, that we will share reasons with the Anselmian being.

But these anti-arbitrariness arguments do not succeed in showing that every rational being must be taken to be valuable by every other rational being in a way that would sustain the view that the Anselmian being must be bound by norms of familiar welfare-oriented moral goodness. I take the Kantian arguments under consideration here to be flawed in numerous ways, but I focus here on the flaw most salient for this context: that the Anselmian being is not simply one 'person among others,' and this vitiates the Kantian argument.

The Kantian argument requires not only the acknowledgment that the agent is committed to viewing him- or herself as valuable, but also that the agent is committed to viewing him- or herself as valuable *in a certain way*: in a such a way as to give that agent reasons to care about his or her rationally willed ends. This poses one obstacle to the success of the Kantian argument, for one might well judge that one's value gives one reason to care about one's rationally willed ends, and take it that consistency, anti-arbitrariness, equality (etc.) requires no more than that one take another's value to give *that other* reason to care about his or her rationally willed ends. But let us spot the Kantian this point, and hold that as none of the ways I am unlike you seem to be relevant differences, my value gives both me and you reasons to care about my rationally willed ends and your value gives both me and you reasons to care about your rationally willed ends. Even granting all this, we have not yet brought the *Anselmian being* into the fold of shared reasons.

The Kantian argument gains what intuitive force it has from the fact that, if we do not take the bare fact that you are not I and I am not you to be relevant, none of the other differences seems to be. That my hair is one color and yours another seems fundamentally unimportant; after all, if I dyed my hair your color and you dyed yours mine, it would not make a whit of difference to the value that should be ascribed to each of us. Thus, each of us is, as Nagel puts it, just one person among others. But it seems plain that the Anselmian being, the absolutely perfect being, is not just one person among others. The difference between the Anselmian being and us is radical, such that it would be very implausible to say that, past the differences in numerical identity between us and the Anselmian being, no other differences could be fundamentally relevant. The differences between us finite rational agents and the unlimited absolutely perfect being are so massive that it seems that any claim that it would be arbitrary to hold that each of us must value him- or herself in a certain way while denying that the absolutely perfect being must value each of us in that way requires further elaboration and defense. What might such a defense look like?

It is hard to say. The Kantian move here is typically to note that since it is one's rational agency that makes one valuable, anyone in whom rational agency is present must be similarly valuable. (Put to the side for now the Kantian's underjustification of the claim that it is one's rational agency that makes one valuable; I will return to this point in a moment.) Even if this is granted, it is not enough to extract the concession that wherever rational agency is present it exhibits that sort of value. For, again, it is not enough that the value be present; it has to give *to the Anselmian being* the same sort of reasons that it gives to finite rational beings. And the massive difference between finite rational agents and the Anselmian being should make one doubt whether one is committed, as a matter of consistency or on pain of arbitrariness, to holding that the Anselmian being must have such reasons.

Look at it another way. Imagine—which seems absurd, and the fact that it seems absurd is revealing—the Anselmian being considering *why* it has good reason to pursue its rationally willed ends. "I suppose," the Anselmian being thinks, "that it must be that I confer value on these ends through my willing them, and thus I must take myself to be valuable." At this point, is the Anselmian being committed to viewing as also valuable, and in a way that would give that being reason to care about their ends, all of the finite rational beings the very existence of which results from the Anselmian being's rational willing? Or isn't it plain that the massiveness of the gulf between the Anselmian being and finite rational creatures—that the Anselmian being exists independently, necessarily, of itself, needs nothing distinct from itself, and so forth—is enough to block the charge that the Anselmian being would be arbitrary to fail to treat the wills of finite rational beings as reason-giving in a way such that the Anselmian being would be governed by familiar norms of moral goodness?[15]

The implausibility of this sort of consistency argument when we are dealing with the Anselmian being—who does not seem to be just "one person among others, all equally real"—can be bolstered by noting another weakness in this sort of Kantian consistency argument. It is crucial to that argument that *being a rational willer of ends* is the description under which one values oneself, for it is only by selecting a description like that one that the Kantian can claim that one is committed to valuing as an end one's fellow human beings—who are, after all, rational willers of ends. But the selection of this description under which one values oneself is itself a contentious question. All that the form of the argument requires is that one value oneself under a description that one does take to be relevant and which must hold of one in any condition in which one takes it that one's willing ends will constitute those ends as reasons for action. But that would allow any *necessary* feature of the agent that the agent judges to be relevant to be able to do the trick. So a theist might well judge that *being made in the image of God* is the relevant description under which one may properly value oneself. Of course, it could not be *that* description under which the Anselmian being values itself and thus takes its ends to be worth furthering. And so the claim that there is some parity between us and the Anselmian being that provides the makings of a consistency

[15] It is important to distinguish these sorts of equality/anti-arbitrariness/consistency arguments that I am criticizing from another sort of argument, one based on an appeal to intrinsic value. The Kantian argument I am considering here runs from *I am committed to viewing myself as valuable in a certain way* to *I am committed to viewing all rational beings as valuable in a certain way* via a no-relevant-differences premise. But one could make a different argument: one might say that the takeaway from the Kantian argument is that we can achieve a rational insight, that rational agency is intrinsically valuable, where to be intrinsically valuable just involves giving reasons of the relevant sort to all possible rational beings. My remarks below (3.5, 4.4) on the appeal to intrinsic value will apply directly to this sort of view.

argument the view that the Anselmian being is subject to familiar welfare-oriented moral norms is rendered even less plausible.

As Schroeder has noted (Schroeder 2007b, p. 19), it is important to remember that *being a reason* is a *three*-term relation, not a *two*-term relation. It is not a relation simply between a fact and an action. It is a relation between a fact, an action, *and an agent*. So it would not be surprising if agents of fundamentally different types stood in different reason-relations. And that suggestion is further supported by the point that characteristic explanations of reason-relations that attempt to account for our shared reasons take the 'our' to concern us humans and our ilk, not agents of all possible kinds. So there seems to be room to take seriously the notion that even though we humans' reasons for action include the reasons presupposed by familiar welfare-oriented moral goodness, the Anselmian being's reasons for action do not include the reasons presupposed by familiar welfare-oriented moral goodness. And when we examine extant accounts of why we humans have those reasons, we can see that no such account suggests that we and the Anselmian being will have common reasons to exhibit familiar welfare-oriented moral goodness.

3.4 What Sorts of Reasons?

Suppose, though, that it is granted that the well-being of humans and other sentient animals gives all agents, including the Anselmian being, some reason to act. That would not be sufficient to ascribe familiar welfare-oriented moral goodness to the Anselmian being. In order for the reasons generated by the well-being of humans and other animals to be those presupposed by familiar welfare-oriented moral goodness, at least two further conditions must be met. First, the reasons must be reasons to *promote* the well-being of humans and other animals, as opposed to reasons to do something else in response to that well-being. Second, the reasons must be what Joshua Gert calls "requiring" reasons rather than merely what he calls "justifying" reasons. And so we have two further potential sources of suspicion regarding the ascription of welfare-oriented moral goodness to the Anselmian being, for we can sensibly doubt whether the Anselmian being's reasons with regard to welfare are both reasons to *promote* welfare and are *requiring* reasons.

On the first condition. There are multiple modes of appropriate response to value.[16] One of them—but only one—is to *promote* that value. Here I understand promotion broadly, to include bringing it about, increasing it, preventing setbacks to it. Another mode of appropriate response is to *respect* it. What respecting involves is less clear, but I have in mind at least refraining from intending to destroy or diminish. It is controversial, but plausible, that one cannot reduce one of these responses to the other, and so one cannot explain the point of the reason to refrain from intending harm solely in terms of promotion. This failure of reducibility makes way for the following possibility: that

[16] See, for a wonderful discussion of this variety, Swanton 2003, pp. 48–55.

even if the well-being of humans and other animals gives an absolutely perfect being reasons for action, the reasons that it gives are, at least in some cases, only reasons to respect and not reasons to promote. Here is a coherent combination of views: I do not have reason that requires me, unless I have more pressing projects, to promote the well-being of each and every spider in the world, but I do have reason (outweighable, but a reason) not to intend to kill spiders. It is a different thing to set oneself to something's destruction and to not promote its well-being, and the importance of the former is not obviously reducible to the latter. (Intending destruction is not simply a particularly reliable way of failing to promote; to intend the destruction of an instance of some good is to be *against* that good in a way that failing to promote it is not. For the idea of being for or against the good, see R. Adams 2006, pp. 15–19; I discuss this issue further in 5.4.) Even if it were granted, then, that an absolutely perfect being would not take death and destruction of humans and animals as an objective, as part of that being's plan of action, without some adequate justification, it is a further step to hold that the absolutely perfect being must take the well-being of all such creatures as to be promoted.

On the second point. Gert makes an important distinction between two kinds of reasons for action: requiring reasons and justifying reasons (Gert 2004, pp. 19–39; see also Kagan 1989, pp. 378–81 on "insistent" and "noninsistent" reasons). (As Gert points out, it is better to characterize this distinction, as he usually does, as between two *dimensions* of normative force that a reason might have, but I will speak in this oversimplifying way.) Roughly, a requiring reason is a reason that is such that if an agent who has that reason fails to act on it, then either that agent is not practically rational or that agent has some superior, incompatible reason that the agent was acting on. A justifying reason is a reason that is such that an agent that acts on that reason acts practically rationally, unless there are some incompatible reasons that render acting on it practically irrational. You might think of requiring reasons as imposing rational *constraints*; you might think of justifying reasons as providing rational *opportunities*. One of Gert's key theses is that a reason can be *purely justifying*, that is, justifying without requiring: it can give an agent a rational opportunity without placing that agent under a rational constraint. A purely justifying reason would be a reason that is such that an agent that acts on that reason acts practically rationally, though that agent may fail to act on that reason without irrationality even in the absence of some other reason that precludes acting on it.

Gert puts this distinction to work in a number of ways, with many of which I disagree. But what is key to my argument here is not any way that Gert uses the distinction but just the distinction itself. For again, suppose that we grant that the well-being of humans and other animals gives an absolutely perfect being reasons for action. And suppose that we grant, further, that the reasons given are reasons to promote that well-being. We still do not yet have enough to ascribe familiar welfare-oriented moral goodness to the Anselmian being. For we could ascribe that sort of moral goodness to the Anselmian being only if the reasons thus provided were all *requiring* rather than *purely justifying* reasons. The goods of well-being and the absence of ill-being may provide, we can grant for the sake of argument, justifying reasons for the Anselmian being to actualize a world with one set of laws rather than another, or for such a being to intervene miraculously. (I give an argument for this thesis in 4.2.) But it is a further distinct claim to say that these are, for the Anselmian being, requiring reasons. Unless these reasons are requiring reasons, though, they are not reasons of the sort presupposed by familiar welfare-oriented moral goodness.

To summarize. The logic of reasons does not require that we humans share reasons with the absolutely perfect being, so we cannot argue from our having those reasons immediately to the Anselmian being's having those reasons (3.2). If we try to explain why the absolutely perfect being has reasons arising from our and other animals' well-being, we are hampered by the fact that extant live explanations appeal to considerations that apply to us humans but not to an absolutely perfect being (3.3). If we allow that well-being does give reasons to the absolutely perfect being, we need further reason to think that the reasons are requiring reasons, and that those requiring reasons are reasons to promote that well-being (3.4). In tandem, these considerations seem to me to constitute very strong reasons to doubt that familiar welfare-oriented moral goodness is to be ascribed to the Anselmian being.

3.5 The Appeal to Intrinsic Value

Well-being is a relational form of value; the fact that something is an aspect of someone's well-being entails that it is good *for him or her*, not that it is good *simpliciter* (cf. Sumner 1996, pp. 20–1; Murphy 2001, pp. 49–50). The value constitutive of well-being is agent-relative rather than agent-neutral value. It is not at all implausible that this is the source of the worrisome gap that I have been considering: even if it follows from something's being good for some agent that it gives *that agent* good, even requiring, reason to promote it, it does not follow from something's being good for some agent that it gives *every* agent good, much less requiring, reason to promote it. Hence the worrisome gap, which generates a good deal of perplexity when we are speaking only of humans and human-like creatures, generates an even greater obstacle for the ascription of a familiar welfare-oriented moral goodness to the Anselmian being.

Given the gap between well-being and reasons and the unsuitability of any of the familiar appeals to close that gap in the case of the Anselmian being, the obvious move is to put the notion of intrinsic value to work. For one might say that even if well-being is a relational form of value, it might nevertheless bear on agent-*neutral* value in a relevant way, one that assures us that, and explains why, the Anselmian being's ethics is an ethics of familiar welfare-oriented moral goodness. One might say that the beings whose well-being the norms of familiar welfare-oriented moral goodness direct us to promote are themselves agent-neutrally valuable, because they are *intrinsically* valuable. And if we think that humans and other sentient creatures are agent-neutrally valuable entities, then we should think that *any* rational agent must have requiring reasons to respond positively to these beings, and to respond positively to them must include promoting and protecting their well-being.[17]

In Chapter 4 (4.4) I will deny the compatibility of creaturely intrinsic value with Anselmianism. (That these are incompatible was Anselm's own view of the matter; see *Monologion*, I, 14.) But it is worth noting now that there would still be problematic gaps in the argument from the intrinsic value of creatures to the Anselmian being's being governed by familiar welfare-oriented moral goodness, even if we were to grant that creatures bear intrinsic value that fixes how agents may reasonably respond to them. Between the intrinsic value of creatures and the right sort of reasons to support familiar welfare-oriented moral goodness there remains a gap. It could be, that is, that some things that have intrinsic value give requiring reasons for every rational being to promote their good. But here are other intelligible views that are consistent with the affirmation of creaturely intrinsic value: intrinsically valuable creatures give *justifying* (but not requiring) reasons for every rational agent to promote their good; intrinsically valuable creatures give requiring reasons to some rational beings, but merely justifying reasons to others; and so forth. Having value of an independent sort is one thing; the particular sorts of reasons to which it gives rise are something else.[18]

Here is a way to think about it. *Bearing intrinsic value* thus conceived is a nonrelational feature of a thing. But *being a reason* is a relational feature—again, following Schroeder, a three-term relation. So even if it is allowed that to be intrinsically valuable is to be *apt* to give reasons, to whom such reasons are given and what sort of reasons are given remain an open question even if a thing is conceded to have intrinsic value.

Nor are matters helped along if one endorses a buck-passing conception of intrinsic value—that for something to have intrinsic value *just is* for, necessarily, all rational beings to have reason to respond favorably to its intrinsic features. For, first, it looks as if one would have to add that the relevant sorts of response are of the promoting, protecting, etc. sort, otherwise one will not be on one's way to an account of the universal applicability of familiar welfare-oriented moral goodness. And, second, one will have to add that the relevant reasons are requiring reasons. And that's just what I claimed that the defenders of the appeal to intrinsic value need to argue for, rather than simply assert. When one is asked to explain why it is true that something stands in a certain relation to all beings of a certain class, it does not help to be told that it does stand in that relation to all beings of that certain class.

So, even without rejecting the idea that creatures bear some sort of intrinsic value, we still face a troublesome gap in explaining the sorts of reasons to which intrinsic

[17] See Davison 2011 for a rigorous account of intrinsic value and a defense of its ubiquity.

[18] So Davison writes that to be intrinsically valuable just is for properly functioning valuers to value something for its own sake, where valuing involves responding to it positively in these ways (Davison 2011, p. 12). But one might ask whether it is possible for there to be valuers of different sorts, with different functions, such that it is possible for properly functioning valuers of different kinds to respond to the same thing in different ways. This is a possibility that Davison notes (p. 12, n. 11), but puts to the side without further comment.

value gives rise.[19] But it is of course open to my opponent to say that I have missed the real point behind the appeal to intrinsic value. The real point is that when one reflects upon human beings and other sentient animals, one can *just see* that the value that these beings bear is such that everyone, even the Anselmian being, must have requiring reasons to promote and protect their well-being. Forget about providing an explanation of those reasons, and an account of why the reasons that we have to respond to these beings in these ways must be shared with the Anselmian being. It is instead just a *datum* that any theory has to accommodate: no being that counts as a rational being could fail to have requiring reason to promote the good of such creatures.

This is the hardest worry to answer, because it does not rely on any argument at all the premises of which could be challenged. For the moment I will be content to raise a skeptical question, a skepticism akin to that to which van Inwagen appeals concerning our capacity to form well-justified modal judgments far outside of the range of our ordinary lives. But my concern is about moral, not modal, knowledge. Our ordinary practical knowledge is knowledge of our form of life, the form of life exhibited by *us humans*. When we form the thought 'of course *everyone* has reason to do *that*' 'everyone' typically ranges over our fellow humans. And so even if one forms the thought, intuitively, that everyone has a requiring reason to promote well-being or prevent setbacks to it, one might well wonder whether the domain within which one can form such judgments reliably really can extend past the case in which 'everyone' includes all of one's fellow humans to the cases in which 'everyone' includes all possible rational beings, even the Anselmian being. I attempt to place quite a bit more pressure on this brute appeal to intuition in Chapter 4 (4.4).

3.6 Moral Goodness as a Perfection Independent of Rationality?

One might wonder whether the view that I have been trying to make room for—that even if we concede that we humans are subject to the familiar welfare-oriented moral standard, the Anselmian being's ethics is not characterized by it—is built around an implausible rationalism about the relationship between morality and practical reason. My worries, which have been framed in terms of whether the Anselmian being exhibits familiar welfare-oriented moral goodness, make use of a strong moral rationalist thesis that for the Anselmian being to act in accordance with a certain conception of moral goodness presupposes that acting in accordance with that conception of moral goodness is a requirement of practical reason (2.2). And so wouldn't the defender of the view that the Anselmian being exhibits familiar welfare-oriented moral goodness be well-advised to register skepticism regarding such moral rationalism? For if the defender of that view were to reject moral rationalism, then he or she could just say: the

[19] In 4.4 I reject the view that creatures have intrinsic value, given an Anselmian conception of God.

Anselmian being exhibits two *distinct* perfections—rationality and moral goodness—and there is no need to give arguments in favor of the view that divine rationality is what entails that the Anselmian being treats these particular morally relevant considerations as decisive reasons. The most salient explanation of why the Anselmian being acts in accordance with these standards is not that being's *rationality* but that being's *moral goodness*. The idea is not that on this alternative view moral goodness and rationality could direct the Anselmian being in *incompatible* ways; that view would be open to devastating objections. The idea would be, rather, that divine rationality is a *thinner* and *more inclusive* notion, and so acting in accordance with moral goodness would be just one, not rationally required but rationally available, option for divine action that nevertheless the Anselmian being, as morally perfect, necessarily chooses.

There is an important point of similarity between this view and the view that I have been proposing. I have suggested that it is possible that favoring human and other animal well-being may be a rational option for the Anselmian being but nevertheless not rationally required, and so a conception of moral goodness that would require favoring human and other animal well-being is not to be ascribed to the Anselmian being as a divine perfection or as an aspect of a divine perfection. This alternative view agrees that favoring human and other animal well-being may be rationally optional for the Anselmian being, but because that being is morally perfect, and moral perfection includes favoring human and other animal well-being, the Anselmian being would have to exhibit familiar welfare-oriented moral goodness.

My first response is simply a reiteration of my defense of the strong rationalist notion of divine moral goodness defended in Chapter 2 (2.2). We do have grounds to assert the strong rationalist thesis generally. But we have special grounds for doing so in the case of the Anselmian being. My argument appealed to divine rationality and divine freedom: affirming a strong rationalist conception of divine moral goodness is the best hope for reconciling divine moral goodness and divine freedom. And so that is my first response: it looks, on this alternative view, that the Anselmian being is not fully free, for the Anselmian being's choices are constrained in certain ways that are independent of what there is good reason for the Anselmian being to do. Though the Anselmian being can see that there are undefeated reasons to act in a way that is incompatible with perfect moral goodness, nevertheless the Anselmian being necessarily does not act in a way that is incompatible with perfect moral goodness. That looks like unfreedom.

I take it that those who are sympathetic with the views of my imagined interlocutor will find this unconvincing. It is not really an affront to freedom, they might retort, if the constraint on action imposed by moral goodness is part of the Anselmian being's nature, which is after all (*ex hypothesi*) a perfect nature. And the interlocutor can ask whether it isn't true that other divine perfections will constrain possible choices of divine action in ways that are not fixed by divine rationality. After all, the Anselmian being cannot choose to perform an action that will result in something that might surprise itself; this is a constraint on divine choice imposed by the Anselmian being's omniscience. So it is not as if we do not already accept that some limitations on divine action that might on their face appear to be incompatible with the divine freedom might nevertheless have to be regarded as acceptable.

My response to this is to distinguish between two ways that divine action might be limited, and to note that one way in which it might be limited seems to pose less of a threat to the divine freedom than the other way. Begin with the ordinary case of human free choice. There seems to be an important difference between the way that, say, the laws of nature impose limits on free choice and the way that, say, inability to take seriously in deliberation an otherwise possible option imposes limits on free choice. We think of proposals for action that involve violations of the laws of nature (forget the possibility of the miraculous for a moment) as being not real options at all, and it might be true that an agent must act only on proposals consistent with the laws of nature while nevertheless being genuinely free. The perfection of freedom, on this view, is about one's practical capacities to respond to a set of possible options, and so is not limited simply by the limits on that set of possible options. By contrast, if there are proposals for action that seem otherwise possible but upon which an agent is unable to act simply because he or she cannot take that proposal seriously in deliberation, no matter that there are good, undefeated reasons in favor of it, then that does seem like unfreedom.

That the Anselmian being cannot perform an action that has results surprising to itself is like my not being able to perform an action that violates the laws of nature. These constraints pertain to what we might think of as the circumstances or context of action; it is how one is able to respond within such circumstances that constitutes one's freedom. If, however, the Anselmian being cannot but act in a certain way, even though that being can see and appreciate that there are good undefeated reasons to act a contrary way, then that seems to me to be unfreedom. For it is as if the Anselmian being cannot take seriously the prospect of acting a certain way, even if there would be adequately good reasons for that being to do so. That would be a deliberative defect and thus a failure of divine freedom. And that's what it seems to me that one is committed to when one ascribes to the Anselmian being a moral goodness that constrains what that being can treat as an eligible option for action, even though there may be good undefeated reasons for acting contrary to what that moral goodness necessitates one to do. So it still seems to me that the notion that the Anselmian being necessarily acts a certain way cannot be sustained unless the Anselmian being has decisive reason to act that way, and so any challenge to the view that the Anselmian being has decisive requiring reasons to promote well-being is a challenge to the view that the Anselmian being's ethics is an ethics of familiar welfare-oriented moral goodness.

The above may still fail to convince. I have an additional challenge to those who wish to defend this alternative view. Everyone working within traditional Anselmianism, and everyone who treats the problem of evil as an argument against the Anselmian being, must take rationality to be a divine perfection. As I argued above, if divine moral goodness involves responding to reasons in a way that is fixed by those reasons, then it is clear why being morally good is an aspect of the divine perfection: being morally good is part of being a perfectly practically rational agent. On the other hand, if one proposes an alternative view on which moral goodness is a perfection distinct from divine rationality, then one has an extra burden of explaining why moral goodness counts as a perfection. If we understand moral goodness in a way that does not presuppose that one has reason to respond to these values, then it is unclear why it is a perfection to respond to these things in these particular ways.

Some defenders of very broadly realist accounts of moral rightness reject rationalism, and they are subject to this same question about human agency. For any set of norms of action and any agent, we can ask two questions: First, is this set of norms of action supposed to guide the action of that agent, and second, is the agent appropriately subject to criticism for failing to act in accordance with those norms? (By 'subject to criticism' here I do not mean anything very substantive, for example, that there are parties with standing to hold them accountable; I mean only that it is correct to judge the agent as being defective, or the action being defective, or something along those lines.) These seem to be distinct questions, even in the moral case. Even granting that morality is supposed to guide the action of each and every rational agent, it seems to remain an open question why we rational agents are subject to criticism, as we seem to be, for failing to act in accordance with the norms of morality. The only answer that seems available is that all of us rational agents are defective for failing to act in accordance with the norms of morality because the norms of morality are norms of human practical rationality.

Now, one might reject this argument, holding that there really is no need to think of a human as defective as an agent for failing to act in accordance with the norms of morality. But note that one cannot avail oneself of the relevantly similar response with respect to the Anselmian being, if one wants also to claim that the Anselmian being's perfection includes moral goodness. For that claim is that one way for the Anselmian being's agency to not be all that it could be would be for that being's agency not to exhibit familiar welfare-oriented moral goodness—that the Anselmian being would not be perfect as an agent unless morally good in this particular way. For a defender of the proposed alternative to make this case, he or she needs to explain why the norms of morality are appropriately applied to the Anselmian being, and this explanation must not advert to a rationalist thesis.

3.7 Where Matters Stand

The argument of Chapters 2 and 3 has been negative. The argument of Chapter 2 aimed to show that the extent to which the Anselmian being acts in a loving way is fixed by the extent to which the Anselmian being exhibits moral goodness of a familiar welfare-oriented sort. The argument of Chapter 3 has been that we have strong reasons to doubt that the Anselmian being exhibits moral goodness of a familiar welfare-oriented sort. The Anselmian being does not exhibit moral goodness of a familiar welfare-oriented sort unless the well-being of creatures provides requiring reasons to promote it. But we have good grounds to doubt that the well-being of creatures provides the Anselmian being reasons of that sort. As the Chapter 2 argument is that the Anselmian being's love need not go beyond what is required by the Anselmian being's moral goodness, the Chapter 3 result is that we not only have good grounds to doubt that the Anselmian being is morally good, but we also have good grounds to doubt that the Anselmian being is loving.

4

The Ethics of the Anselmian Being I (Promotion)

4.1 The Central Theses regarding the Ethics of the Anselmian Being

The aim of Chapters 2 and 3 was to unsettle the common conviction that the ethics of the Anselmian being is of the familiar welfare-oriented sort, whether on account of that being's having a necessary love for all sentient creatures (Chapter 2) or on account of that being's adhering to a standard of moral goodness regulated by the value of those creatures and their good (Chapter 3). The aim of this chapter and Chapter 5 is more positive. Here I want to provide an account of the ethics of an Anselmian being.

I am going to speak of a creature's exhibiting to some degree the perfections appropriate to its kind as its 'perfection,' and I am going to speak of a creature's being well-off to some degree its 'well-being.' There are disputed questions about how perfection and well-being are related in creatures for whom the realization of both of these sorts of value is possible,[1] questions that I want to avoid for the most part. But it is plausible enough to say that when we invoke a formulation of the problem of evil concerning God's failing to bring about some particular level of goodness in God's creatures, or God's failing to prevent some setback to the good of creatures, what we have in mind is either the perfection of those creatures or their well-being. So I will, somewhat cumbersomely, be framing my theses about the Anselmian being's ethics in terms of that being's reasons with respect to the 'perfection/well-being' of creatures.

There are two central theses that I aim to defend regarding the ethics of the Anselmian being. The first of these, defended in this chapter, is that the existence and perfection/well-being of creatures provide justifying, but not requiring, reasons for the Anselmian being to promote their existence and perfection/well-being. The argument for this conclusion proceeds in two stages. First, I offer reasons from the absolute perfection of the Anselmian being, along with Anselmian methodology (1.4), to find this a promising conception of the ethics of an Anselmian being (4.2–4.3). Second, I appeal to an account of the nature of the value of creatures in relation to the Anselmian being that is plausible in itself and is an instance of that conception (4.4–4.5).

[1] For the view that these are distinct values, the realization of which in some subject is a contingent matter, see Sumner 1996, pp. 21–4; for the view that they are to be identified in beings capable of well-being and of perfection, see Murphy 2001, pp. 46–95.

The second of these theses, defended in Chapter 5, is that the Anselmian being takes the due perfection/well-being of creatures to provide requiring reasons, even decisive requiring reasons, not to intend their loss and destruction. In short, the Anselmian being does not intend evils. I explain there what reasons we have both for thinking that this thesis is true and for taking there to be no tension between the absence of requiring reasons to promote creatures' good and the presence of requiring, even decisive, reasons not to intend evils.

In Chapter 6, I will turn to an account of how this understanding of the Anselmian being's ethics should transform our understanding of what is problematic about the problem of evil.

4.2 The Existence and Perfection/Well-Being of Creatures Give the Anselmian Being Justifying Reasons for Promotion

The existence and perfection/well-being of creatures give the Anselmian being justifying reasons to promote that existence and that perfection/well-being. What this means is that bringing into existence a creature, and bringing about a creature that is to be better- rather than worse-off, is something that makes rational the Anselmian being's acting to bring about that outcome.

That the existence and perfection/well-being of creatures provide the Anselmian being with justifying reasons for promotion is suggested by two features that must be ascribed to the Anselmian being. The first of these is that, as the Anselmian being is absolutely perfect, the Anselmian being must be rational. But a being who is rational, if it is to act, must have a reason for doing so. Otherwise the act would be entirely pointless, and a perfectly rational being would not act in an entirely pointless way. The second of these is that, given the metaphysical possibility of Anselmianism, then the Anselmian being possibly brings about the existence of creatures who are to some degree well-off. If this is not obvious, recall that while truths about what the actual being who qualifies as the Anselmian being is like do not entail that an Anselmian being is like that (for example, that the actual being who qualifies as the Anselmian being spoke from a burning bush does not entail *an Anselmian being speaks from burning bushes*; see 1.1), such truths do entail that an Anselmian being is *possibly* like that (e.g. that the actual being who qualifies as the Anselmian being spoke from a burning bush entails *an Anselmian being possibly speaks from burning bushes*). Anselmianism entails that for anything that exists and is distinct from the absolutely perfect being, then an absolutely perfect being creates it (van Inwagen 2006,[2] Murphy 2011a, pp. 6–12). But there exists something that is distinct from God: you, I, and all other finite beings. Given the metaphysical possibility of Anselmianism, then a being who

[2] Note, though, that van Inwagen embraces a weaker version of this view, one that does not cover abstracta, in van Inwagen 2009.

qualifies as an Anselmian being created these things. Thus it follows that *an Anselmian being possibly creates* is true.

It is not possible that an Anselmian being acts unless that Anselmian being has reason to do so. And it is possible for an Anselmian being to create. Thus the Anselmian being has reasons to create, reasons of the sort that make possible rationally creating. It is also possible for an Anselmian being to provide a greater level of perfection/well-being rather than a lesser for the creatures that exist. Thus the Anselmian being has reason to bring about a higher level of perfection/well-being, reasons that make possible rational action for the sake of providing creatures with greater perfection/well-being. And so we must hold that the Anselmian being has, at least, justifying reasons to bring about the existence and perfection/well-being of creatures.

Must we hold that the justifying reasons to bring about the existence and perfection/well-being of creatures in some sense have their source in the value of those creatures? For, after all, it does not follow from the Anselmian being's having reason to bring about creaturely existence and perfection/well-being that those reasons are in any way rooted in the value of those creatures and their condition, any more than my reason to drop and do twenty pushups must be rooted in the goodness of my dropping and doing twenty pushups. It may be rooted in the requirement of obedience to my drill sergeant, who gave me the command because of the disvalue present in dropping and doing twenty. The answer to the question "Must the reasons for the Anselmian being to create be based in the value of the creatures and their good?" is Yes and No, or, better, No and Yes and No and Yes: (1) No, inasmuch as the source of these reasons cannot be the intrinsic value of creatures. (2) Yes, as there could be no other adequate explanation of why the Anselmian being has justifying reason to create that does involve creatures as loci of value, valuable beings, even if not intrinsically so. (3) No, for although the creaturely order must include a locus of value for the Anselmian being to have justifying reason to create, it might not be 'individualistic,' but in terms of the whole created order, with individual creatures having value that gives the Anselmian being justifying reasons wholly in terms of their being a part of that order. (4) Yes, because even though the 'locus in creation' view does not rule out the thesis that God's justifying reasons for creating include only the whole of creation, the most plausible view is that for each creature that can exhibit some level of perfection/well-being—I think that is every possible creature—then that creature's existence and perfection/well-being are a justifying reason for God to bring it about. To elaborate:

(1) If what is being asked is whether the Anselmian being's justifying reasons to bring about creaturely existence and perfection/well-being are rooted in the intrinsic value of those creatures, then we must say No: for Anselmianism about God entails that no creature has intrinsic value.[3] I make the argument below (4.4).

[3] Note that by 'intrinsic value' I mean value that a being has that is independent of any relations that it stands to other things. I don't mean the looser sense, in which intrinsic value is just final, non-instrumental value.

(2) Nevertheless, we must take the explanation of God's having justifying reasons to create to include the goodness of creaturely existence and perfection/well-being. Creatures need not exhibit intrinsic value in order to be agent-neutrally valuable. (To be intrinsically valuable entails that the value exhibited is borne in virtue entirely of one's intrinsic features; to be agent-neutrally valuable does not imply this.) And this agent-neutral value must be realized by the existence and perfection/well-being of creatures. For everything that is not a creature already exists absolutely and perfectly without any creative act. The only possible locus of value that would account for the Anselmian being's reasons would be in the creaturely order, in the beings to exist and realize some level of perfection/well-being through divine action.

(3) That this locus of value is in the creaturely order does not itself entail that each creature's existence and perfection/well-being are a source of justifying reasons for the Anselmian being. It is compatible with the argument that the locus of value must be in the creaturely order to hold that what gives the Anselmian being a justifying reason is the created universe as a whole, or some section thereof, and individual creatures are merely parts that have no reason-giving force on their own but only as a part of some wider creaturely order.

(4) Nevertheless, this is an implausible view. For it seems that any basis for holding that the created universe as a whole is good in a way that gives the Anselmian being reason to bring it about would be something that also held of individual creatures, even if in a dramatically lesser degree.[4] And it seems that there are some ways in which at least some individual creatures would do better (for example, with respect to exhibiting unity, or with respect to being in the image of God). The upshot is that the prospect of a creature's existence, and to a greater level of perfection/well-being rather than lesser, is something that the Anselmian being has justifying reasons to promote.

4.3 The Existence and Perfection/Well-Being of Creatures Do Not Give the Anselmian Being Requiring Reasons for Promotion

But it does not follow from the Anselmian being's having *justifying* reason to create beings, or beings with a certain level of perfection/well-being, that the Anselmian being has *requiring* reasons to do so. (For this distinction between justifying and requiring reasons, see 3.4.) We cannot conclude merely from the fact that creatures

[4] For a similar sort of argument to the conclusion that everything must exhibit some intrinsic value, see Davison 2011, pp. 61–78. I reject Davison's view, for I take no creature to have intrinsic value in the strict sense. But I accept as plausible his view that all creatures have a certain sort of agent-neutral value, though in my own view this value is necessarily present in virtue of the necessity of their standing in a certain relationship to God (4.4).

and their good give an Anselmian being rational *opportunities* for action that they place any sort of rational *constraint* on an Anselmian being's actions—that the Anselmian being must create, or create with a higher level of well-being/perfection, unless the Anselmian being has sufficient reason to the contrary.

That the existence of requiring reasons to promote creaturely existence and perfection/well-being does not follow from the existence of justifying reasons to promote creaturely existence and perfection/well-being does not show, of course, that there are no such requiring reasons. But this is the true view. The Anselmian being could refrain from creating anything at all, and *requires no reason* for so refraining. This also means that for any additional increment of well-being or perfection that the Anselmian being could provide to some creature, the Anselmian being *needs no reason* for failing to confer that additional increment of well-being. The Anselmian being did not have to create you, or me, or any of the creatures that that being created, nor did the Anselmian being have to create at all; and that being's failure to create would need no justification, would require no further rational account. And whatever level of well-being the Anselmian being conferred upon you, me, or anyone else, the Anselmian being, even if possibly conferring an extra increment of well-being upon us, needed no reason not to; and that being's failure to confer greater perfection or a higher level of well-being would need no justification, would require no further rational account.

The first points to make in favor of this view are that room was cleared for it by the arguments of the first three chapters and that nothing in section 4.2 in any way calls this view into question. The Anselmian being's being possibly a creator and being rational entails that there are good reasons for the Anselmian being to create, but they do not entail that these reasons are requiring reasons. All that is needed is that creation be a worthwhile opportunity for the Anselmian being, not that it be something that it must do unless there are sufficient reasons to the contrary.

We have seen that there is room for the view that the existence and perfection/well-being of creatures do not give requiring reasons to the Anselmian being to bring them about. To go past this point, we need some positive reasons for the denial that creaturely existence and well-being give requiring reasons to the Anselmian being to promote them. As I mentioned above (4.1), I will make this argument in two stages. I want first to give a couple of arguments in this section that there is some pressure, given Anselmian methodology, to deny that the existence and perfection/well-being of creatures give requiring reasons for the Anselmian being to bring them about. I will follow this (4.4) with a more substantive argument that the best account of the nature of creaturely value given the Anselmian conception suggests an account of the Anselmian being's reasons that fits with this denial.

Among the perfections typically ascribed to the Anselmian being is *sovereignty*. The Anselmian being's stance with respect to the world is active rather than reactive: the Anselmian being is fully in charge, such that all facts about creation are ultimately to be explained by God and facts about God. Sovereignty involves *dependence upon* and *control by* that which is sovereign. That what exists depends on God and its features are controlled by features of God seems central to our conception of God as sovereign. (See Murphy 2011a, pp. 6–12, 61–8.) But one might also think that the Anselmian being exhibits greater sovereignty to the extent that the Anselmian being has *discretion*, that the Anselmian being is free to settle by that being's own choices the way that the world will be.

Now there is no simple way to settle the extent of the discretion that the Anselmian being has. It is relatively uncontroversial, though not particularly informative, to say that the Anselmian being's discretion does not go beyond the metaphysically and practically necessary. If some proposition's truth is metaphysically necessary, then the Anselmian being's discretion does not extend to its being false. If some act of bringing about the obtaining of some state of affairs is necessarily such that the Anselmian being has decisive reasons to perform it, then the Anselmian being's discretion does not extend to that state of affairs' not obtaining. So the Anselmian being's discretion does not extend to *2+2's not equaling 4*, or to *the Anselmian being's not being loved by the Anselmian being*. On the other hand, if some proposition's truth is contingent, and it is not the sort of proposition that it is logically incoherent that God bring about its truth, and the practical reasons at stake do not necessitate God's not bringing it about—well, if that proposition's truth were not a matter of some being's discretion, then that would disqualify that being from counting as absolutely sovereign and thus from counting as an Anselmian being.

To say more, we need to return to the earlier methodological reflections on how Anselmianism about God is to be deployed. Our conception of the divine perfections should press outward (1.4), and that is because our conception of an absolutely perfect being is not simply that of a being whose perfection expands to fill metaphysical possibility space, whatever size that space is, but has an absolute character, so that if those perfections are not good enough, we should deny that there is any such being as God. Let's think a bit about the cash value that this sort of methodological stance has.

Suppose we resume an inquiry suggested in 1.3 by considering how to spell out in more detail a relatively uncontroversial divine perfection—say, omniscience. One will have at least a rough-and-ready conception of what is involved in omniscience—say, knowing all truths. (I said it was rough-and-ready.) One will have some uncontroversial cases that fall within the divine perfection so conceived—say, that the divine being knows that water is H_2O, and that humans are mammals, and so forth. Now: suppose that there is some case with respect to which it is controversial whether it falls within the divine perfection so conceived—say, whether the divine being knows counterfactuals of freedom. Here is the question: Does the fact that we are working out the substance of a divine perfection provide any rational pressure toward a 'Yes' answer? Or are formal characterizations of divine perfections rationally neutral between 'Yes' and 'No' answers? Do not misunderstand. I am not asking whether there is *irresistible* pressure originating within perfect being theology toward a Yes answer. That would obviously have absurd implications, leading to ridiculous characterizations of divine perfections and making the inquiry into the intrinsic impossibility of counterfactuals of freedom having truth-values irrelevant. What I am asking is, again, about rational pressure. Does the fact that we are talking about an absolutely perfect being provide some 'outward pressure' on the contours of a divine perfection, so that our characterization of it should be expanded? Or should our characterization of a divine perfection be entirely subordinated to our understanding of its limiting factors?

Suppose that one has investigated counterfactuals of freedom and has come to the following provisional conclusion. There does not seem to be any incoherence in the idea of a counterfactual of freedom or in the idea of its having a determinate truth-value. But one does not judge oneself to be in a position to pronounce on the issue of whether there are any true counterfactuals of freedom. The question is whether one's position on this issue should be altered at all if one adds to the background the fact that there exists an absolutely perfect being, a being who has, among other features, the perfection of knowledge—that is, having knowledge to the maximal value limit of having knowledge. To have knowledge to the maximal value limit of having knowledge is not, recall, simply having as much knowledge as possible. It is that there is an intrinsic maximum of the value of knowledge that is characterizable independently of what is metaphysically possible (1.3); the importance of what is metaphysically possible is simply that, if the intrinsic maximum of the value of knowledge is not possibly realized by any being, then there is no Anselmian being. But now if one thinks that we should ascribe knowledge of a greater value to a being who knows counterfactuals of freedom than to a being who does not know them, then our earlier reflections on Anselmian methodology suggest that this provides us reason to believe that the Anselmian being knows counterfactuals of freedom.

Consider another perennial issue, that of God's involvement in the ordinary course of nature. There are a number of views available, and it would not serve our ends to formulate them too finely. But we might arrange such views on a continuum with respect to the extent to which divine action is to be invoked in accounting for the action of creatures in the natural order. *Deists* hold that divine action is necessary to bring the created order into existence, but that creatures can remain in existence and exercise their causal powers without further divine involvement. *Mere conservationists* hold that divine action is necessary to create and conserve in existence the creaturely order, but creatures can exercise their causal powers without further divine involvement. *Concurrentists* hold that divine action is necessary to create and conserve creatures and to cooperate in the exercise of their causal powers. *Occasionalists* hold not only that divine action is needed for creation and conservation, but that there are no creaturely causal powers; all creaturely change is immediately and completely accounted for by divine action (see Freddoso 1986, 1987, 1991, and 1994).

Consider Suárez's position and arguments on this issue. He judges the occasionalist position to be plainly false and philosophically and theologically unmotivated. He endorses the concurrentist view, and offers a number of considerations in its favor. But he saves what he calls his "best argument" for last:

This manner of acting [i.e. divine concurrence in the ordinary course of nature] in and with all agents pertains to the breadth of divine power, and on God's part it presupposes a perfection untainted by imperfection; and even though it does bespeak an imperfection on the part of the creature,...this imperfection is nonetheless endemic to the very concept of a creature or participated being as such....For the rest, there is in this way a perfect and essential ordering between the First Cause and the secondary cause, and there is nothing impossible here...therefore, this general influence should not be denied to God (*Disputationes Metaphysicae*, 22, 1, 13).

I understand Suárez here to be making an argument from the perfection of the divine nature to the concurrentist account of divine action in nature. It befits the perfection of the divine nature to be involved in this intimate way in the bringing about of events in the natural order.[5] While it correspondingly involves some imperfection in creatures—just as creatures must be created and conserved by God, and are not self-existent as God is, they are also unable to act on their own—this is an imperfection that befits the created condition. And as nothing precludes this relationship between God and creature in the bringing about of events in the natural order, then, that relationship ought to be affirmed. Suárez suggests that the best argument appeals primarily to God's nature—it speaks to the "breadth of divine power" and is possible only for a being whose "perfection [is] untainted by imperfection." And so we should take God's involvement in nature to be that characterized by the more extensive concurrentist account rather than that characterized by the less extensive conservationist or deistic accounts. Suárez invokes our methodological principle, that the nature of God as absolutely perfect gives positive reason to ascribe an absolutely greater degree of the good-making properties to God, rather than simply to ascribe to God whatever degree of such good-making properties we have independent grounds to think are within the scope of the metaphysically necessary.

I have offered a couple of case studies in which we might appeal to the absolute greatness of the Anselmian being as a way of tipping the scales toward a certain view of what is metaphysically possible. But it seems to me that these considerations are relevant also when thinking about the practically possible, that is, that which practical rationality permits. And this bears directly on the range of divine discretion, the scope for divine choice in fixing on what world to create, or to create at all. What we saw in Chapter 3 was that most views on why human beings are properly governed by familiar welfare-oriented moral goodness, on which the existence and well-being of sentient creatures provide requiring reasons for action, fail to apply to the Anselmian being. I conceded that one might dig in and hold that, even though we lack anything like a persuasive account of why the Anselmian being's ethics would be the ethics of familiar welfare-oriented moral goodness, such an ethics must be ascribed to the Anselmian being (3.5). But what the defender of this view should concede, I think, is that one who is uncertain about whether, or even denies that, the Anselmian being's ethics is characterized by familiar welfare-oriented moral goodness has not been shown to be in any sort of logical or metaphysical muddle. No inconsistency or

[5] I have argued that it is an aspect of divine sovereignty; see Murphy 2011a, pp. 61–8.

argumentative tension of any sort has been revealed in the view of one who grants that humans, and perhaps any rational creature, have requiring reasons to promote the existence and well-being of fellow rational (and perhaps also sentient) creatures, but that the Anselmian being need not have such reasons—that for the Anselmian being, such reasons are justifying only.

It is in such contexts as these that the methodology of Anselmianism, that the Anselmian perfections press outward (1.5), plays an important role in determining how we should fix the range of the divine perfections. Divine discretion as to how the world is fashioned is something that belongs to the divine perfection, as an aspect of divine sovereignty. Like knowledge and power, its excellence has an absolute character, such that our understanding of its goodness is not simply that of filling in whatever space the modal contours of reality leave to the Anselmian being, but being simply absolutely good. But the presence of requiring reasons limits divine discretion, by narrowing the range of what is practically possible for the Anselmian being to do. But with so little basis for holding that the existence and well-being of creatures give the Anselmian being requiring reasons for action, I say that we should hold that the perfection of divine sovereignty, including discretion, gives us reason to hold that the existence and well-being of creatures give the Anselmian being no such requiring reasons.[6]

4.4 The Value of Creatures and the Reasons of the Anselmian Being

The reasons for affirming that the existence and perfection/well-being of creatures do not give the Anselmian being requiring reasons to promote them were built on a piece of methodology, the move from the Anselmian being's absolute perfection to our having reason to support a more extensive interpretation of the great-making properties. These reasons, I think, do support the conception of the Anselmian being's ethics that I am putting forward. But we might nevertheless remain unsatisfied unless we had a plausible account of why the Anselmian being's ethics has that shape. To be told (to put it crudely) that the divine perfection requires rationality and sovereignty, and the

[6] The notion that the value of humans gives the Anselmian being justifying, not requiring, reasons enables a response to Nygren's criticism of rival Christian accounts of divine love. Nygren claims that divine love must be thought of as spontaneous and entirely unmotivated. He considers the view that divine love is motivated by something like the intrinsic value of creatures, but rejects that position:

> If this interpretation...were correct, God's love would not be in the last resort spontaneous and unmotivated but would have an adequate motive in the infinite value inherent in human nature. The forgiveness of sins would then imply merely a recognition of an already existing value. But it is evident enough that this is not the forgiveness of sins as Jesus understands it. When He says, 'Thy sins are forgiven thee,' this is no mere formal attestation of the presence of a value which justifies the overlooking of faults; it is the bestowal of a gift. Something really new is introduced, something new is taking place (Nygren 1969 [1938]).

But on the view of divine love suggested by the view that I am defending, divine forgiveness would not be a required response to existing value. Though justified, it would still be free, and fully retain its character as a gift. For more thoughts along these lines, see 9.4.

only way to get a sufficient measure of both is by holding that the Anselmian being's reasons to bring about creatures that exhibit a certain level of perfection/well-being are justifying rather than requiring, does not tell us *why* those reasons are as they are for the absolutely perfect being. An analogy: it may be important for us to know that if we are under genuine moral requirements, then those requirements must be backed by decisive reasons for us to comply (2.2); and so, since we are under a moral requirement to keep our promises, there must be decisive reasons to keep our promises. But that does not tell us what those reasons are, what their source or nature is, and so forth. So even if we are persuaded of the existence of such reasons, we lack an explanation of them. Similarly, even if we are moved by the view that the reasons of the Anselmian being are as they are, we as yet may lack any understanding of those reasons, why they are as they are.

It is useful to begin by considering an argument for the denial of the position that I am putting forward here. In 3.5 we considered the obvious argument that creaturely good must give requiring reasons, those based on the notion of intrinsic value. The idea, recall, is that the beings whose perfection/well-being the Anselmian being has reasons to promote are themselves agent-neutrally valuable, because they are *intrinsically* valuable. And if we think that these creatures are agent-neutrally valuable entities, then we should think that *any* rational agent, including the Anselmian being, must have requiring reasons to respond positively to these creatures.

There are various ways to formulate the view just described, and I will consider others. But it seems to me that the present formulation is frequently endorsed and worth discussing. Noteworthy about the present formulation is its treating the intrinsic value of certain creatures as explanatorily prior to the agent-neutral value of those creatures, and the agent-neutral value of those creatures as explanatorily more basic than the reasons to respect that value by promoting those creatures' well-being. So I begin with this basic appeal to intrinsic value, and why we should reject it, and why that rejection leads to a more adequate characterization of creaturely value.

For a creature to bear intrinsic value is for it to have value that holds independently of the relations in which that creature stands to other things.[7] Any value that a creature has that it might lack were it to stand (perhaps counterpossibly) in different relations to other beings is not intrinsic value. But I say that, given the existence of an Anselmian being, there could not be a creature with intrinsic value.

This was Anselm's own view of the matter (*Monologion* I, 14). Anselm held that the absolutely perfect being's perfection involves its being the *sole* being the value of which exists of itself, and not in relation to anything else. So while the absolutely perfect being bears its goodness *a se*, creatures have their goodness in relation to the absolutely perfect being, by way of *participation* in that being's goodness. I will say a bit more

[7] I am taking for granted Korsgaard's distinction between *intrinsic* value, the value that a being has solely on account of its intrinsic properties, and *final* value, the value in virtue of which one may properly act for something's sake (Korsgaard 1983, pp. 169–73).

about this notion of participation below in this section, but whatever we say about it, it is obviously an essentially relational notion, and so participated goodness is necessarily not intrinsic goodness. I make this appeal to authority only for the sake of noting that, whatever contemporary Anselmians think, there is one possible view on what Anselmianism entails about the realm of value that was taken seriously by an (!) important Anselmian and that precludes creaturely intrinsic value. Those of us sympathetic to Anselmian thinking about God should, then, at least take this possibility seriously.

We can make this argument also from the point of view of the divine perfections themselves. Consider again the perfection of sovereignty. For the Anselmian being to be *sovereign* is at least for the existence and character of all beings not identical with the absolutely perfect being to depend on and have their features fixed by the absolutely perfect being. Such sovereignty, further, seems more fully and valuably realized when the relations between these facts about God (for example, facts about God's nature, or about God's will) are immediate rather than fully mediated by non-divine facts. So it seems that divine sovereignty over the normative order would be more fully and valuably realized if facts about God contribute to fixing the value of creatures, and in an immediate way (for example, by the value of creatures being in part fixed by their being likenesses to God, or by their being loved or wanted or approved of by God, or something along those lines).[8] Given the methodological point that the divine perfections should be conceived as pressing outward (1.4), we have reason to ascribe this sort of extensive sovereignty over the normative order to the absolutely perfect being (Murphy 2011a, pp. 61–8).

That which is not only good in itself but is the source of any goodness of other things is greater than that which is simply good in itself. But if so, then a being would be greater if it were not only good in itself but also the source of any goodness in other things that might exist. And that the goodness of other things is derivative in this way seems not to be impossible. So we should say that the Anselmian being is not only good in itself but the source of the goodness of any beings that are distinct from the Anselmian being. So, given Anselmianism, there is no creature that is intrinsically good.

But one sympathetic to the appeal to intrinsic value as an account of the Anselmian being's reasons may feel that what is being objected to here is not what is essential to the argument. It is true that it is a commonplace to appeal to the intrinsic value of creatures as a justification for the Anselmian being's bringing into existence, and for promoting the perfection/well-being of, those creatures.[9] But it is not crucial for this explanation of the Anselmian being's reasons that the value of creatures be *intrinsic*

[8] As is clear from these examples, the facts about God that fix these normative facts need not be facts about what God wills or wants; on a view like Adams's (1999, pp. 34–6) or my own (2011, pp. 148–80), they may be fixed by some necessary relation to the divine nature. For a view on which what fixes such normative facts are facts about what God loves, see Wolterstorff 2008, p. 352.

[9] For a particularly straightforward example, see Dougherty 2014, pp. 130–1.

value in this strict sense. Notice that as the appeal to intrinsic value is formulated, the intrinsic value of creatures is invoked simply to explain their agent-neutral value. But one might drop the appeal to creaturely intrinsic value and just say: creatures are agent-neutrally valuable, and so they should be assessed as valuable by all reasonable agents, including the preeminently rational Anselmian being. It does not particularly matter whether this value is intrinsic or conferred (or otherwise present in virtue of some relation), so long as it is agent-neutral and necessarily exhibited. And so even if the value of creatures is possessed in virtue of their relation to the Anselmian being, nevertheless that value can do the work of explaining why the Anselmian being has reasons to promote their existence and perfection/well-being. It does not matter *why* creatures are so good; what matters is that they *are* good, and necessarily so, and thus give the Anselmian being reason to look after them.

As is clear from 4.2, I have no quarrel with the notion that the agent-neutral value of creatures makes it the case that the Anselmian being has reasons to promote their existence and perfection/well-being. And allowing that they have such value necessarily and that such value necessarily gives the Anselmian being reasons to promote their existence and perfection/well-being does not require us to take back anything that we said above about the sovereignty and discretion of the Anselmian being. If the value that creatures have is due to some relation that they stand in to the Anselmian being—for example, as on Adams's view,[10] *being like the Anselmian being*—then facts about creaturely value are controlled by relevant facts about the Anselmian being. And the Anselmian being's discretion is not limited, not yet, by the concession that these creatures necessarily give the Anselmian being reasons to act, for such reasons may be justifying reasons only, and justifying reasons do not require divine action of any sort, even in the absence of considerations to the contrary.

We should not say, though, that the agent-neutral value of creatures gives the Anselmian being *requiring* reason to promote their existence and perfection/well-being. Note again the point made above (3.5) in discussing the proposal that the intrinsic value of creatures entails that their good gives requiring reasons for every agent; the same holds for the proposal that agent-neutral goodness of creatures entails that their good gives requiring reasons for action for everyone. That is, even if we grant for the sake of argument there is some agent-neutral value necessarily borne by creatures of some kind, it does not follow that such agent-neutral value gives requiring reasons for every rational being to promote the good of creatures of that kind. It may be that their agent-neutral value gives justifying reasons for every rational being to promote their good, but not requiring reasons; it may be that it gives requiring reasons to some

[10] Actually, this is not quite Adams's official view. Adams's official view is that creatures are good when they resemble God in a way that gives God reason to love them (R. Adams 1999, pp. 34–6). But that would render useless this conception of creaturely goodness for explaining why God has reasons to protect, etc. creatures that are good in this way. I think the considerations that Adams invokes for modifying his account of creaturely goodness to include a reasons condition should not have moved him in that direction; see Murphy 2011a, pp. 156–7.

rational beings, but merely justifying reasons to others; and so forth. Having agent-neutral value is one thing; the particular sorts of reasons to which it gives rise are something else.

Nor must this remain merely a skeptical point. Consider the following conception of the value borne by God and creatures, a conception that was a familiar feature of high medieval thinking about God and creatures and which affirms that creatures themselves are bearers of agent-neutral value while denying that the value that they bear entails that their existence and/or perfection counts as a requiring reason for God to promote it. No one, according to this conception, should deny that there is some sort of agent-neutral goodness borne by creatures: after all, God made the world, and saw that it was good. Yet God was not rationally necessitated to create by the prospect of creaturely goodness. Nor does the creaturely goodness, even considered as already existing, rationally necessitate God to promote creatures' perfection to a certain level, or to add further perfection when possible. The idea that the absolutely perfect being could be made to act by some creature as final cause is as contrary to that being's sovereignty as the idea that the absolutely perfect being could be made to act by some creature as efficient cause. The sovereign absolutely perfect being is not necessitated into action for the sake of creatures.

Aquinas's view is instructive here. In the *Summa Theologiae* Aquinas poses the question whether God loves all things. A defender of the appeal to the intrinsic or agent-neutral value of creatures might suppose that Aquinas would argue in the following way: Creatures' existence and well-being are good; so God, being perfectly responsive to the good, must desire that existence and well-being in the absence of adequate reasons to the contrary; and so, absent such reasons, God desires the existence and well-being of creatures, and that counts as God's loving every creature.[11] But, although Aquinas does affirm that God loves all things, this is not Aquinas's argument. Here is what Aquinas says:

God loves all existing things. For all existing things, insofar as they exist, are good, since the being of a thing is itself good, and likewise, whatever perfection it possesses. Now it has been shown above that God's will is the cause of all things. It must needs be, therefore, that a thing has being, or any kind of good, only insofar as it has been willed by God. To every existing thing, then, God wills some good. Hence, since to love anything is nothing else than to will good to that thing, it is manifest that God loves everything that exists (Aquinas, *Summa Theologiae* Ia 20, 2).

Note how different Aquinas's argument is from that suggested by the appeal to intrinsic (or agent-neutral) value. Aquinas's argument is that God's being loving is to be *consequentially* ascribed to God in virtue of all creatures' exhibiting some level of goodness and God's being creatively responsible for their exhibiting that level of goodness.[12]

[11] See, for example, the arguments in Pruss 2012a, p. 22 and in Dougherty 2014, pp. 130–1.

[12] I don't think Aquinas's argument in this passage is successful as it stands; he needs to add that God wills the creature's being *for its own sake* (even if it is also for God's sake, or for other creatures' sake).

Here is a comparison. Thomas Nagel, in asking whether all motivation proceeds from an agent's desires, says that this is true, but notes that this concession does not imply that desire is explanatorily prior to motivation; we can ascribe a desire to x to an agent simply in virtue of the fact that an agent was motivated to x, and so we can as a consequence ascribe to the agent the desire to x (Nagel 1970, pp. 29–30). Similarly, Aquinas's answer here does not suggest that God's loving creaturely goodness is explanatorily prior to divine action in response to creatures; rather, we can ascribe love of creatures to God in virtue of the fact that God acted to bring about creatures' being to some degree in act. Such lovingness would be ascribable to God *whatever* choice God made about whether to bring *whatever* creatures into existence and to *whatever* level of perfection.

Aquinas does not think that God can be rationally necessitated by creaturely goodness. But he does think that God can be rationally necessitated. God, on Aquinas's view, necessarily wills God's own goodness, because God is absolutely, completely, exhaustively good (*Summa Theologiae* Ia 19, 3). Now one might think that if God wills God's own goodness, then God should necessarily will creaturely goodness, at least in the absence of competing considerations. A perfectly good will wills all good, one might say. But this is not Aquinas's view. For—and this is the crucial point—it is not just that creatures exhibit *less* of that goodness that God exhibits, so that they are on the same scale, but God is just higher up on it. It is, rather, that creaturely goodness is a lesser *kind* of good, goodness *by participation*. That some being is good by participation does not concern merely whether that being's goodness is intrinsic or extrinsic. It concerns the very kind of goodness exhibited, and affects the sort of reason-giving force that this goodness has.

Suppose that we consider a world that includes one intrinsic good, and then we suppose that a distinct, further intrinsic good is added to that world.[13] It is part of the logic of intrinsic value that by adding this second intrinsic good, one adds *further goodness* to that world. And if one supposes that intrinsic goodness is requiring-reason-giving, one has *additional requiring reason* to bring about that second good. But the view of Aquinas, and of the high medievals who shared Aquinas's view, is that the world of God alone and the world of God along with God's creation do not follow this logic. When God creates, God does not bring about *further* intrinsic goodness or even further agent-neutral goodness of the same sort that God has. Creatures are agent-neutrally good, but there is no *further goodness* brought about by creating. For God alone realizes all good. How could a being who is absolutely perfect

A willing of some creature's good that were absolutely instrumental could not count as loving that creature. (If I give you some good in order to make you trust me so that I can cheat you out of everything you own, that I willed good to you does not count as my loving you. Matters would not be helped if I give you some good to get someone else to trust me, so that I can cheat that other person of everything he or she owns.) This does not make any problems for my own argument, for one can rationally will something for its own sake without having requiring reasons to do so; one needs only justifying reasons.

[13] Never mind that this is impossible on the Anselmian picture, for reasons we considered earlier in this section.

not exhaust all the possibilities of goodness? And so the fact that agent-neutral goodness is indeed exhibited by creatures does not give God requiring reason to bring those creatures into existence. This is because all creaturely goodness is goodness by participation.

On this view, then, the Anselmian being's bringing about some set of creatures to some level of perfection, though a choice to bring about more *good things*, is not a choice to bring about more *goodness*. Bringing about more goodness is impossible, on this view. All goodness is realized by the Anselmian being. The choice between there being only the Anselmian being and there being the Anselmian being and creatures as well is a choice between two ways that the divine goodness can be manifested, not a choice between there being divine goodness alone and there being divine goodness and some more goodness besides. The divine goodness can be manifested wholly in itself, or in itself *and* by participation. But these are two ways for the divine goodness to be manifested; it is not that the divine goodness is manifested the same way in both cases, with additional goodness realized in one of them, in creatures as well as in the Anselmian being.

Here is an analogy. We might consider different ways in which one party who is justified in holding some belief might bring it about that some other party is justified in holding that belief. You might prove some theorem, and so be justified in believing it; and then you teach me the proof, I understand it, and come to hold the corresponding belief. This is a world in which there is not only one more *justified believer* in that proposition than a world in which you alone know the proof, it is also a world in which there is, in a straightforward sense, more *justification*. Compare this to a case in which you simply report to me that the proof is successful, and I believe you on the basis of your testimony. This is a world in which there are more justified believers in that proposition, but not more justification. (One could rightly take the former world to be one in which there is more evidence for the truth of the proposition from both parties' having justification for believing it; one could not rightly do so in the latter case.) This is what goodness by participation is like. If one being is intrinsically good and another is good simply because it participates in the intrinsic good's goodness, there is an additional *good* (and even agent-neutrally good) *thing*, but there is no more *goodness* than if the intrinsically good thing alone existed.

The explanation of the reasons for promoting the existence and perfection/well-being of creatures in terms of creatures exhibiting goodness by participation only is superior, I think, to rival accounts of why God is under no rational necessity to create. One prominent strand of anti-necessitarianism about creation is formulated in terms of a certain view about practical reason: eudaimonism. According to eudaimonism, the foundational principle of practical reason gives the realization of one's own good as the overall aim of action. The eudaimonist account of practical reason was, as a matter of history, typically coupled with a perfectionist account of the good, on which the realization of one's own good was identified with or constituted by one's becoming perfected, actualizing the capacities appropriate for the sort of being that one is. Given this sort of view, it is clear that one could be rationally necessitated to perform some action only if that action were necessary for the achievement of one's own good—if one needed to perform that action to realize one's good. But given such a view, it seems clear that an absolutely perfect being could not be rationally necessitated to create. For an absolutely perfect being does not have to, it does not need to, create in order to realize its good, at least if its good is understood in perfectionist terms. This argument holds a fortiori for creation to any level of perfection/well-being for creatures—the absolutely perfect being does not need to create, and does not need to create to any degree of perfection/well-being, and so could not be rationally necessitated to do so.

Put as strongly as this, the argument seems to prove too much. Rational necessity is to be understood in terms of what is necessary for the realization of one's own good, understood in terms of one's perfection. But to have any sort of reasons at all would be understood in terms of furthering or promoting in some way one's perfection, even if not necessary for such. But this would seem to make creation not only rationally unnecessary, but in principle rationally inexplicable. Since the Anselmian being is already completely perfect, any creative act would seem to be pointless. But pretty plainly it has *some* point, for here, after all, is creation. So there must be an error in the argument somewhere. And once we identify the error in the argument, it is possible that correcting the error will enable us to see that creation, and perhaps even creation to a certain level of perfection/well-being, is rationally necessary, even for an Anselmian being.

One might challenge this argument by denying that eudaimonism, or eudaimonism coupled with perfectionism about one's good, is the right model for thinking about the reasons of an Anselmian being, or by claiming that one has made illicit further assumptions about what eudaimonism-cum-perfectionism entails for practical rationality. Kretzmann (1991) challenges Aquinas's anti-necessitarianism, claiming that on Aquinas's own principles, he should be a necessitarian about creation. But Kretzmann does not challenge Aquinas's eudaimonism. Instead, Kretzmann holds that Aquinas's affirmation of the 'Dionysian principle'—that good is diffusive of itself—commits him to holding that failing to create is not a real option for God, while not challenging eudaimonism. The best way to reconcile these is to hold that there is an error in the argument from eudaimonism and perfectionism to the conclusion that God need not create. Perhaps the error is to assume that *promotionism* comes along with eudaimonism: that is, that if one's own good is the basis of all of one's practical reasons, then all actions that are reasonable for one to perform are acts of *promoting* one's own good. And Aquinas is, in any case, committed to denying promotionism. For Aquinas thinks that God's loving God, though it does not promote God's goodness, is rationally necessary for God.

The appeal to creaturely goodness as participated goodness provides a better way to explain, contra Kretzmann, why God is not rationally necessitated to create. Kretzmann appeals to the Dionysian principle, holding that goodness must be diffusive of itself. And perhaps it must be, if the diffusion of intrinsic goodness were a real possibility. But it is not a real possibility. God can create more beings, and these beings will indeed be good. But God cannot create more goodness. Even considered apart from creation, there exists all the goodness that is or ever could be.

4.5 Does the Appeal to Creaturely Goodness as Participated Goodness Undermine the Justifying Reasons to Create?

Creatures' existing and exhibiting perfection/well-being is agent-neutrally good, but their participated goodness, and thus the coming into existence of creatures or their gaining some perfection/well-being, does not add goodness to the world. This is my explanation of why the defensible (4.3) thesis that creaturely goods do not give the Anselmian being requiring reasons to promote them is true. But one might think that the view that I have defended falls prey to a problem with Aquinas's anti-necessitarian eudaimonist argument that I identified above: it proves too much. In making participated goodness look unable to *require* the Anselmian being to act for its sake, at least in the absence of considerations to the contrary, I have also made participated goodness look unable to *justify* the Anselmian being in promoting it. For what would be the point of God's creating unless further goodness will be brought into the world thereby?

Consider an analogy that has the potential to be very misleading. Suppose that all the members of some population equally merit and have an equal share of the goods worth having. This situation is about to change, though. There is an additional good that will drop onto half of the population, like manna from heaven. You can see who will receive this good, though the parties who will receive it merit it no more and no less than those who will not receive it. That this good is coming is inevitable, and once received it cannot be added to or destroyed. But: you have the power to alter *who* receives it. You can intervene so that it is received by a different set of people than those who will receive it if you do not intervene, and you have the ability to determine which particular, identifiable individuals receive this bonus. Do you have any reason to exercise this power, to change which set of individuals receives this extra, unmerited benefit?

There is a straightforward case that you have no such reason. You are not going to add any more good to the world by so doing. All you will be doing is moving a good from one party to another, without improving the situation with respect to equality (the same levels of equality/inequality will result) or merit (all equally merit/fail to merit the relevant goods). In this scenario it seems pointless to put in any effort, however trivial, to make such a transfer, as pointless as it would be to ensure that the number of hairs in your eyebrows is even rather than odd—as no good turns on it, making the effort is action without reason, unintelligible. (I suppose there may be *some* reason here—perhaps you're bored, and looking for something to do—but the central point is that reasons are not given by the features of the situation that you will be changing by intervening.)

There is some analogy to the divine case as I've characterized it. By creating, I have argued, the Anselmian being is not adding goodness to the world; the Anselmian being is (and this is the very misleading part about the analogy)[14] adjusting how that goodness is manifested. In the case I described, the question is whether the fixed-sum, transferrable good will show up in one random group or some other; in the creation case, the question is whether the divine goodness will be manifested in God alone or in God and (as participated goodness) by creatures. Just as it might seem pointless to move the transferrable good around, it might seem similarly pointless for the Anselmian being to act so that the divine goodness is manifested in one way rather than another.

But it seems plain that the lack of agent-neutral goodness added in the good-transfer case does *not* entail that one would not have reason to transfer some of these goods from one set of parties to another. If some of those who would otherwise miss out on extra goods are friends of yours, then you obviously *do* have a reason to make the transfer—the agent-*relative* reason to benefit one's friends. You can acknowledge and act on that reason even while acknowledging that *the world* is not made better from a neutral point of view by transferring the goods from non-friends to friends. (This case requires no view on whether it would be wise or just to make this transfer—only that there are reasons that are agent-relative in play.)

This explains why there can be justifying reasons for God to create, and to some level of perfection/well-being, even if God does not add goodness to the world, but only affects how that goodness is realized in the world. It is to create for the reason of the agent-*relative* value that creation will have for the beings who are created. There is no additional value *in the world*. There is no additional value *for God*. There is no requirement that one take up this perspective in creating, or to do so to a certain extent. It is, rather, a *generosity* that may be freely exhibited and which rationalizes the choice to come.

4.6 Reasons to Promote and Reasons to Respect

I have so far argued for two theses about the ethics of the Anselmian being: the Anselmian being has justifying reasons to promote the existence and perfection/well-being of creatures, and it is not true that the Anselmian being has requiring reasons to promote the existence and perfection/well-being of creatures. But there are multiple sorts of appropriate response to value, and *promotion* is only one of these; *respect* is another, and the appropriateness of respect as a response to the good is not obviously reducible to the appropriateness of promotion as a response to what is good (3.4). It may be, then, that there are further informative theses about the Anselmian being's ethics that concern the reasons that the Anselmian being has to respect creaturely good. In Chapter 5 I will argue that the Anselmian being has not only requiring reasons, but even decisive requiring reasons, to exhibit a certain sort of respect for creaturely goods.

[14] What is misleading is that it is not as if God loses some of God's own goodness by creating, which is then relocated into creation—that is what the analogous case suggests. But at a relevant level of abstraction, these are both cases in which the amount of goodness is not what is up to the agent; what is up to the agent is how that goodness will be manifested or realized.

5

The Ethics of the Anselmian Being II (Respect)

5.1 The Anselmian Being Does Not Intend Evil

In 3.4 I claimed that there are multiple ways of appropriately responding to value. I also claimed that the response *respect* is not reducible to the response *promotion*. What I had in mind is that goods often make intelligible a certain way of acting with respect to them: acting so that those goods are more likely to be realized. This is *promotion*, and there are many sorts of action in response to goods that have their appropriateness as species of promotion. If there are any responses to goods that seem *not* to involve making it more likely that some good will be realized—because the good at stake is not of the sort that could be promoted; or even if it is of the sort to be promoted, such promotion is not in the circumstances a real possibility; or even if it is of the sort to be promoted and such promotion is in the circumstances a real possibility, there are ways to respond to the good in question that do not make it more likely that the good will be realized, yet still seem appropriate in light of it—then it is prima facie plausible that there are some responses to the good the appropriateness of which is not reducible to the appropriateness of promotion. I now stipulate that any such responses are 'respect' responses to the good.

In contrast to promotion, this *respect* category of responses to the good looks gerrymandered. Philosophers have appealed to different sorts of response that could be lumped in here. The Kantian point that persons, though not the right sort of thing to be promoted by action (states of affairs' obtaining can be promoted; substances cannot), are nevertheless due a certain response (not being treated as mere means, but as ends-in-themselves) is an instance of this notion (Donagan 1980, pp. 62–6, 224–39 and Anderson 1995, pp. 8–11, 17–30). But so too is the natural law theorist's account of the doctrine of double effect, on which human goods are such that we are to refrain from intending the destruction of those goods, even when other important goods can be brought about thereby (for example, Murphy 2004); and so too are most accounts of symbolic action, action that is appropriate because of its expressive relation to the goods on which it bears (R. Adams 1999, pp. 214–30). I am not going to defend some unified theory of respect responses to value. My aim is to defend the view that a specific respect response is one that the Anselmian being has requiring reason to perform, and indeed that this requiring reason is decisive in the case of the Anselmian being. My thesis is that the Anselmian being has decisive requiring reasons not to intend the absence of due perfection/well-being in creatures. I will call absence of due perfection or due well-being 'evils,' and I will summarize my thesis as *the Anselmian being does not intend evils.*

I earlier (4.1) clarified my use of the term 'perfection/well-being' with respect to creatures with the aim of avoiding some controversial issues about the relation between perfection and well-being. I now note that I include 'due' in my formulation of this thesis in order to avoid taking a stand on another controversial issue. What I have in mind by the well-being or perfection that is 'due' to some creature is that which it is supposed to have. I will leave this 'supposed to have' vague for the moment (I return to it in 6.5), except to make the following brief remarks. The 'supposed to have' here is a *local* notion, involving what perfections or aspects of well-being it is fitting for this creature of this kind in these circumstances to exhibit. This is *not* a notion by which we appeal to *global* considerations to determine what features it ought to exhibit—I do not, for example, have in mind by 'supposed to have' some moral sense, in which the well-being or perfection that something is supposed to have is what it would have if things were morally best in the world, or if agents were acting as they should, morally speaking. Rather, what constitutes a creature's due perfection or well-being is determined by more local factors, factors simply about the appropriateness or fittingness of this creature or a creature of this kind exhibiting that perfection or that aspect of well-being. (So it would be coherent to say that it is for the best that some creature be subject to some loss of well-being, which loss is nevertheless an evil.) One might think that the relevance of some or all of these local factors is just part of the concept or nature of well-being and perfection, and thus 'due perfection' and 'due well-being' are pleonasms. Or one might deny that.[1] In any case, I do not wish to take a stand on it at the moment. My claim is that the Anselmian being does not intend the absence of such appropriate well-being or perfection for any creature, because there are not only requiring but decisive requiring reasons against doing so; and as the Anselmian being is perfectly rational, the Anselmian being would never do what there is decisive reason not to do.

I first argue for the distinction between what is intended and what is foreseen (5.2), and argue that this distinction is a real one even in the case of the absolutely perfect being (5.3). I then articulate why the Anselmian being has requiring reason not to intend evil (5.4), and why we should think that in the case of the Anselmian being,

[1] Suppose that a human being who is not subject to accident or disease will typically die after one hundred years or so of life. While a typical year of human life is good for the human who lives it, one might think that one who does not enjoy a 101st year of life is not subject to an evil, whereas one who does not enjoy a 51st year of life is subject to an evil. The idea would be that while a (pain-free, etc.) year of life is a good for the human being who lives it, it is only failure to get what instances of one's kind are typically allotted in terms of this good that counts as being *deprived* of something. But I am not defending this position. I mean to take no stand on it.

these reasons are decisive (5.5). Though the presence of requiring reasons to promote creaturely perfection/well-being would compromise the Anselmian being's sovereignty (4.3), the presence of requiring, even decisive, reasons not to intend the absence of due creaturely perfection/well-being does not (5.6).

5.2 The Intended/Foreseen Distinction

Here is a quick argument that the Anselmian being has reasons not to intend evil. The Anselmian being has reasons to promote the good of creatures, and by intending evil, the Anselmian being would be, in some way, setting back that good. So there is at least some reason for the Anselmian being not to intend evil.

Though some can avail themselves of this argument, I cannot, for I want to show that there are *requiring* reasons for the Anselmian being not to intend evil, and I have argued that the Anselmian being has only justifying, not requiring, reasons to promote the perfection/well-being of creatures (4.2–4.4). But even putting that point to the side, the aim here is to show that there is a distinctive reason not to intend evil that goes beyond any reasons provided by reasons to promote the relevant values. The idea, as noted in 5.1, is to explain how there are reasons not to intend evil that are irreducible to the reasons entailed by the reasons to promote the good. That there is a reason not to intend evil is not supposed to be simply an implication of the fact that when one intends evil, then one is likely to bring about something that there is a reason not to bring about. There is supposed to be something *special* about intending evil, such that acting with that intention makes the action—partially constituted by the having of that intention—subpar, defective, in some way not all an action can be.

It is thus particularly important to make a distinction between acting with the intention of evil and acting in other ways that involve the possibility, probability, or even certainty of evil resulting. As the most salient of such ways is acting with the *foresight* of such a possibility, probability, or even certainty, it is important to ward off objections to the very idea that there is a conceptual or real distinction between what is intended and what is foreseen.

The prominent claim that there is no real intended/foreseen distinction is not the claim that if an agent foresees that p the agent intends that p. I foresee that Jimmy's Old Town Tavern will be populated tonight. I do not intend that Jimmy's be populated tonight. So there is obviously *some* conceptual difference between intention and foresight. Critics of the intended/foreseen distinction want to say, rather, that somehow, *with respect to action*, there is no such distinction: to act with the intention to bring about some outcome is not to be distinguished from acting with the foresight that some outcome will (may? probably will?) occur when one acts. But we obviously cannot read this as the claim that action with foresight entails action with intention. Again, in writing this sentence, I foresee that Jimmy's will be populated tonight. But in writing this sentence, I do not intend that Jimmy's be populated tonight.

What critics of the very existence of the intended/foreseen distinction have in mind is a much more plausible thesis: that an action's being performed with the foresight that its being the case that p will result (either logically or causally) from that action entails that action's being performed with the intention that its being the case that p will result (either logically or causally) from that action. So Sidgwick, who was extremely careful about what he published and who put *The Methods of Ethics* through a half-dozen editions in his lifetime, says in that work that "it is best to include under the term 'intention' all the consequences of an action that are foreseen as certain or probable" (1981, p. 202).

Why would one fold what is foreseen as a result of one's action into the intention of the action? Once we allow that there is not even the least reason to believe that action with foresight that p entails action with the intention that p, why would we think that a special case of this—action with the foresight that its being the case that p will result from the action entails action with the intention that its being the case that p will result from the action—is true? There must be something special about this *particular* sort of foresight about the action, foresight about *what results* from the action. But no one has given any adequate account of what is special about that sort of foresight that would show that what is foreseen with respect to the results of an action is an intended result of that action.

And it is not just that this burden has never been discharged: there are strong reasons to deny the entailment. Taking the low road, that of counterexample, we can provide cases in which it is obvious that some consequences of one's action, while foreseen, are not intended. Joseph Boyle and Thomas Sullivan (1977, p. 358) describe a case of a person who wishes to defend his family honor by oratory, knowing that his speech difficulties are almost certain to make his words come out with a serious stutter. It would be very peculiar to say that the person intends to stutter his way through his speech. He does not intend to stutter. He aims not to stutter, and is trying not to.

Taking the high road, that of explanation, it seems clear that intention and foresight are different kinds of mental state, and thus must be conceptually distinguished. Foresight is a kind of belief: to foresee something is to believe that it will (or will likely) occur. Intention is, while not a kind of desire, akin to it: to intend something is to seek its realization, to have it as a goal that regulates deliberation and action. But belief and desire have different 'directions of fit.' Belief aims at fitting the world: so if one believes that p, and that p is not the case, one should revise one's belief so that it fits with the world. Desire aims at fitting the world to it: so if one desires that p, and it is not the case that p, one should revise the world so that it fits with one's desire. Since foresight and intention have distinct directions of fit, there must be a difference between them. So it is possible to foresee that some state of affairs will obtain as the result of one's action without that state of affairs' obtaining being the intended result of one's action. (See also Aulisio 1995, pp. 345–7, which is indebted to Anscombe 1957.)

5.3 Intention and Foresight in the Anselmian Being

Now, even if it conceded that there is such an intended/foreseen distinction, one might think that this is a distinction that dissolves in the context of fully rational beings, or in the context of a being that is not only a fully rational being but unlimited in any other respect relevant to the excellence of agency. But this is false: even in the case of the Anselmian being, we have reason to distinguish between what that agent intends by acting and what that agent foresees will result from acting.

Consider the thesis that the intended/foreseen distinction breaks down in the context of fully rational agents: while it is possible for what is intended and what is merely foreseen to be distinct for agents generally, it is not possible for *rational* agents, for that a rational agent foresees a certain result from his or her action entails that by choosing that action the agent intends, in part, that result. As Chisholm claims—he calls this the "principle of diffusiveness of intention"—"if a rational man acts with the intention of bringing about a certain state of affairs p and if he believes that by bringing about p he will bring about the conjunctive state of affairs p and q, then he does act with the intention of bringing about p and q" (1970, p. 636). So, even if there is a conceptual distinction between intention and foresight, in rational agents the foreseen effects of what one intends 'flow into' one's intention, leaving the category of the foreseen but unintended meaningful but empty. And as the Anselmian being is not just minimally but perfectly rational, we should hold that any truth that is constitutive of rationality will hold of the divine rationality. So if Chisholm's diffusiveness-of-intentions principle is correct, then what is intended by the Anselmian being will be just what is foreseen (in the relevant sense) by the Anselmian being.

But it seems to me that there is little warrant for Chisholm's principle. Again: the low road. Suppose that I intend to change lanes on the highway leading into Washington, D.C. I foresee that by changing lanes, even using my signal and allowing plenty of room, my action will cause the driver in the next lane to make an obscene gesture at me. According to the view that rational agents enfold the foreseen into their intentions, I must intend that I change lanes and be the recipient of the obscene gesture. This is silly enough. But suppose that driver in the next lane, feeling cheerier than usual, does not make the obscene gesture. Must I then try to provoke the driver into doing so, so that my intention will be satisfied? This is even sillier.

Again, still on the low road. The principle that rational agents enfold the foreseen into their intentions would make a solution to the paradox of happiness impossible, at least for rational, informed agents. It turns out there are some activities from which one cannot derive satisfaction—or the most satisfaction available from that activity—unless one performs the activity without attempting to derive satisfaction from it. With some activities, this is a merely contingent feature—it may just be an interesting feature of some people that they cannot derive full enjoyment from chess if they play the game while intending to get satisfaction from it. With some activities, the possibility of enjoyment in that activity is excluded by the aim of enjoying it, because the activity is essentially altruistic, e.g. selflessly helping others. But the principle of diffusiveness of intention would make these activities impossible for rational agents. Suppose that I intend to help others without regard to promoting my own good. Suppose that I also foresee that performing this action will lead to my enjoyment. So according to the principle, if I am rational, I will intend to help others without regard to promoting my own good and to gain enjoyment from doing so. Since this is incoherent, if I am rational, I will never intend to help others without regard to my own good, at least so long as I believe that I may well end up enjoying it.

The principle of diffusiveness of intentions is just false. The low roads clearly lead away from its acceptance. And Chisholm gives little argument for it. It is true that there is a fairly widely acknowledged principle of rational intending of the form *if A is rational, and A intends that p, and A believes that q, then A intends that r.* It is the necessary means principle: if A is rational, and A intends that p, and A believes that its being the case that q is a necessary means to its being the case that p, then A intends that q.[2] But aside from the fact that the necessary means principle is not subject to the embarrassing counterexamples to which the principle of diffusiveness of intention is subject, it is clear that there is a rationale for the necessary means principle, a rationale that is absent in the case of the principle of diffusiveness of intention and explains why it is, on reflection, so implausible.

The necessary means principle has its plausibility in virtue of the fact that to intend an end is to set oneself to the achievement of a certain goal, and thus to commit oneself to taking a path that, so far as it is in one's power, leads to that goal. So if a rational agent comes to believe that there is only one available path to one's intended end, then that rational agent will either take that path or give up on the goal. The subordinate intention for the means is needed to guide one's conduct on the path to one's intended goal; the rational agent forms that intention because of the need to guide his or her action in pursuit of the end. But in the case of the principle of the diffusiveness of intention, there is no practical need to expand one's intention to include within it all manner of foreseen consequences of the pursuit of one's end. The point of expanding one's intention to include within it not only the goal, or the means to reach that goal, but also the further consequences, is—what? It is pointless, as the highway case shows. It requires as a matter of rationality for one to include in one's objective matters in which one takes no interest, and indeed in which one may have an interest that things turn out the opposite way from what one foresees. There is, then, an important distinction between intention and foresight, and the distinction is maintained even in the case of fully rational agents.

There is, nevertheless, some justified uneasiness at thinking that this distinction between the intended and the foreseen holds so neatly in the divine case. I do not think that the fact that the Anselmian being is omniscient is a plausible source of this uneasiness.

[2] This isn't quite right. We need to add, at least, that A believes that A's intending that q be the case is necessary for q's being the case.

It is true that the Anselmian being knows exactly what will result from any choice that the Anselmian being makes, and so the Anselmian being's foresight is maximally certain.[3] But this does not seem to me to be anything that could give us a reason to think that the intended/foreseen distinction collapses in the divine case. Given the above point that intention and foresight have different directions of fit, it would be very strange that a movement from lesser to greater certainty about the outcome of one's action is, in all rational beings, a movement from what may be merely foreseen but unintended to what is intended. My thinking that by bombing a munitions dump I am likely to cause harm to some civilians is not enough to make the harming of those civilians part of my objective; being brought from likelihood to certainty is not going to make such harming of civilians any more part of my objective. And so the fact that the Anselmian being has such knowledge of the outcome of divine action is not any reason to think that the intended/foreseen distinction is going to break down in this case.

Perhaps more plausible is the idea that because the Anselmian being is sovereign over creation, then everything that occurs within creation, having been foreseen by the Anselmian being, must be something that this sovereign being aims at, intends. But that is a mistake, even on the very strong conception of divine sovereignty that I am working with in this book. According to the doctrine of divine sovereignty that I am employing, every fact in the created order is explained by facts about the Anselmian being. Some of these facts may be explained by facts about the divine nature. But even for those explained by the divine will, not all of the facts about the created order that are explained by facts about the divine will need be explained by the fact that the Anselmian being intends that *those* facts obtain. They may (for example) be explained by their being consequences of a conjunction of the laws of nature (arguendo, intended by the Anselmian being) and some other fact (arguendo, intended by the Anselmian being), and consequences of such conjunctions may be foreseen by the Anselmian being without being intended. I am happy to say that for every contingent truth, its complete explanation includes facts about what the Anselmian being intended, but that complete explanation may not include that the Anselmian being intended that contingent fact.

In my view, the most serious worries here result not from divine omniscience or divine sovereignty but from divine simplicity. (Some do not think that Anselmianism entails divine simplicity; they do not need to worry here.) Given divine simplicity, there are bound to be difficulties involved in the ascription of distinct mental states to the Anselmian being that are not involved in the ascription of such distinct states to us complex beings. And one might well think that the distinction in the Anselmian being between *choosing with the intention that* and *choosing with the foresight that* is likely to present such difficulties.

[3] I reject open theism's limitations on divine foreknowledge. The only arguments for open theism that I find initially plausible are those based on a tension between human freedom and God's omniscience, should God have foreknowledge of future free actions, and I take those arguments to have been laid to rest by Merricks 2009.

I am not going to pretend that I do not find this all very puzzling, and I am not going to attempt to sort out the general problem of how we are to ascribe to the Anselmian being meaningfully a variety of distinct mental states though that being is entirely simple. But I do want to comment on the more specific problem of how we distinguish between the Anselmian being's intending and merely foreseeing, on the assumption that we have an available solution to the general question of how to ascribe distinct mental states to a simple being. The idea is that, given a solution to the general problem of the ascription of distinct mental states to the Anselmian being, we face no *further* obstacle to using the rough-and-ready tools by which we distinguish between intention and mere foresight in our fellow human beings.

For example: one of the premier tests of intention as opposed to mere acting with foresight is a counterfactual test. The test asks whether one would have performed the relevant action if the given outcome were not foreseen to come of the action. (So: if we are wondering whether the bomber intended to kill those civilians that the bomber in fact foreseeably killed by dropping the bombs, ask whether the bomber would have carried out that bombing if killing of civilians were not a foreseeable result.) This test is only a test, not a criterion; and it is not infallible. It works well only if one employs multiple formulations of the test for a given putative intention. And like counterfactual tests for causation, it is subject to problems from finks and antidotes. I doubt that these problems can be fixed in a non-ad-hoc way. But as merely a rough-and-ready way of getting a hold of what intentions to ascribe to the Anselmian being, it would be extraordinarily helpful if we knew what counterfactuals held: if some outcome results from the Anselmian being's action, but the Anselmian being would have performed that action even had some outcome not come from it, then it is prima facie plausible that this outcome was not intended by the Anselmian being. How we know such counterfactuals in the divine case is not really to the point: perhaps the Anselmian being has a track record; perhaps the Anselmian being tells us; perhaps there are some value judgments that we are confident in ascribing to the Anselmian being that would explain the truth of various counterfactuals.

It is worth commenting in more detail about this final point, about the value judgments to be ascribed to the Anselmian being. Different platitudes hold of the intended and the foreseen, in the case of a fully rational being. To put things relatively uncontroversially for the time being, that some outcome is intended by a fully rational being entails that that being judges it to be *good* in some way—good in itself, or at least as a means to what is good, or bearing some other positive relevant relationship to the good. No such entailment holds with respect to what is foreseen, even by a fully rational, fully knowledgeable agent. So we have reason to judge at least of things that happen that they are intended by the Anselmian being only if they are themselves good or serve something good.

The point that I am making here is that our standard ways of ascribing intentions to agents—either more directly, by way of the counterfactual test, or more indirectly, by way of the assumption that the agent in question is a reasonable agent and that reasonable agents do not intend certain things—do not seem to be particularly threatened by divine simplicity. To put the point another way, even granting for the sake of argument the usefulness of introspection into one's own complex inner life as a way of knowing one's own mental states and the distinctions between them, no such complexity-presupposing ways of knowing are employed by us in ascribing intentions, and distinguishing between the intended and the foreseen, with respect to other agents. So it does not seem to me that divine simplicity, puzzling as it might be, poses a *special* problem with respect to the distinction between the Anselmian being's intention and the Anselmian being's foresight.

There is a difference between what one intends in one's action and what one foresees to be a result of one's action. This difference has application even in the case of a fully rational, fully knowledgeable, fully sovereign being. And so we can ask whether there are reasons for a fully rational, fully knowledgeable, and fully sovereign being not to intend evil, reasons that go beyond whatever reasons there are for a fully rational, fully knowledgeable, and fully sovereign being not to act in a way that that being foresees will have evils among its results.

5.4 The Anselmian Being's Requiring Reasons against Intending Evil

The claim that the Anselmian being has a requiring reason not to intend evil is the claim that there is some consideration against acting with the intention that some aspect of a creature's due perfection/well-being be absent that is not a consideration against acting with the mere foresight that some aspect of a creature's due perfection/well-being will be absent, and, further, that in the absence of other relevant considerations it would be unreasonable for the Anselmian being to act with such an intention.[4] In this section I argue that there are such requiring reasons; in the next section (5.5) I argue that there are no relevant considerations that would make it reasonable for the Anselmian being to act with such an intention, and thus these reasons are decisive.

The argument for there being a requiring reason for the Anselmian being not to intend evil rests on the connection between the intention of an action and what makes for that action's success. My thesis is that an agent's intention in acting—both with respect to the end of the action and with respect to the means that the agent will take to achieve that end—defines the *success conditions* of the action, what it is for the action to be a success and for the agent to be successful as an agent in acting. By contrast, what is merely foreseen does not at all define the success conditions of the action. These differences between intention and foresight provide the basis for an explanation of why the Anselmian being has requiring reason not to intend evil.

[4] The further condition is necessary to ensure that this reason not to intend evil is not merely justifying.

Suppose that I intend to drive from Washington, D.C. to Dallas, Texas, leaving at approximately a certain time and arriving at approximately a certain time. I go to Google Maps and devise an effective route to follow to get from Washington to Dallas within these parameters. I now have a highly detailed plan of action that I mean to carry out, an ordered sequence of actions which if followed will take me from Washington to Dallas. Lacking a smartphone, I print up the directions and hop in the car. I proceed to follow the plan *exceedingly poorly*. I take left turns where I should take right turns. I take exits that I should not take. It is not as if I have abandoned my plan for a new one, or have decided to give up my aim to get to Dallas for the sake of a spontaneous, go-where-you-wanna-go see-America road trip: I've set my plan, and I'm screwing it up. Yet, miraculously, at approximately the time I had planned to arrive in Dallas, I end up in Dallas. I have screwed up my plan at various points. But I achieve my intended end (more on this in a moment), or, better, the end in light of which I selected my means in deliberation.

My claim is that my action in getting from D.C. to Dallas was not successful, and that I was as an agent unsuccessful in acting. It was, obviously, successful in *one* sense. I ended up in Dallas. But it was not successful in an important way. I failed to carry out the plan of action that I had set for myself. I had decided to execute a certain plan of action, and I did not execute that plan of action. So my action was unsuccessful, and I was a failure as an agent.

One might respond: Look, you got what you ultimately cared about getting. You wanted to get to Dallas on time; you got to Dallas on time. How you got there was a mere means. But a mere means, by definition, is something you care about only insofar as it conduces to the end. Since you attained the end, your action was successful in the only sense that counts.

But this is a bad argument. When one is deliberating among various courses of action in light of some intended end, it may well be that all that matters with respect to these actions is how effective each is in helping one to realize the desired end. To call a proposed action a mere means is, first and foremost, to describe what counts as a merit or demerit of that action from the point of view of deliberation: it is to say that there is no reason to choose that action except for a certain sought end or ends, and whether there is reason to choose that action depends on how well the action conduces to that end. But that a proposed action is a mere means in this sense does not imply that its successful execution is in itself indifferent. For once the proposed action is decided upon, it has a feature that it previously lacked: it is now *intended*. And what I am saying is that through being intended, an action chosen merely as an effective means becomes more than a mere means; the successful execution of those means as one's route to one's sought end, along with the realization of the sought end, defines the success of one's action.

I have appealed so far directly to the judgment that my action in getting to Dallas was unsuccessful in important ways. Let me try to add some support for this. I think that, if I arrived in Dallas in the way described, I would have some reason to regret the various mistakes that I made—the turns that were not according to plan, the mile markers that went unnoticed, the lane changes that were performed late or not at all. "I'm such an ass," I might justly castigate myself. "I screwed things up, not paying attention, not following the directions properly. That (and by 'that' I take it to be obvious that what I am referring to was the set of concrete actions that took me from D.C. to Dallas) was a disaster. What a *lucky break* that I ended up here on time." That this response is perfectly sensible suggests that I am right to think of my action as unsuccessful, though very, very lucky. I need not claim, and am not claiming here that it would be reasonable for my overall attitude toward my trip to be one of regret: after all, I made it, and I'm lucky that I made it, and my enjoyment in having achieved my end and my thankfulness to divine providence for getting me here on time might swamp the reasons I have for regret about the haplessness of my attempt to execute the plan. All I claim is that I have some reason to regret my misadventures, and this reason for regret shows that the intended means define in part the success conditions for my plan of action.

Further: think again of the way that direction-of-fit considerations define intention. Just as the world's being a certain way defines what makes a belief true, the world's being a certain way defines what makes an intention satisfied. But I did not just intend the end, getting to Dallas: I intended a set of means for achieving that end. Thus, even if the intention were satisfied with respect to the end, the intention is not satisfied with respect to the means. If successful belief is true belief, successful intention must be satisfied intention. So, insofar as this intention is unsatisfied, it is unsuccessful. So the unsatisfied intention with regard to the means is sufficient to make my action unsuccessful.

Further: think of the close analogy between success in coming to a true belief and success in coming to a satisfied intention. In aiming to coming to a true belief with respect to some proposition p, one's evidence with respect to the truth or falsity of p is a mere means. In looking to form an opinion about p, and knowing that the truth of q would be relevant to the truth of p, we treat the truth of q as a mere means. But if we come to form a true belief about p on the basis of screwy evidence, we do not treat our belief that p as fully successful; it falls short in some way. We mark this falling short by denying the title of 'knowledge' to such beliefs, noting that the true belief in such cases is merely accidental or lucky. If we allow that belief, be it ever so true, can be less than fully successful on account of its evidentiary shortcomings, we should be willing to allow that action, be its end ever so realized, can be less than fully successful on account of its designated means not being properly executed.

Here is another way to criticize the view that an action in which the intended end is satisfied while the means are unaccomplished is successful: it is plausible even to deny in such cases that the intended end is realized. For when an end is an object of intention, one does not simply want it, or wish for it. One aims at it as at least the partial product of the execution of these means. Think of the way that deliberation characteristically proceeds: one settles tentatively on an end to be pursued, and casts about for different ways to realize it; only when one determines that there is an acceptable route to the end does the end become a fully fledged intention, something that one is set on achieving. To be set on achieving an end is to cleave to it as something to be realized, in part, through one's deliberate efforts. But in the D.C.-to-Dallas example I did not realize the end through my deliberate efforts: I realized it through fortuitous circumstances arising partially out of and partially in spite of my deliberate efforts. So I am not altogether confident in the case that the intended end really was achieved.

So I say that in a chosen plan of action, which involves both an intended end and means intended to realize that end, both the end and the means set the success conditions for action meant to execute that plan. By contrast: with respect to my trip to Dallas, there were a variety of things that I could foresee with some certainty. I could foresee very clearly that there would be traffic on the highway getting out of D.C. I could foresee that a number of people would fail to yield in traffic, and that some of them would actually accelerate to cut me off when I signaled a lane change. I could foresee that there would be litter on the highway, and that there would be plenty of garish billboards. But if there is no traffic, everyone yields properly, there has been a recent cleanup, and all the billboards have been taken down, that would not make my action unsuccessful. The most that it would show is either (a) that my beliefs were false, and so my beliefs about my action were unsuccessful, or (b) that my beliefs were true, and so we have decisive *evidence* that my action was unsuccessful. (There should be no temptation to confuse the satisfaction conditions of an intention with evidence that the satisfaction conditions have been met.)

So the success conditions for an action are defined by the intention, both the intended end and the means intended to realize that end. The success conditions for an action are not defined by the merely foreseen. These theses serve as the basis for the explanation of the Anselmian being's having requiring reasons to refrain from intending evil.

It is commonly accepted that there is something extra shady about intending evil *as an end*. Pursuing an evil for its own sake is bad, and it seems clear that the Anselmian being would not take evil as the justifying objective for some action. It does not seem, then, very controversial to hold that the Anselmian being would not aim at evil for its own sake. Those who would argue that the Anselmian being might intend evil would want to focus on cases in which the Anselmian being might intend evil *as a means*, a means to some worthwhile good. Leibniz, for example, did not think that the absolutely perfect being could will moral evils. But he did think that nonmoral evils—pain, injury, and so forth—were the sort of thing that the Anselmian being could intend for the sake of more valuable goals to be realized thereby (*Theodicy*, I, §§23–6).

But intending evil as a means is a lot more like intending evil as an end than we tend to think, and this similarity suggests an account of why there are distinct reasons not to intend evil, even as a means. I am not saying, of course, that there is no difference between promoting some state of affairs for its own sake and promoting it as a means to realizing some other state of affairs. The promotion of a state of affairs for its own sake regulates the promotion of states of affairs sought as a means to it, so there must be some difference. But I think that it is important to stress the similarities between pursuing a state of affairs as an end and pursuing it as a means. Seeing the similarity between these will bring out a *pro tanto* undesirability of intending evil, one that goes beyond the *pro tanto* undesirability of acting in ways from which one foresees that evil will result.

When one settles on an end and grasps that some sequence of actions is an effective way to realize that end, it is not as if one is then whisked along by the motivational tug of the end into adopting the means. This is true even if the proposed means are the only ones available for achieving the end. One reason for this is the straight Kantian point that ends are revisable: when one sees that a proposed course of action is the only one available to realize an end, one nevertheless might choose to reject pursuit of the end instead of adopting those means. One must *cleave to* the means; one must *choose* them. That means as well as ends are chosen is the reason, I think, why achievement of the means enters into the success conditions of an action. They are no longer mere means, in the sense that they have importance only as conducing to the end.

When one chooses evil, even if only as a means, one sets oneself to its achievement. It is now, as we saw above, a defining success condition of one's action or of oneself as an agent: one's action is successful only if, and just because, the evil is brought about, and one is successful as an agent only if, and just because, the evil is brought about. But this is not the case with merely foreseen evil. When one acts with the mere foresight that evil will result, one's action does not get defined in terms of it. Even if the presence of evils is a marker of one's success, evidence of it, it is in no way constitutive of that success. One's goodness as an agent does not include one's success in aiming at evil, when the evils that result from one's action are foreseen only.

In defending the double effect principle and its presupposition that there is a morally relevant distinction between the intended and the foreseen, Thomas Nagel writes:

> The difference [between intending evil and acting with mere foresight of evil] is that action intentionally aimed at a goal is guided by that goal. Whether the goal is an end in itself or only a means, action aimed at it must follow it and be prepared to adjust its pursuit if deflected by altered circumstances—whereas an act that merely produces an effect does not follow it, is not guided by it, even if the effect is foreseen....
>
> ...But the essence of evil is that it should *repel* us. If something is evil, our actions should be guided, if they are guided by it at all, toward its elimination rather than toward its maintenance. That is what evil *means*. So when we aim at evil we are swimming against the normative current (Nagel 1986, pp. 181–2).

But while Nagel thinks that this explains why, as a matter of moral psychology, intending evil exerts severe pressure on the agent, it is not clear why, as a matter of *justification*, intending evil is unjustifiable when carried out as a means to a greater good. My argument provides the basis for a further defense: we should not, I say, overstate the difference between intending evil as an end and intending it as a means. For once intended, the evil is no longer a mere means, one among perhaps many paths that one might follow to achieve a good; it becomes something whose obtaining is defining of one's successful action.

It remains to link this point about intention and success conditions with the reasons of an Anselmian being. One thing that seems clear about the agency exhibited by an Anselmian being is that we must hold that the Anselmian being has decisive requiring reasons not to exhibit agency that is worse than that being might exhibit. For the Anselmian being necessarily exhibits agency such that there is no agency better that that being might exhibit. Even if it is a necessary truth that there is no best world that the Anselmian being actualizes, we should say, as we said in 2.4, that the agency exhibited by the Anselmian being's bringing about a less-than-maximally-good world is nevertheless unsurpassable agency. And, as we saw in 2.2, we must hold of any agency exhibited by the Anselmian being that that agency is exhibited by the Anselmian being necessarily only if there are decisive reasons for the Anselmian being to do so. So we should say that there are decisive reasons for the Anselmian being not to exhibit less than maximally good agency.

Here, then, is the argument that the Anselmian being has requiring reasons not to intend evil. The Anselmian being has decisive requiring reasons not to exhibit agency worse than that being might exhibit. In the absence of considerations that would justify it, one's agency is made worse by having evils among the success conditions for one's action. But by intending evil, either as an end or as a means, evils become part of the success conditions for one's action: one's agency is made successful by evil's coming to obtain as a result of one's action. The Anselmian being must, then, have decisive requiring reasons not to intend evil in the absence of considerations that would justify so intending. But if one has decisive requiring reasons not to intend evil in the absence of considerations that would justify so intending, then one has requiring reasons not to intend evil. For to have a requiring reason to perform some action is to have a reason that would be decisive in favor of that action in the absence of relevant counter-considerations.

Note that this argument clearly does not generate the result that the Anselmian being has requiring reason not to act with the foresight that evil will result. Such a result would contradict my claim from the previous chapter (4.3), that the Anselmian being has no more than justifying reasons to promote the perfection/well-being of creatures. But the argument here does not generalize to cover the Anselmian being's acting with foresight of resulting evil. For, as I argued above, that one foresees evil resulting from one's action does not make those evils success conditions of one's action, and the argument that the Anselmian being has requiring reasons not to intend evil essentially relies upon the claim that for one's success to be constituted by evil makes one's agency, ceteris paribus, worse than it could be. Thus, the argument does not generalize in a way that calls into question the argument of Chapter 4.

5.5 The Anselmian Being's Decisive Reasons against Intending Evil

The fact that the Anselmian being has requiring reasons not to intend evil does not entail, of course, that the Anselmian being never intends evil. Requiring reasons' presence entails that one who is rational and aware of those reasons will act in accordance with them unless there are considerations to the contrary. But we have not yet seen why there could not be any considerations to the contrary that would render the Anselmian being's intending evil rational.

To make a case that there could not be considerations that adequately justify the Anselmian being's intending evil, one could proceed in either of two ways. One could claim either that the intending of evil is just not the sort of thing that there could be adequate reason for the Anselmian being to do, and thus any alleged considerations that one might put forward in favor of such a course of action must be failures. Or one could proceed comparatively, considering the sort of reasons that one might offer for the Anselmian being's having reason to intend evil, and arguing that no such reasons manage to justify the Anselmian being's intending evil. I will proceed in both ways, making the case both that the intending of evil is incompatible with the absolute perfection of the Anselmian being and that no creaturely good could justify it.

It seems to me that there is a strong case simply in terms of the absolute perfection of the agency of the Anselmian being that the Anselmian being must have decisive reason not to intend evil. Recall on the Anselmian view that I defend, it is not enough to count as God that one be the greatest possible being; the range of the greatness that is possibly realized must be adequately great, such that there is no way in which the value of the absolutely perfect being is held back merely by the contours of what is possible (1.3). But it seems to me that any being who goes for evil—any being who commits to the bringing about of evil, whether as an end or as a means, so that that being's success as an agent is constituted by privation and loss—has introduced a limitation into its agency, and thus would not count as an absolutely perfect being.

Now one might think that this puts the cart before the horse. The limitation present in one's agency by the intending of evil counts as a defect in one's agency, one might say, only if it is not otherwise justified. So this cannot be an independent line of argument for the Anselmian being's never intending evil; we have to proceed to the other line of argument, the comparative line, to see whether there could be justified intending of evil by the Anselmian being.

But this is not right. Even if the intending of evil might be justified in relation to the promotion of certain goods—that is, if nothing about the badness of intending evil explains why this evil could not be intended for the sake of some particular creaturely good—the intending of evil might nevertheless remain unjustified because of its relation to some other goods. The relevant good here would be the perfect goodness of the Anselmian being. It could be unfitting for the absolutely perfect being to have evil as its good, so to speak—for the perfect good to set a course for evil. The notion of fittingness here is a familiar one. We often do think that there are certain actions that are not in themselves wrong but are not appropriately carried out by certain classes of persons. So Aquinas argues, for example, that there is nothing wrong with fighting just wars, but nevertheless clerics are not to be warriors, because it is not fitting for one in the cleric's role to be involved in the shedding of blood (*Summa Theologiae* IIaIIae 40, 2). This is the kind of argument at work here. It is not fitting for the absolutely perfect being to set itself on evil, which is what intending evil is. The reason for not intending evil is the absolute goodness of the Anselmian being—we might think of this as the *holiness* of the Anselmian being, that it is to remain untouched by anything evil.

Consider now the other way of arguing for the decisive character of the Anselmian being's reason not to intend evil. One might be tempted by the point that any creaturely goods to be realized by the obtaining of some evil are goods that the Anselmian being has only justifying, not requiring, reason to bring about, and so the Anselmian being could not be bound to realize those goods by intending evil. But this would be a very bad argument. The whole idea of a justifying reason, after all, is that it justifies action that would otherwise be contrary to reason. So even if it is no more than rationally optional for the Anselmian being to realize some creaturely good by intending evil, that would be plenty to show that it is false that the Anselmian being does not intend evils.

What suggests to me the inability of the promotion of creaturely goods to justify the Anselmian being's intending evil is not the sheer fact of these goods providing the basis of only justifying reasons for the Anselmian being to promote them, but what explains their providing only justifying reasons—that these goods are goods by participation only. We have allowed that in the absence of adequate justification, the presence of evil among the success conditions for the Anselmian being's agency would be a blight on that agency and so could not be present. But now we should ask whether some good that is merely a good by participation could justify the presence of what would otherwise be a marring of the Anselmian being's agency. It seems to me that the answer is No. If being for the sake of promoting some creaturely good were sufficient to make it no longer the case that the Anselmian being's intending evil involves having evil as a success condition for the Anselmian being's action, then one could see how the participated good could be enough to make the relevant difference. But if the difference is being made only by somehow making it worthwhile for the Anselmian being to include that mark in its agency, that is what seems to me deeply implausible.

Another way of getting at my worry is by contrasting this case with the standard sort of case in which it is argued that intending evil is justifiable by appeal to greater goods. The standard case involves one human intending harm to one human for the sake of greater benefit to be realized for some other humans. To defend this view, one might deny the special relevance of intention, or argue that the special relevance of intention is outweighed by the greater goods to be gotten. Now, I have already defended, and have no more to say about, the special relevance of intention. But on the outweighing notion: While I would not endorse the view that the benefit brought to one human can simply outweigh the harm inflicted on another, incommensurability being what it is (see Murphy 2001, pp. 182–7), one can surely see the force of this sort of consequentialist weighing and be tempted by the position. By contrast, though, what are being set against each other here are a reason for the *divine* goodness not to be marred by an intention for evil and a reason that favors the realization of some *creaturely*, participated good. And so I find the view that the Anselmian being can intend evil even less plausible than I find the view that some human may aim at harm to another human simply for the benefit of some third party.

5.6 An Objection from Divine Sovereignty

Aside from worries about the cogency of the arguments offered above for the view that the Anselmian being does not intend evil, there are a number of objections that one could raise with respect to the implausibility of the conclusion. The central objections with which I am concerned are those that hold that the God of orthodox Christian theism has intended evils (as I have defined 'evils'; 5.1), and since God is an Anselmian being, it must be false that the Anselmian being never intends evil (or true that orthodox Christian theism is incoherent when it holds that God is absolutely perfect and God intends evil). I will treat such objections as versions of the argument from evil (6.5), and I reserve for Chapter 6 discussion of the ways in which the conception of the Anselmian being's ethics defended here transforms the problem of evil.

There is an objection that I want to consider here, though, concerning the compatibility of the argument for the Anselmian being's not having requiring reasons to promote creaturely good defended in Chapter 4 and the argument for the Anselmian being's having requiring (5.4), even decisive (5.5), reasons not to intend creaturely evil defended in this chapter. The objection is this. One important strand of the argument for the Anselmian being's not having requiring reasons to promote the perfection/well-being of creatures is that such a view better captures the perfection of sovereignty, in particular, the discretion that the Anselmian being has regarding whether there will exist a created universe and what its character will be. Because we should conceive the Anselmian being's perfection as pressing outward (1.4), the absence of good reasons to hold that the perfection/well-being of creatures gives requiring reasons is a basis to hold that the excellence of sovereignty includes the discretion for the Anselmian being to create without necessitation—that while the existence and perfection/well-being of creatures provide rational opportunities for the Anselmian being to act, the Anselmian being needs no reason not to take these opportunities, and so is in no way necessitated by creatures. But one might think that the Anselmian being is necessitated by creatures and lacks important discretion on the view that I have defended in this chapter: for the Anselmian being, I have claimed, never intends the absence of due perfection/well-being.

The first response to this objection is that the arguments here are not on a par. As I noted, what we think about the extent of the Anselmian being's discretion is going to depend on our other arguments about what reasons we have independent grounds to ascribe to the Anselmian being. And my view is that we have no good grounds to hold that the Anselmian being has requiring reasons to promote the perfection/well-being of creatures but there are good grounds to hold that the Anselmian being has requiring reasons not to intend evil. So there are reasons to deny that the discretion ascribed to the Anselmian being should be expanded outward to allow for the possibility of the Anselmian being's intending evil.

This first response, though correct, is unsatisfying. What is unsatisfying is that we should like to have an account of *why* it is that the rejection of the view that the Anselmian being can intend evils does not commit one to the view that valuable discretion is denied to the Anselmian being. The second response is to note the differences between the cases and why the discretion to intend evil is not a valuable feature that divine sovereignty should be redescribed to accommodate. Here is what seems to me the key difference. The denial that the Anselmian being has requiring reasons to promote creaturely well-being was primarily for the sake of ensuring that the Anselmian being is in no way necessitated into action by the prospect of creaturely good. The Anselmian being is sovereign, and there is nothing about the goodness of creatures that can make necessary the Anselmian being's doing anything to bring about their existence or that of any of their goods. The affirmation of the Anselmian being's not intending evil was primarily for the sake of preserving the holiness of the Anselmian being, of ensuring that the Anselmian being's agency is in no way marred by taking on evil as an objective that would be defining of the Anselmian being's success as an agent. That the Anselmian being's own goodness necessitates the Anselmian being not to act in certain ways, should the Anselmian being choose to act at all with respect to creatures, does not seem to me to be a limit to the Anselmian being's valuable discretion; that creaturely goodness necessitates the Anselmian being to act at all does seem to me to be such a limit.

The Anselmian being has reasons to promote the existence and perfection/well-being of creatures, but they are justifying, not requiring reasons. The Anselmian being has reasons not to intend the absence of due perfection/well-being of creatures, and these reasons are decisive; the Anselmian being does not seek evil, whether as a means or as an end. The Anselmian being thus possibly creates, and possibly creates beings who realize their good better rather than worse, but it is false that the Anselmian being creates unless there is good reason not to or makes creatures better-off unless there is good reason not to. The Anselmian being is never set on creaturely evil. But it is not true that the Anselmian being is set on creaturely good.

6

The Argument from Evil and the Ethics of the Anselmian Being

6.1 The Failure of Arguments from Evil against the Existence of the Anselmian Being

My main aim in providing an account of *the Anselmian being's* ethics is as part of the task of getting at *God's* ethics: God is necessarily an Anselmian being, so any truths about the Anselmian being's ethics are necessary truths about God's ethics.[1] But as I noted in the Introduction, the issue with respect to which the question of God's ethics has most obvious and dramatic application is the problem of evil. In this chapter I will make explicit how the problem of evil and its seeming force against the existence of an Anselmian being is dramatically transformed by the account of the Anselmian being's ethics in the previous five chapters: recent formulations of the problem of evil have little force against the existence of an Anselmian being, given the conception of the Anselmian being's ethics that I have defended (6.2–6.3). I show that the force of this view is similar to that which is provided by a distinct response to the argument from evil, that of skeptical theism, though the ways in which my view is more radical than skeptical theism enable it to avoid some objections to which skeptical theism is subject and the ways in which it is less radical than skeptical theism enable it to avoid some objections to which it is subject (6.4). I will then turn to what I take to be a distinct argument from evil that could target my view, an argument based not on the existence of evil, but on God's intending it (6.5). The final section is a transition to the second Part of this book. The argument from evil against the existence of an Anselmian being is effectively defanged by a proper understanding of the ethics of the Anselmian being. But the view of the Anselmian being's ethics that undercuts the argument from evil against the existence of such a being allows a new argument from evil to arise—one that does not deny the existence of an absolutely perfect Anselmian being, but denies that we should worship or have allegiance to any such being, if it does exist (6.6).

[1] This is why it is very important to distinguish between the theses *it is false that the Anselmian being is loving* and *the Anselmian being is not loving*. I affirm the former, and it is compatible with the former that God's ethics is in fact an ethics of love (though this would have to be a contingent truth about God). I reject the latter, for it would entail the falsehood *God is not loving*.

6.2 The Logical Problem of Evil

The formulation of the idea that there is a logical inconsistency between the existence of evils and the existence of God in contemporary discussions of the argument from evil is due primarily to Mackie (1955). Mackie takes it that by 'God' we mean a being who is omnipotent and morally perfect. Mackie holds that employing no more than basic logic and expansions of the concepts 'omnipotent' and 'morally perfect'—respectively, there are no limits to what an omnipotent being can do, and a morally perfect being eliminates evil so far as it can (Mackie 1955, p. 26)—we can reach the conclusion that there is no evil. But there is evil. So there is no God.

There is some reason to doubt that Mackie really thought that the logical problem of evil as formulated above really is a devastating argument against theism, given some of the concessions that he makes in that paper. But put that interpretive issue to the side. There are numerous ways to respond to this version of the logical problem, the most prominent of which is Plantinga's, which runs by noting an obvious revision that would have to be made to Mackie's expansion of the notion of moral goodness and providing a model on which there is evil and yet it would not have been possible even for an omnipotent being to eliminate it without an unacceptable loss of great goods (Plantinga 1974, pp. 164–93). While there are, as is typical, some dissenters (see, for example, DeRose 1991, Howard-Snyder and O'Leary-Hawthorne 1998, and Pruss 2012b), the consensus that Plantinga's response to the logical problem of evil successfully undermines it is one of the strongest consensuses to be found in philosophy.

The acknowledged strength of Plantinga's response to the logical problem may seem to make spending any more time discussing it pointless. But, as I noted, there are dissenters even to Plantinga's overwhelmingly accepted free will defense, and so it is worth considering what alternative responses there are to the logical problem. Further, and more importantly, note that to count as a 'logical problem' of evil depends on a certain way of laying out the argument, along with certain presuppositions for what would count as success and about how devastating the argument would be if successful. It does not seem to depend on the sort of evil invoked. So, as Draper has noted, one can run a logical problem of evil not just about the existence of evil, but also about a type of evil, a particular evil, the distribution of evil, and so forth (Draper 2009, p. 334). And so even if Plantinga's central free will defense is powerful against a logical argument that takes simply the existence of evil as its premise, it may be less successful against other such arguments. So it is worth commenting a bit on how the conception of the Anselmian being's ethics defended here can be invoked against this, or any plausible, version of the logical problem.

First, one can challenge the conception of God offered by the standard version of the logical problem of evil. Some ask whether it is appropriate to take God to be omnipotent, for example, or whether it is appropriate to interpret God's omnipotence in some particular way. What is crucial to such challenges is that one have a principled, compelling account of why omnipotence should not be considered part of the concept of God, and so why one is not cheating or simply changing the subject when attempting to evade the argument from evil by appealing to an alternative conception. Thus, my appeal to the Anselmian character of God is not a cheat, because it is very plausible that what justifies the ascription of these features to God is that they are taken to be perfections (0.1). It is therefore worth asking whether the existence of evil is in logical tension with the existence of an Anselmian being.

Second, the standard logical problem appeals to the existence of evil. It is assumed that evil does not exist necessarily. It is also assumed that the relevant relation in which God stands to evil is that God has the ability to see to it that it does not obtain, that is, that God can successfully promote, at will, the nonexistence of evils.

But it is now pretty obvious why the standard logical problem of evil is unproblematic for the prospects of the existence of an Anselmian being. For we are being asked whether the Anselmian being must see to it that no states of affairs including evils obtain. As I have argued, though, the Anselmian being's ethics is not an ethics of familiar welfare-oriented moral goodness, and so any expansion of 'moral perfection' that presupposes that God is morally perfect in the familiar welfare-oriented sense is irrelevant in making the case that the existence of evils is incompatible with the existence of God. The excellence that the Anselmian being exhibits vis-à-vis creaturely goods and evils is not moral goodness in the familiar welfare-oriented sense, but rather perfect rationality, meaning that the Anselmian being acts perfectly on all of the reasons that the Anselmian being has with respect to those goods and evils. But the reasons that the Anselmian being has to promote the nonexistence of creaturely evils are not requiring reasons, but only justifying reasons (4.2–4.3). Since one can exhibit perfect rationality with respect to some justifying reason without acting on it, even in the absence of reasons to the contrary, the fact that there are evils that God has justifying reasons to prevent but does not prevent does not count in any way against God's being absolutely perfect.

So here is a model for the consistency of the existence of evil with the existence of the Anselmian being. Consider some evil, say, the pointless suffering of a deer in a forest fire (Rowe 1990 [1979], pp. 129–30). The Anselmian being might fail to prevent this evil, for no reason at all, because acting so as to prevent that suffering provides the Anselmian being only justifying reasons for acting.

Note also that this account of why the Anselmian being's existence is compatible with the existence of creaturely evil is obviously generalizable to any particular evil that one might wish to invoke against the existence of the Anselmian being. For all of these evils are such that the Anselmian being has only justifying reasons to prevent them, and so the Anselmian being's perfectly rational agency is compatible with the presence of any such evil. So Draper's point—that one can formulate a logical problem of evil that is framed in terms of some particular evils rather than the existence of some evil or other—generates no concerns given the ethics of an Anselmian being.[2]

6.3 The Evidential Problem of Evil

The more interesting question is what we should think about the evidential problem of evil, for there is far less consensus about the extent to which the evidential problem of evil can be answered well by the theist. My aim in this section is not to evaluate the state of the discussion on this issue, but to argue that when we formulate the evidential argument as an argument against the existence of an Anselmian being, we can see that it is gutted by the understanding of the Anselmian being's ethics that I have offered. I will take as my paradigm the well-worked-out version of the evidential argument offered by Draper (1989, 2009, 2013). I will argue that Draper's argument is a failure when taken as an argument against the existence of the Anselmian being. I will also argue that this failure is not due to any eccentric feature of Draper's argument, but instead is due to features that we should expect any evidential argument from evil to exhibit.

Evidential arguments do not proceed by trying to establish some logical inconsistency between some known fact about the existence of evil, or of some specific evil, kind of evil, or distribution of evil, and the existence of God. They proceed by trying to show that such evils make the existence of God significantly less likely. Some proceed simply by arguing that it is unlikely that there exists a justification for God's allowing some particular evil, and so, since God is morally perfect, it is unlikely that God exists. Some proceed comparatively, by considering theism and some rival thesis, and attempt to show that theism is rendered much less likely than the rival hypothesis by some fact about evil.[3]

I take such comparative arguments, which Draper labels "Humean" arguments, to be the most perspicuous form for the evidential argument to take, and I will consider Draper's formulation of it as an exemplar. Seeing how the view of the Anselmian being's ethics that I defend makes possible a response to Draper's argument will enable us to see how a generalized response to such arguments from evil might go.

Draper takes theism to be the hypothesis that there exists a being that is omniscient, omnipotent, and perfectly morally good, and is creator of the world. The 'hypothesis of indifference' is the rival hypothesis that "neither the nature nor the condition of sentient beings on earth is the result of benevolent or malevolent actions performed by a nonhuman person" (1989, p. 13). Now consider O, the set of observations made by oneself or others concerning sentient beings' experiencing pain and pleasure. How

[2] What about the *distribution* of evils? Could not some distribution of evils suggest that it could have come about only by God's intention, and thus God must have intended some such evils—contrary to what I have argued an Anselmian being could do? I will treat the question of whether there is evidence that God intends evils in 6.5.

[3] For an account and defense of this distinction between the logical and evidential arguments, see Howard-Snyder 1996b, p. xiv; for a rejection of the relevance of the distinction, see Dougherty 2014, p. 45.

likely is it that O would be true given the hypothesis of indifference, and how likely is it that O would be true given theism? Draper's conclusion is essentially comparative: the hypothesis of indifference explains the facts O reports much better than theism does, or, equivalently in Draper's framework, the probability of O given the hypothesis of indifference is much, much greater than the probability of O given theism. What drives this result is what Draper takes to be the dual nature of pleasures and pains: that they are biologically useful and intrinsically[4] morally important. That pleasures/pains are biologically useful plays an important role in explaining why they would be present both on the hypothesis of indifference and on theism. But that they are intrinsically morally important makes no difference to their likelihood given the hypothesis of indifference while driving the likelihood down massively given theism.

Draper's strategy is to help us see the truth of his conclusion by slotting the pleasures/pains reported in O into three categories, and thus offering three propositions regarding those pleasures/pains that, conjoined, are equivalent to O. We are to consider (1) those observations regarding moral agents' pleasure/pain that is known to be biologically useful, (2) those regarding the pleasure/pain of sentient beings who are not moral agents, which pleasure/pain is known to be biologically useful, and (3) those regarding the pleasures/pains experienced by sentient beings, which pleasures and pains we do not know to be biologically useful.

Consider the first category. On the hypothesis of indifference, we would expect pain and pleasure, if moral agents experience them, to contribute to biological goals. But given this second feature, that pleasure and pains have intrinsic moral importance, it is far less likely, given theism, that pleasure and pain would be employed to serve biological goals.

Now suppose that we assume the presence of biologically useful pleasures/pains in moral agents, and ask which hypothesis makes the presence of pleasures/pains of the second category more probable. Again, it would not be surprising on the hypothesis of indifference for pleasure and pain to have this role for sentient beings that are not moral agents. But it would be much more surprising given theism, for God would have extra motivation to preclude pain in sentient beings that lack moral agency, as such pains cannot even serve the morally useful roles that they can sometimes play in moral agents. Thus, with respect to the second category, the presence of such pleasures and pains is more probable given the hypothesis of indifference than given theism.

Now, take as given the pleasures/pains that are biologically useful, and ask on which view biologically useless pleasures/pains seem more probable. It seems clear that they are much more likely given the hypothesis of indifference than theism. Biologically useless pleasure/pain nevertheless typically bears an obvious explanatory relation to that pain which is biologically useful: that nature cannot be fine-grained, and so forth.

[4] Draper doesn't mean by *being intrinsically morally important* what I mean by it. He does not mean *being morally important apart from all relations to other things*; he means *having agent-neutral, non-instrumental moral importance, such that agents will have good reasons to do something about it.*

But why there would be biologically useless pleasure/pain on theism is much harder to see. It looks pointless unless there is some moral goal being served, but its distribution does not seem to support such an understanding. So the pattern of biologically useless pleasures/pains we encounter seems far better explained given the hypothesis of indifference than theism.

The upshot is, of course, that the facts about pleasure and pain are much more probable on the hypothesis of indifference than on theism, and thus we have strong—albeit defeasible—reason to endorse the hypothesis of indifference over theism (Draper 1989, pp. 15–19). Now there have been multiple lines of response to Draper, many of which he anticipates in the original paper in which the argument is formulated. (Among these is the skeptical theist's response, which I discuss in 6.4.) But I am not interested in pursuing such lines. For recall that my aim here is to consider my own view of the Anselmian being's ethics as a response to formulations of the argument from evil. And there is an obvious point of entry here: Draper's argument is explicitly formulated in terms of God's being perfectly morally good, where the moral goodness in question is of the familiar welfare-oriented sort (Draper 1989, pp. 12–13). As I have claimed that all of God's necessary features are perfections or implications of perfections, and I have denied that love and moral goodness are Anselmian perfections, I would reject this starting point. But of course the key question then becomes whether the ethics that I have ascribed to the Anselmian being, and thus which must be God's ethics as well, is something that one could make use of in an evidential argument similar to Draper's.

Suppose we are considering now the relative probabilities of the hypothesis of indifference and Anselmianism, understood as the thesis that there is an absolutely perfect being, where this being is sovereign over the created world. This Anselmian being, if my earlier arguments are correct, has justifying but not requiring reasons to bring about creaturely existence and perfection/well-being. What difference does this make to Draper's argument, now read as an argument for the superiority of the hypothesis of indifference to Anselmianism?

The existence of an Anselmian being with the ethics that I ascribe to that being can be considered as a sort of middle point between a God whose ethics is of the familiar welfare-oriented sort and the hypothesis of indifference. Draper's argument is driven by the fact that God will treat the intrinsic badness of pain as being something that gives God requiring reasons to eliminate it. Thus its very presence in some state of affairs counts against that state of affairs' probability, assuming God's existence. If it is to be present, it is because it can serve some important role, some end that God has reason to promote. The hypothesis of indifference is not burdened by those commitments, and thus has an immediate leg up on theism in accounting for evil. But note that the Anselmian view that I have defended shares with the hypothesis of indifference *the denial* that there is a being with the power to do something about pains and pleasures who has requiring reason to prevent these intrinsically bad states of affairs from obtaining. So any maneuver that Draper makes to hold that the hypothesis of indifference has an easier time with the distribution of pain that relies on the requiring-reason-giving character of pain is going to be unsuccessful.

But, of course, there is a relevant difference between the hypothesis of indifference and the Anselmian thesis: the Anselmian thesis holds that there is a being with the power to do something about pains and pleasures and who has *justifying* reasons to do something about them. Does that enable Draper to revive his argument?

It does not allow Draper to maintain the form of his earlier conclusion, which is that the observed distribution of pleasure and pain is *much more probable* on the hypothesis of indifference than on the Anselmian thesis, or even that it is more probable. For it seems to me that the probability of this distribution of pains is just *inscrutable* given my account of the Anselmian being's ethics. Given that whether to act on these reasons is, by hypothesis, not required by rationality, and nothing in the Anselmian being's nature disposes that being to act on that reason or not, we have no basis at all for making an assessment on the extent to which the Anselmian being will take the pleasures and pains of creatures as reasons to promote their obtaining or their not obtaining.

One might retort that at least the hypothesis of indifference gives predictions about the likelihood of this state of affairs, and so it is on that basis preferable to a view that yields no result at all (Dougherty 2014, p. 23). But I find this response unpersuasive, both because it overstates what we learn about the merits of the hypothesis of indifference from Draper's argument and it understates what we learn about the merits of the hypothesis of Anselmianism from my argument.

First, Draper's argument does not claim that we can make solid predictions about the likelihood of O given the hypothesis of indifference; what we are given is the thesis that, *whatever* that likelihood is, it is *many times greater* than the likelihood of O given theism. The entire argument is run comparatively and reaches a comparative conclusion. So any inscrutability that infects our assessment of the probability of O given the existence of the Anselmian being infects our assessment of the probability of O given the hypothesis of indifference.

Second, it seems to me that the Anselmian thesis should not be criticized, even in relation to some other hypothesis, simply for having the implication that the probability of a certain outcome is inscrutable on it. It is a different thing for a thesis to be so uninformative that it does not yield information about how likely something is—that it is just silent on it—and for a theory to be so informative that it entails that no such likelihood could be sensibly given. My claim is not simply that we have no basis to affirm any particular probability that some evil would exist given the Anselmian being's existence, though there may be some such probability to detect. It claims, rather, that there is no such probability to detect. As the features of the created world are a matter of divine discretion, there are no such reasons that so much as dispose, however mildly, the Anselmian being to create one way or another.[5]

[5] Thus, my view differs from skeptical theism, discussed in 6.4, which has the resources to claim only that we lack a basis for forming a justified judgment of probability, not that there is no such fact to detect.

6.4 Skeptical Theism

My appeal to inscrutability in 6.3 may call to mind what seems to be becoming theists' go-to defense against the argument from evil, some form of what is now called "skeptical theism." (For surveys, see Bergmann 2009 and McBrayer 2010.) I want in this section to consider the relationship between the defense against the argument from evil that I have offered, based on an account of the Anselmian being's ethics, and the skeptical theist's approach to defending against that argument. I will describe the skeptical theist strategy, noting that my response to the problem of evil shares some of skeptical theism's thrust, while also showing that there are ways in which my own view is more radical and ways in which my own view is less radical than skeptical theism. This is not just for the sake of a proper understanding of how my view differs from skeptical theism. I think that the ways in which my view is more radical than skeptical theism enable it better to keep the problem of evil at bay, and the ways in which my own view is less radical enable it better to avoid some of the objections that have been pressed against the skeptical theists.

I take the skeptical theists to endorse the view that God acts in accordance with familiar welfare-oriented moral goodness. They affirm that God acts to prevent setbacks to creaturely well-being unless there are sufficient considerations to the contrary. What they say, though, is that we have good reason to believe that we have only the most meager insight into what are those other considerations to the contrary that God might have. The claim that our insight into these other considerations is likely to be incredibly meager is not supposed to be some further ad-hoc posit to avoid the evidential problem of evil. Rather, it is supposed to be something that we should recognize as a simple implication of the enormous epistemological gulf between God and us. To put it another way, the skeptical theists should acknowledge that even if there were no initially plausible argument from evil—either the world did not present itself such that evil's presence called into question God's existence, or we took ourselves to have other sufficient arguments to rebut the problem—the thesis that our understanding of the goods and evils upon which God acts would still have to be taken to be extremely limited and possibly unrepresentative of what goods and evils there really are.

Now, the response to the evidential argument from evil that I defended in 6.3 shares some of the thrust of the skeptical theist response. The shared strategy is to argue that we have grounds to think that the way that we have good reason to respond to evils may well not be the way that God has good reason to respond to evils. When confronted with some evil, we humans think that, if we had the ability to do something about it, then we should, and so, since God has the ability to do something about it, God should. The skeptical theist notes that we should run this inference only if the reasons upon which we base the correct judgment that we should do something about it if able are the same reasons upon which God would base God's judgment about what is to be done. And I would make the same response.

But my view differs from the skeptical theists'. I agree with the skeptical theists' strategy, at that level of abstraction. And I agree that this sort of skepticism is an entailment of the gap between God and creatures. But there are important differences, and these differences make a difference in the extent to which our responses to the evidential argument from evil are open to serious objection. So let me say something about those differences, describe what I take to be the key objections to skeptical theism, and explain why the differences between my view and the skeptical theists' help to avoid these objections.

Skeptical theism is built on an *epistemological* thesis: that we should not take our knowledge of the goods and evils upon which God might act to be representative of what those goods and evils really are. In its use, skeptical theists have taken for granted some moral theses and remained noncommittal about others. So, as I noted, skeptical theists have generally taken for granted the standard view that God is governed by familiar welfare-oriented moral goodness. They have also remained generally silent about the various ways that goods and evils might bear on action, and the various ways that these can justify or fail to justify particular kinds of responses to those goods. By contrast, the view that I have defended is built on a set of theses of *ethics*, not epistemology: the Anselmian being does not have requiring reasons to promote creaturely perfection/well-being, though the Anselmian being does have justifying reasons to do so; the Anselmian being does, however, have requiring, even decisive, reasons not to intend creaturely evil. Note that these theses are not theses only about the Anselmian being's reasons in relation to the promotion of creaturely goods and evils; they are theses about the different responses—not just the particular response of promotion—to those goods and evils that the Anselmian being has reason to have.

Thus, the view that I have defended is somewhat more radical than the skeptical theists' view in one way and less radical in another. It is more radical in that it denies that God is necessarily bound by familiar welfare-oriented moral goodness. Not only might God have *more* reasons than those that are within our grasp; God has *less* stringent reasons to promote the good of creatures than we humans have. It is less radical in that on the view that I have defended, God's nature precludes God's intending evil, and so there are no goods that could justify God's intending evil for the sake of those goods. Thus, we should not leave open the possibility that there might be goods outside our ken that justify God's intending evil; there are no such goods. Skeptical theism, articulated simply as an epistemological view about the unrepresentativeness of our knowledge of goods and evils, does not have the resources to rule out that possibility.

As I said, I am interested in cataloguing these differences between my own view and skeptical theism as responses to the problem of evil not simply to gain clarity about the distinctiveness of these positions but to see how the further theses that I endorse enable one who accepts the skeptical theist's epistemological thesis and who is broadly sympathetic with the strategy to answer some worries that have been leveled against it. These worries are of two sorts. The first concerns whether the skeptical theist account really does block the argument that the evils of this world lower the likelihood of theism in comparison to other relevant hypotheses. The second concerns whether the skeptical theist account yields unacceptable implications, regardless of its success in responding to the argument from evil.

One claim leveled against skeptical theism is that the epistemological claim upon which it rests its defense against the argument from evil is not strong enough to do the necessary work in responding to that argument. That claim is that we do not know that the goods and evils with which we are familiar are representative of the goods that there are. But one might retort that this claim is not strong enough. It is not sufficient for one to dismiss the fact that there are goods and evils that God would not be justified in allowing without adequate reason that we do not know that there are not goods and evils that might justify God's allowing those evils. Rather, one would need to know that one's knowledge is not representative. The skeptical theists' actual claim is sufficient to make one open to the possibility that one might have to update one's judgments of the relevant likelihoods in the face of further information. But it is not enough to give one reason to dismiss the fact that the goods and evils with which we are familiar do not give an adequate basis to justify God's allowing the evils that we know of. And so the skeptical theist thesis is not sufficient to beat back the evidential argument from evil. (See, for example, Draper 1989, pp. 24–5 and 2009, p. 344.)

There is some force to this objection to skeptical theism. As Draper powerfully argues, accepting this sort of argumentative move may leave one open to a variety of skeptical hypotheses massively undermining our knowledge, when such hypotheses should do no more than leave us open to the possibility of updating in light of future confirmation of the skeptical hypotheses. But I will not attempt a full evaluation of this criticism here. The important point for my purposes is that the objection is not even plausibly applicable to my account of how we should respond to the evidential problem of evil. For though my view, like that of the skeptical theists, appeals to the notion that we should doubt that the way that we have good reason to respond to evils is the way that God has good reason to respond to evils, my view is not based on skeptical theses. It is not based on possible limits to our knowledge, but on truths that we have good reason to endorse regarding reasons for action and the divine nature. What we have reason to endorse is that there is no default setting for God to act in accordance with the norms of familiar welfare-oriented moral goodness. Because the skeptical theists affirm that default setting and try simply to supplement that with a skeptical claim about what further reasons God might have, they are open to Draper's objection. By rejecting the view that God is necessarily bound by familiar welfare-oriented moral goodness, my view is in no way open to that objection. This is one way that my view is more radical than the skeptical theists', and thus it is insulated from the objection that skeptical theism is an insufficiently strong thesis to do the work it needs to do.

A seemingly distinct set of concerns for skeptical theism is about the further implications of the view, in particular, whether there are objectionable practical implications to the epistemological thesis upon which the skeptical theist response to the problem of evil is based. I say 'seemingly' because it may not be that thesis that makes trouble, but only that thesis along with the concession that it generates the sort of strong reason to withhold judgment about whether God has reason to permit the various evils of which one knows. (It may be that so long as one takes only the moral from the fact of the epistemological gap between God and humans that Draper urges us to take, then these practical implications do not straightaway follow; but if one grants for the sake of argument that skeptical theism's epistemological thesis does generate the needed result, then the implications will be too much to accept.) At any rate, the establishing of these unfortunate practical implications would be bad news for the skeptical theist, insofar as skeptical theism puts itself forward not merely as an implication of theism that gives us reason to be open to our value judgments being overturned, but as a reason to refrain from making judgments about whether God has reason to permit various seemingly gratuitous, and even horrendous, evils.

One set of practical implications that objectors have invoked against skeptical theism concerns how we human beings ought to act with respect to each other. The basic idea is this. We seem to be under moral requirements with respect to our fellow human beings to prevent their undergoing certain evils. But if we are skeptical theists, we should hold the following view: our fellow humans' undergoing some evil may in fact be a constituent part of some good that is outside our ken. And thus, when faced with a situation in which one can easily prevent another human being from suffering some evil—say, one can save an infant from drowning without risk or any cost whatever to oneself—one's skeptical theism will render the clear moral requirement murky. As Almeida and Oppy argue, if we are skeptical theists, and we encounter someone who will undergo some evil unless we intervene,

> we should insist that it is not unlikely that there is some good which, if we were smarter and better equipped, we could recognize as a reason for a perfect being's not intervening to stop E. Plainly, we should also concede—by parity of reason—that, merely on the basis of our acceptance of [the skeptical theist's theses], it is not unlikely that there is some good which, if we were smarter and better equipped, we could recognize as a reason for our not intervening to stop the event. That is,...it is not unlikely that it is for the best, all things considered, if we do not intervene. But...it would be appalling for us to allow this consideration to stop us from intervening. Yet, if we take [the skeptical theist's theses] seriously, how can we also maintain that we are morally required to intervene? (Almeida and Oppy 2003, pp. 505–6)

This sort of argument strikes me as having little force against the skeptical theist. First, commonsense morality is, and is for good reason, not entirely objective in its content, fixing the moral requirements that we are under with respect to others without regard to considerations about what is within or without our ken. The fact that a certain set of considerations is simply inscrutable to us gives us second-order reason to treat them as irrelevant in determining what we are to do. Second, it is tremendously misleading to think that what we owe to our fellow humans with respect to protection from harm is to be explained in terms of something that is good from the point of view of the universe; it is better explained in terms of the harm that will befall the other person—an agent-relative evil—and the relationship that holds between the parties. In such cases, the sorts of goods or evils that the skeptical theist is contemplating as justifying divine action are not on the scene justifying my action in saving or failing to save another human from harm. (This is the point, I take it, of Trakakis and Nagasawa's (2004) distinction between "us-justifying" and "God-justifying" reasons; it is not just that all reasons are goods that we are better or worse at recognizing, it is that some are goods and reasons that apply to some of us in virtue of where we stand in the web of relationships, others not.)

I take it that these are responses to the claims about skeptical theism's alleged counterintuitive practical implications for us that are well-known, and I think when properly developed they show that the practical implications objection goes nowhere. (See also Bergmann 2009, p. 392.) Of course there are some views that would be threatened: if one held a view on which the requirements that one is under are fully objective, in the relevant sense, and fully controlled by the overall consequences of one's action, then that would be a view on which skeptical theism would make trouble for ordinary morality. But the fact that there are implausible moral theories on which skeptical theism would have implausible implications about the moral reasons we have is not much of an objection to skeptical theism.[6]

Nor does the view that I defend introduce some new consideration that would render my view susceptible to this objection, even if standard skeptical theism is not. Recall that my argument proceeds by taking for granted the substantial correctness of our views about our reasons for action, and then arguing that there are grounds to hold that the Anselmian being's reasons are importantly different from our own. This takes for granted the distinction between us-justifying and God-justifying reasons, which is the fundamental basis for denying that untoward implications result for our reasons by affirming skeptical theism. And since the content of our reasons includes reasons that are partly subjective and are not fully consequence-governed, there is no threat to sensible interpretations of our reasons for action by affirming the view I have defended.

Far more threatening, both to skeptical theism and to my view, are the alleged implications about *God's* reasons, or about what we know about those reasons, and the conclusions that we can no longer draw about divine action. Erik Wielenberg (2010) has argued that we cannot rationally rely on divine testimony if we accept the truth of skeptical theism. (Hudson's later (2014) argument makes fundamentally the same point; earlier work by Maitzen (2009) also discusses the issue briefly.) The argument is straightforward. The whole thrust of skeptical theism is that, given our lack of knowledge of the

[6] Jordan (2006) claims that a host of standard moral theories would be undermined by skeptical theism. As far as I can tell, with the exception of the grunting flatfooted objective impartial consequentialism that I conceded might be rendered problematic by skeptical theism, none of his objections to these views hits its target. Two examples: Jordan's claim that Kantian theories would be undermined misunderstands the way in which Kantian views really are insensitive to overall consequences; his objection that natural law theories are undermined misunderstands the way in which natural law theorists take overall consequences of actions to justify allowing particular evils.

range of divine reasons, we should not expect to be able to identify the point of some existing evil. But this should apply to possible evils as well as actual ones. Suppose that we accept that lying to someone is an evil. Nevertheless, because we do not have a grasp of divine reasons, for all we know it could be the case, for any act of divine testimony, that it might be not an instance of truth-telling but a lie that is an evil but nevertheless justified by the promotion of some good or the prevention of some evil that is beyond our ken. Thus, we cannot rationally rely on the veracity of divine testimony if we also accept skeptical theism as a response to the problem of evil.

I think that, articulated in the minimal way that skeptical theism is articulated, this objection is extremely powerful against the combination of views that skeptical theism functions as a response to the evidential argument from evil and that we can gain knowledge by God's testimony to us *qua* testimony.[7] (There might be deviant ways that divine testimony could give us knowledge on this view.) One might be unconcerned with this result, if one is inclined to a theism that does not include revelation by testimony as part of its picture. That is not my inclination, nor is it that of the run-of-the-mill skeptical theists. So this argument is indeed problematic for actual skeptical theists on the ground. Is it a problem for my own view?

No. Because there is at least one way in which my own view is less radical than the skeptical theists'. My own view distinguishes between the Anselmian being's reasons to *promote* the good of creatures, including improving their perfection/well-being or preventing setbacks to it, and the Anselmian being's reasons to *respect* the good of creatures, including not intending the absence of due perfection/well-being. Even though the Anselmian being has merely justifying reasons to prevent setbacks to creaturely well-being (4.2–4.3), the Anselmian being has decisive requiring reasons not to intend creaturely evil. That is because intending evil involves taking on evil as part of the success conditions for one's action, which is not fitting for the agency of the absolutely perfect being (5.5). This is obviously not based on any sort of skepticism; it is based on our understanding of the holiness of the absolutely perfect being.

But this commitment enables a response to Wielenberg's argument that is not among the resources of skeptical theism. For to be intentionally deceived by divine testimony is to be betrayed by God. For in assertion the speaker assures the audience that what is being said is true, and can be counted on. And so lying always involves an intended evil (see Garcia 1998, and Murphy 2002a, pp. 29–30). But, as I have argued, the Anselmian being does not intend evil. So the Anselmian being never lies. (I would say similar things about other intentional deceptions—that they, objectionably, involve

[7] McBrayer and Swenson argue that this objection to skeptical theism is a bad one, because we think that we can rely on the testimony of other humans, and "In many cases we cannot tell whether they are being deceitful in a given instance" (2012, p. 148). But I don't see that this helps. With humans, we have general background reasons to take humans to tend inertially to truth-telling and to take them rarely to have adequate reason to tell lies. But God will not tend inertially to any action—God does what God has most reason to do, and otherwise chooses freely—and, given skeptical theism, we will be far from clear on what the relevant goods and evils are that bear on God's choices. For further discussion bearing on this issue, see Murphy 2002a, pp. 33–8.

intending evil, though not necessarily the evil of betrayal that I invoke here. But the casuistry of distinguishing between intention and foresight in considering actions that result in others' holding false beliefs generally raises difficulties that do not arise when one is dealing with assertion of known falsehood.) Thus, if the Anselmian being addresses one, then one can count on that being's assertions' being true.

Note that this view is not dependent on an objection that Wielenberg dismisses, that is, that it is absolutely wrong to lie, and so no divine reasons could justify it. While I do reject lying entirely as a permissible option (Murphy 2001, pp. 234–8, and Murphy 2002a, pp. 29–30), it is not on that basis that I argued for the Anselmian being's never intending to assert falsehoods to us. It is compatible with my view as defended in this book that it is not always wrong for us to lie, but that God never would do such a thing. Perhaps—though this is not my view—we are permitted to lie in various sorts of circumstances. But we are not absolutely good beings, and what is fitting for us beings of limited goodness may be entirely unsuitable for the absolutely perfect being.

The skeptical theist conclusion regarding the mere presence of evils in the world that the Anselmian being could do something about is correct: we have no grounds to think that the Anselmian being's existence is in tension with the presence of that evil. But we know that the Anselmian being is not the sort of being who would be set on, who would aim at, the existence of those evils. So even if the skeptical theist lacks the resources to avoid implications of the form *we cannot know that an absolutely perfect being would not aim at x*, where x is some creaturely evil, my own view would deny all such implications, and on principled grounds.

6.5 An Argument from Evil Based on Divine Intentions

I emphasize in the previous sections (6.2–6.4) the ways in which the account of the Anselmian being's ethics that I defend can be put to work as a response to versions of the argument from evil. I have claimed that this view of the Anselmian being's ethics takes the heart out of standard formulations of that argument, logical (6.2) and evidential (6.3), at least if they are conceived as arguments against the existence of an absolutely perfect being. I have argued also that my account of the ethics of an Anselmian being succeeds in avoiding the objections that have plagued a somewhat similar strategy employed by the skeptical theists (6.4). There is only one way in which my account of the absolutely perfect being's ethics contains a new vulnerability that one could exploit to provide an argument against the existence of such a being, for there is only one way that the view that I provide ascribes a less discretionary ethics to the absolutely perfect being than is identified by one who ascribes familiar welfare-oriented moral goodness to that being. Common understandings of familiar welfare-oriented moral goodness seem not to be as rigorist about the proscription of intending evil. Even if these rule out intending evil as an end, they seem to leave open the possibility that one might have sufficiently good reason to aim at some evil—say, by telling a lie—for the sake of some sufficiently worthwhile end. (As I noted in 6.4, I think that commonsense morality is not sufficiently rigorist about such acts of intending evil.) But I have denied that the Anselmian being could have such reasons to do evil, and so the Anselmian being never intends evil (5.5).

To exploit this thesis in formulating an argument from evil, one could not simply invoke the *existence* of evils that the Anselmian being would very well know about in creating the world. The fact that people would die young of terrible diseases is something that the Anselmian being must know would happen, but unless the *intention* that people die young from disease can be ascribed to the Anselmian being—that such was the absolutely perfect being's aim, as an end or as a means—no argument based on the fact that the Anselmian being does not intend evil gets off the ground. So unless the defender of the Anselmian being's ethics can be shown to be committed to the view that there are evils in this world that that being must have intended, there are no grounds to get this alternative argument from evil going.

I am not sure what grounds there are, on grounds of natural knowledge alone, to make a case that any evil or combination of evils is intended. Perhaps if the evils exhibited in this world displayed some sort of pattern that could be only the work of a providential evil-intender, a case could be constructed—a sort of argument from evil design—but that is not our world. Thus, just as with the worry about divine lies noted in 6.4, the problem is not my account of the Anselmian being's ethics together with some set of uncontroversial facts about the natural world; it is that account in tandem with some view, given or implied by revelation, of what the Anselmian being has intentionally done.

Here is one such argument. It might be taken to be a datum of revelation that God intended the existence of rational animals, and it is a fact that the existence of rational animals was the result of a process a crucial aspect of which was that innumerable living beings died young. (They in fact died painfully in many cases, but this might be merely foreseen.) One might argue, then, as follows. As a matter of revelation, God intended that rational animals exist. The evolution by way of natural selection that brought about the existing of rational animals, though not the only way that rational animals could be brought into existence by God, was the way that they actually were brought about by God. Because natural selection involves creaturely evils, and God obviously intended natural selection as a means to bring about rational animals, then God intended evils. Not as ends were they intended, but as means—but that is sufficient, on the view defended above (5.4), for evil to be among the success conditions for divine action, and thus enough to be a basis for an argument from evil against the existence of the Anselmian being.

I do not think that this argument is successful, though I concede its initial plausibility. There are various ways to trim back the claim that the Anselmian being does not intend evil to avoid the argument—to claim that the relevant evil includes only setbacks to the good of *rational* beings, say, and so to hold that though God intends harms to nonrational creatures in the bringing about of rational creatures, God never intends harm to rational creatures. I will not pursue such a line here. My aim is instead to explain why this argument fails, why the fact that the process by which rational animals came to exist includes evil and that God did intend the coming into being of rational animals does not show that God intended evil.

Begin by considering the following possibility.[8] One might intend that some end be realized, knowing that some evil will result from it, but judging it to be worthwhile overall to bring about that good even with the side effect of that evil. One later forms the intention to bring about some other end, making use of the evil that resulted from one's prior intention being realized in order to bring it about. Obviously, in so acting, one did not *intend* the evil in question. For by hypothesis, when one formed the aim of bringing about the first good, the evil was a foreseen consequence of it, not at all intended. And one could not have intended it after the fact in bringing about the second good, for one cannot intend what has already come to pass.[9] So the following is a possible pattern of action that does not involve intending evil: intending a good G_1; evil E resulting from the bringing about of G_1; intending G_2; making use of E in the bringing about of G_2.

So there is such a thing as 'making use' of an evil that does not involve intending it. This is not an invention of casuistical philosophy, but is part of our everyday repertoire of distinctions regarding how we agents relate to the evils that bear on our actions in some way. What is important is whether or not this distinction breaks down when we are considering the ways in which the Anselmian being would be acting to create the world with all consequences of various courses of action known to that being and all intentions—or perhaps, better, all aspects of one grand intention—fixed together, not serially in time. My view is that this distinction does not break down, and that is why this argument from natural selection that the Anselmian being must intend evils fails.

What is crucial in the standard case is not the fact that the intentions are formed at distinct times, but that each of the intentions is itself taken to be worthwhile, aimed at a valuable end, and assessed as justifiable on its own. That these intentions are formed at different times in my initial case serves merely to ensure that each of these intentions is independently justified. While counterfactual tests are not fully reliable here, as they are not fully reliable generally in thinking about intention and foresight (5.2), we might say that what is important is that G_1 is judged to be a worthwhile end, such that it is worth seeking even though E flows from it and even apart from G_2 being able to be realized through E, such that the agent would (or might well, or could) aim at G_1 even apart from the prospects of G_2 being realized thereby.

Suppose that, on a brutally hot day, I am considering whether to ride my bike to work or to drive. I consider that I will in fact suffer some significant discomfort by riding my bike, though the goods of cycling would make it worthwhile. I also note that

[8] Many of these ideas are clearly related to F. M. Kamm's work on what she calls "the Doctrine of Triple Effect," which makes similar distinctions in a much more sophisticated way; see Kamm 2007b.

[9] Except, perhaps, in those deviant cases in which one has some sort of counterfactual control over the past; for example, one can pray now for something to have happened in the past, and God's foresight that one would offer that prayer could have contributed to the explanation of its having happened.

I need a subject for a first-person essay on cycling, and the discomfort of riding on a brutally hot day would make a serviceable subject.[10] I say that I can intend to ride to work on the hot day and to intend to get a subject for a first-person essay without intending to undergo discomfort during this ride. I intend to ride, and I intend to make use of my discomfort as a subject for my essay.

One might think that this must be wrong, or at the very least, it is wrong if what I have said about the connection between intention and success conditions for action is right. Experiencing discomfort on the ride is necessary for getting the subject for my essay, and so if I misread the weather report or happen to feel cooler than usual, then my action will not be successful. But this is not the relevant sense of success. There are lots of factual predictions on the basis of which one forms intentions, the falsity of which will undercut success. I intend to buy life insurance, and I intend that my survivors be paid when I die. But I do not intend my death; taking for granted that I will die, I intend that my survivors be paid. I may indeed make lots of plans about the future financial security of my progeny premised on my death. If God miraculously keeps me alive until I am older than Methuselah, my intention to provide for their financial security via life insurance will not be a success, but not because I intended my death and failed to die; it is because I expected to die and did not. Similarly, I intend to ride my bike, and I intend to get a subject for a first-person essay by riding. But I do not intend the discomfort; given that I will be very uncomfortable, I intend that I will get an essay topic from it. Thus, just as I make use of rather than intend my death in the life insurance case, I can make use of rather than intend my discomfort in the hot weather cycling case.[11]

To return to the case at hand: The pattern of deliberation that I am going to describe is not anything that goes on within the mental life of the absolutely perfect being (0.3), but going through it will help us to see the difference that I am trying to get at. Suppose that the Anselmian being has in mind some species of being that it intends to exist. It judges the existence of that species to be good, as a distinctly valuable way of imitating the divine nature, and it judges the existence and perfection/well-being of whatever members of the species that exist to be good. Now, the Anselmian being could bring that species into existence immediately. But the Anselmian being also judges the following. If some other form of life exists for a time, then under certain circumstances (random to our eye, but known to the Anselmian being) there will be evolution resulting in the existence of the species that the Anselmian being intends to exist. If the Anselmian being judges that that other life form's existing for a time in those circum-

[10] Trust me that it is a serviceable subject; I am a David-Foster-Wallace-caliber essayist in this example. This is not a nearby possible world.

[11] The harder sort of case is that in which the intention to bring about the good would not be worthwhile unless the evil results from which one could make use in bringing about a further end. There is some pull in such cases in thinking that for such action to be rational, the evil must be intended. There is some disagreement about this. But I need not enter into it. For given my expansive account of the way that the Anselmian being can act on the justifying reasons given by creatures' existence and perfection/well-being, I need only this weaker account of the way in which one can make use of evils without intending them.

stances is good, and something that the Anselmian being would have justifying reason to bring about, then the Anselmian being may choose to bring that other life form into existence in those circumstances, both for its own sake and to make use of the fact that it will lead to the species that the Anselmian being intends to exist.

If this is right, then this argument from evil based on the Anselmian being's intending evil is a failure. I agree that as a matter of revelation God intended that rational animals exist. I agree that the evolution by way of natural selection that brought about existing of rational animals, though not the only way that rational animals could be brought into existence by God, was the way that they actually were brought about by God. But even though natural selection involves creaturely evils, I deny that God intended the early death of nonrational animals that drives evolution by natural selection as a means to bring about rational animals. I say, rather, that God *makes use* of the early death of creatures rather than intending it. And so we have no basis here for an argument from evil against the existence of an Anselmian being.

There are other appeals to revelation upon which one might rely in order to make an argument from intended evil against the existence of the Anselmian being. The most prominent of these are particular divine actions involving punishment, or for smitings or directives to smite, the divine motivations for which are unspecified or only partially specified. I think that the way in which punishment is connected to the intention to harm is actually a more difficult question than it may appear: punishment is paradigmatically about the authoritative directive for one to set oneself outside of the goods of common life, not about one party inflicting a harm on another (Murphy 2006a, pp. 152–9). But let us consider the starker understanding here, and suppose simply that God deprives some persons of life or limb as a matter of punishment. Those who affirm the *God does not intend evil* thesis have three responses available. The first is that God does not really intend the deprivation of life or limb in such cases. The second is that, even if God does intend the deprivation of life or limb, it does not count as intending evil, because of the way that the evil is situated with respect to some good. The third is that, even if God does intend the deprivation of life or limb, it does not count as intending evil, because the conditions of justified punishment ensure such deprivations are not evils in the relevant sense.

Tollefsen (2013), taking himself to follow Aquinas, appeals to the first option. Here is what Aquinas says: "God in inflicting punishment does not intend the evil for those punished but intends to imprint the ordination of his justice on things, just as the water's privation of its form results from the presence of the fire's form" (*De Malo* I, 3, ad 10). The analogy is that, although fire's presence predictably and necessarily results in water's withdrawing to some extent, it is not an 'aim' of the fire that water so withdraw. But I confess that I do not understand how this is supposed to be a relevant analogy. Here is something that strikes me as analogous: the enforcing of norms of justice by good, intelligent people will result in the wicked feeling dismayed, though the good and intelligent may not at all intend the dismaying of the wicked by ordaining justice. But when punishment is being imposed, part of what *constitutes* its success is the deprivation of aspects of well-being of those punished. So I do not see how this is a plausible strategy for dealing with the issue.

Others might claim that it is crucial that when God deprives the punished of life or limb, the deprivation is not instrumentally but constitutively related to the goods of justice to be brought about. The idea is that what is involved in intending the deprivation of life or limb as a matter of punishment does not fall within the scope of the rejection of intended evil, or within the scope as it should be characterized: for when the deprivation of some good is for the sake of justice, then it is not an evil in the relevant sense. One might treat this difference—that the deprivation is *constitutive* of a good—as itself dispositive, but I do not think it is. Even if we were to make a game out of harming, a very exciting and challenging game, that play is a fundamental human good would not imply that the harming that takes place as part of the game would count any less as the intentional infliction of creaturely evils.

A better option, I think, is that there is a clear sense under such (retributive) justice accounts of punishment in which the good of which the party is deprived is no longer 'due' to that person, and given our characterization of evil as the absence of *due* perfection/well-being in a creature, intending harm to a person as a (correct) application of justice in punishment is not the intending of evil.

One might object that this is hogwash, the worst sort of special pleading. By making a move like this, one opens the floodgates to not counting as 'due' to a creature any good that God has reasons to take away. If all it is for a good to be due to a creature is for it to be one that God thinks is a good idea, or not a bad idea, to let that creature enjoy, then the claim that God does not intend evil of course amounts to nothing. But I deny that any floodgates have been opened. The key point in spelling out the idea of a due good is that it is *local*, not responsive to the overall situation, but something specific about the creature or its kind. But whether one has acted wrongly in a way that makes one deserve punishment is local in this way; whether one deserves punishment is fixed by what one has done, what one is responsible for. The requirement that due goods are due in virtue of local features is satisfied in this case, and would not be in cases in which (for example) God might want to harm someone, say, simply for the sake of setting an example for the rest of the world.[12] So while God's lying to someone simply for the sake of fulfilling some wonderful divine purpose would count as God's intending evil, God's putting an evildoer to death for his or her offenses need not.

[12] Here is a rough-and-ready way to think about it. In cases in which the local features of the case make the deprivation of well-being/perfection not an evil in the relevant sense, we might well deny that it is a 'bad thing' if the deprivation takes place. (Indeed, this is just how van Inwagen characterizes evil in his 2006; in the context of the argument from evil, he says, 'evil' just means "bad things" (p. 4).) So while it might be bad for a justly convicted prisoner to be imprisoned for his or her offenses, it is not a bad thing that he or she is imprisoned. But in other sorts of cases, such as a case in which an innocent is harmed for the sake of bringing about great goods or preventing worse evils, we would still say that it is a bad thing that the innocent suffers, even if we, or some of us, judge it worthwhile overall. The thought, then, is that while God might intend setbacks to well-being that are not 'bad things' in this intuitive sense, God would never intend setbacks to well-being that are 'bad things' in this intuitive sense.

I think that the point that not all evils that the Anselmian being makes use of need be intended by the Anselmian being and the point that harms inflicted for the sake of justified retributive punishment may not count as intended evil together put paid to the most worrisome issues about whether revelation makes trouble for the existence of a perfect being who never intends evil. In the former case, the alleged intended evils are not intended; in the latter case, the alleged intended evils are not evils. One may raise problematic texts where it seems that God goes beyond that, but these are themselves cases in which what is being asserted, what is supposed to be literally true, what are supposed to be the motivating reasons of God, and so forth are up for serious dispute, even among those who take the authority of revelation extremely seriously. (See, for example, Swinburne 2011 and Wolterstorff 2011.) If one must defend a particular reading of (e.g.) the book of Joshua as the best of many contentious readings for the sake of making trouble for the claim about the Anselmian being that I have defended, I will take that as a sign of progress and an invitation to engage in further casuistry about the Anselmian being's ethics.

6.6 The Arguments from Evil That Remain

There is no good argument from evil against the existence of the Anselmian being. The standard forms of that argument, which appeal to the existence of evil or evils, falter in the face of the fact that the Anselmian being's reasons to prevent such evils are justifying, not requiring (6.2–6.3). The clearest vulnerability of the thesis that there exists an Anselmian being is evil that is intended by the Anselmian being. But the existence of evil does not entail that God intends it, and even granting for the sake of argument certain theses drawn from revelation about God's will, we do not have a successful argument that there does not exist an absolutely perfect being who is not only all-knowing and all-powerful but also never intends evil (6.5).

But while a better understanding of the ethics of the Anselmian being renders the argument from evil against the existence of an absolutely perfect being ineffective, one might plausibly claim that I have not made any progress on the *real* problem of evil, or that I have made the *real* problem of evil worse. The worry is that even if one decisively shows that the absolutely perfect being's existence is not called into question by evil, the problem of evil that this objector is concerned with is directed against *God*—the object of worship by Jews, Muslims, and Christians. And regardless of what we should think about the ethics of an absolutely perfect being, this objector may point out, we are supposed to know something more than that about God's ethics: we are supposed to know, by revelation at least, that to this being are correctly ascribed a variety of moral virtues and a great deal of love for creation. We are also, this objector reminds us, supposed to know something about *our* ethics with respect to God: we are supposed to worship God, and we are supposed to be loyal to, to be obedient to, to be allied with God. And so even if we are convinced that there is no good argument from evil against the Anselmian being, there may be good arguments from evil against *God*, understood as an absolutely perfect being who, as a matter of fact if not a matter of necessity, is characterized by a familiar welfare-oriented ethics and understood as a being whom we are supposed to worship and to whom we are supposed to show complete loyalty, obedience, and allegiance.

I think that there is a good deal to this challenge, and that is why this book has two Parts. But I also think that we should be a bit clearer than this objection is both on what the precise objections are supposed to be and about the extent to which the conclusions of this Part have allowed us to make some progress even on what the objector considers the 'real' problems of evil.

Here is one way to make matters more precise. "What you have shown, if anything," the objector might claim, "is that the familiar welfare-oriented moral goodness and/or love that characterizes God cannot be necessary to God. For all that is necessary to God is God's perfection, and neither familiar welfare-oriented moral goodness nor the sort of love for us often ascribed to God is an implication of the divine perfection. But those who advance the problem of evil are, or should be, content to show that there does not exist a being who is omniscient, omnipotent, and *at least contingently* morally good and/or loving in the relevant way—that's what the God of Abrahamic theism is supposed to be like, and that's what the problem of evil is really supposed to be a problem for. Since all you have done is to show that God does not exhibit these features necessarily, not that God does not exhibit these features even contingently, you have done nothing to blunt the real problem of evil."

Not quite. Putting to the side the question of whether the 'real' problem of evil is only that directed against the God of Abrahamic monotheism,[13] it seems to me that this objection misses an important result of showing that the extent to which God exhibits welfare-oriented moral goodness or love is contingent at most. It is this: any feature that is ascribed to God as a necessary feature is ascribed to God as an entailment of a divine perfection; but divine perfections must be ascribed to God at their intrinsic maximum (1.4). Thus, if we are to ascribe some conception of moral goodness or love to God as a matter of necessity, we must do so in a way that pegs out the goodness or love meter at its highest level of value. And that is an important part of how arguments from evil work—by noting that God must be *maximally* concerned for our well-being. But once we give up the notion that God's welfare-oriented moral goodness or love is part of God's perfection, we should no longer feel any pressure to interpret God's concern for our well-being in a way that is, along the relevant practical dimensions, maximal. Thus, there may be a theologically acceptable account of God's love for us that does not make such love maximal, and so does not serve nearly so easily as a premise in an argument from evil.

[13] The argument from evil is not supposed to be simply an *ad hominem* against a particular group of theists, holding that there is no being that has all of the features that they ascribe to a being that they call 'God.' The argument from evil is supposed to be an argument that there is no God. But if the best understanding of *being God* is *being an absolutely perfect being*, then the argument from evil is a failure, because that argument is wholly unsuccessful in giving us reason to believe that there is no absolutely perfect being.

My response, then, is that as a response to the problem of evil not as posed against the existence of an Anselmian being but as posed against the God of traditional Abrahamic monotheism, what I have shown in Part I does not fully solve *that* problem, but it does open up new possibilities for a persuasive response. And I will attempt to fulfill that promise in Part II, where I argue for an account of the contingent norms to which an Anselmian being might subject itself that is compatible with the features of the God of traditional Abrahamic monotheism but is not subject to a persuasive argument from evil.

There is a second challenge, one that is framed in terms of our ethics with respect to God. For consider the two main formal understandings of God that are alternatives to the Anselmian formulation within standard theism: that God is the being supremely worthy of worship and that God is the being perfectly worthy of supreme allegiance (0.2). We will have to say more later (7.1–7.3) to provide a specification of these conceptions, but the idea is that God is a being who deserves one's full admiration and support—one should admire God, one should ally oneself with God, one should be on God's side, one should be loyal to God, one should be obedient to God, one should trust God, one should defer to God, and so forth.

But here is the problem. Grant that there is no conflict between the evil of the world and the existence of an absolutely perfect being. The way that we secured that lack of conflict was by prying the Anselmian being's reasons apart from our reasons—by making the Anselmian being's ethics very different from our own, so that there is a vast run of reasons that we do not share with the Anselmian being. But it is a pointed question how we could possibly treat God as supremely worthy of worship, alliance, devotion, loyalty, obedience, and so forth if we and God do not share reasons for action—share them in the way that we would if God exhibited familiar welfare-oriented moral goodness.[14] It is one thing to think that, even if we are having trouble seeing why God does and allows what God does and allows, God is nevertheless acting on a set of reasons that we and God share, and acting on them better than we ourselves are able to. It is quite another to think that, even though God is perfect at acting on all of the reasons that God has, nevertheless how God appropriately values our ends could be massively at odds with how we appropriately value our ends. (See also Gale 1999, pp. 210–11.)

We could put this argument from evil in the following way. Perhaps it is true that a putatively absolutely perfect being would exhibit no *rational defect* by allowing the evils that we find in our world. So there is no good challenge from evil to the existence of an Anselmian being. But any being whose reasons do not preclude that being from

[14] I think that this is the moral of M. Adams 1999. Adams in fact follows Scotus in holding that creaturely good does not necessitate divine action, and so it is possible for there to be an absolutely perfect being who does not treat our good as giving requiring reasons for action. Her concern is that such a being is not a being who is good to us, and to whom we could have the right sort of allegiance. I am in fundamental agreement with her on this point, and I take Part II of this book to be working out exactly what this problem is and what the contours of a solution would have to be like.

allowing such evils is not a being to whom we could be bound to give supreme worship and show supreme allegiance. So even if the argument of Part I were a singular success in establishing that the argument from evil is ineffective against the existence of an Anselmian being, this is of no help in showing that we could owe our allegiance to a being who is not disposed to oppose those evils. Indeed, one might think we have made this problem of evil *worse*, by rendering in principle unintelligible how we could ally ourselves with such a being. And since it is clear that the God of orthodox Abrahamic theism is not only perfect but a being to whom such full allegiance is owed, the way that we solved the problem of evil as posed against the existence of an Anselmian being makes the problem of evil as posed against *God*, to whom we owe complete allegiance, worse, much worse.

One might think that I am being too hard on the Part I view, and offer the following defense. Some writers, harkening back to a distinction made in Plantinga (1974, p. 195), distinguish between the problem of evil in its theoretical form and the problem of evil in its practical form. In its theoretical form, the problem of evil is concerned simply with the way that evil presents an epistemic challenge to reasonable belief in God. The practical form, by contrast, concerns how theists are to respond to evil—that is, how theists' attitudes and actions with respect to God should be affected by their encounters with evil (van Inwagen 2006, pp. 4–5). Now, relying on this distinction, one might say that all of my concerns about worship-worthiness and allegiance-worthiness should just be folded into this *practical* problem of evil; putting to the side the questions about specifically Christian views of God noted above in this section, the *theoretical* problem of evil is adequately dispensed with once we show that evils do not pose any evidential threat to the existence of the Anselmian being.

I reject the offer of help, for I reject the view that these questions about God's worship- and allegiance-worthiness do not belong to the investigation of the theoretical problem of evil. Those who distinguish the practical problem from the theoretical problem must presuppose that it is *God* one's response to whom might be appropriately or inappropriately transformed by one's encounter with evil. But what I am noting is that some very plausible conceptions of God just *include* certain responses to God being appropriate, and even required, as part of the formal characterization of what it is to be God. So when one raises challenges to the view that the Anselmian being merits our worship or allegiance due to the Anselmian being's not sharing our ethics with respect to the elimination of evil, one is raising a theoretical problem of evil concerning God's existence, an objection to God's existence given a conception of God on which worship- or allegiance-worthiness is at least partly constitutive of *being God*.

The consideration of whether and how the Anselmian being is supremely worthy of worship and allegiance is the task of Part II.

PART II

God's Ethics

The first Part of this book asks what we can say of God's ethics simply insofar as God is an Anselmian, that is, absolutely perfect, being. The central conclusions were that (1) the existence and perfection/well-being of creatures provide justifying reasons for the Anselmian being to promote them (4.2); (2) it is not true that the existence and perfection/well-being of creatures provide requiring reasons for the Anselmian being to promote them (4.3–4.5); (3) the Anselmian being has decisive requiring reasons not to intend creaturely evil (5.2–5.5); and (4) given this conception of the Anselmian being's ethics, there is no plausible argument from evil against the existence of the Anselmian being (6.2–6.3, 6.5).

The aim of Part II is to ask further questions about how we are to relate to the Anselmian being, given this conception of the Anselmian being's ethics. In Chapter 7, I will argue that while the perfection of the Anselmian being entails that being's necessary worship-worthiness, the perfection of the Anselmian being does not entail that being's allegiance-worthiness, especially given the conception of the Anselmian being's ethics defended in Part I. I also argue that the contingency of the Anselmian being's allegiance-worthiness is not itself an objectionable implication of my account of the Anselmian being's ethics.

But God is supposed to be worthy of complete allegiance. So one must be able to provide an account of how an Anselmian being, though not necessarily allegiance-worthy, could be allegiance-worthy, and if we are not immediately to reach skeptical conclusions about the existence of an allegiance-worthy Anselmian being, this account must be plausibly true of the actual world. In Chapter 8 I exhibit this plausibility by exhibiting the conditions under which the Anselmian being could be worthy of our complete allegiance. Central to this account are theses concerning the possibility and value of entering into a relationship with the Anselmian being by which one subordinates one's will to that of the Anselmian being—this is the good of 'religion'—and concerning the sort of ethics that an Anselmian being would have to have to in order for us to enter into that friendship-like relationship. This contingent ethics is, in keeping with divine sovereignty, self-imposed: the Anselmian being comes to be under further norms, in addition to those described in Part I, only by subjecting itself to them.

In Chapter 9 I consider whether the argument from evil can be revived against the existence of an Anselmian being who has taken on the contingent norms considered in Chapter 8. I say No: I say that the existence of evil is the basis for no argument against the existence of an Anselmian being whose contingent ethics makes that being fully worthy of allegiance. I also deny that the specific ethics that is ascribed to the Anselmian being by Christian theism in particular changes the prospects for this revived argument from evil. I conclude by considering the objection that the conception of divine ethics defended in this book is a rearguard action, a retreat from advancing and strengthening formulations of the problem of evil. I of course deny this. My view is that the conception of divine ethics presented here is independently attractive. A central insight of this account, an insight not adequately captured by now-standard views, is that God loves us though God does not have to.

7

Worship-Worthiness and Allegiance-Worthiness

7.1 Worship-Worthiness

Suppose that the Anselmian being's ethics are as Part I claims them to be. We should think of that being as absolutely perfect (1.3), but should not take the Anselmian being's agency with respect to us to be governed by familiar welfare-oriented moral goodness. Does this give us any reason to doubt that the Anselmian being is a being that is necessarily worthy of worship, indeed necessarily supremely worship-worthy? As I noted in 0.1, there are multiple reasonable conceptions of God, and one of the crucial questions in fundamental theology concerns the relationship between these conceptions. It may be supposed that an absolutely perfect being will be supremely worship-worthy. But one might judge that, if the ethics of the Anselmian being are as I have argued, this supposition needs to be reassessed.

Let me begin by distinguishing two questions. The first is the question of *worship-worthiness*, its basis, and its applicability to the Anselmian being; the second is the question of the *obligation to worship*, its basis, and its applicability to us with respect to the Anselmian being. There has been some recent discussion about how to explain the obligation to worship God, some of that discussion skeptical (see, for example, Bayne and Nagasawa 2006). Without commenting at all on that discussion, I note only that the question of the worship-worthiness of God and the question of the obligation to worship God are distinct, as different as the question of whether a joke is funny and the question of whether one should laugh at it.[1] Worship-worthiness is our central concern here, though I will also briefly comment on the further question of the obligatoriness of worship.

Worship-worthiness involves—I will not claim that this is an analysis—the potential worshipper having reasons of the right sort[2] to worship the potential object of worship.

[1] This distinction is not the same as the distinction, noted by Bayne and Nagasawa in their article on the obligation to worship God, between the reasonableness of worshipping God and the obligation to do so. A joke may be such that it is funny but never reasonable to laugh at.

[2] The notion of 'reasons of the right sort' has a prominent role in contemporary discussions of normativity, and it is an open question how far we can analyze this notion rigorously. Here I leave matters intuitive. If a powerful person can credibly threaten me with all sorts of terrible evils if I do not worship him, that does give me reason to worship him: the reasons to avoid these terrible evils. (Of course, I should not worship

Worship is a phenomenon involving beliefs, attitudes, and actions. To worship some being presupposes and is partially constituted by having a set of beliefs and attitudes toward that being. The actions that worship involves are actions that express, in more or less direct ways, those beliefs and attitudes. Thus, we can ask a variety of questions about worship-worthiness: first, what are the beliefs and attitudes presupposed by acts of worship; second, what sorts of actions constitute fitting or unfitting expressions of those beliefs and attitudes; and third, what sort of normative force do these relationships of fittingness and unfittingness have in the practical lives of those for whom such beliefs, attitudes, and actions are open possibilities?

Worship-worthiness is fundamentally a relational notion. For a being to be worthy of worship is for that being to be worthy of some person's worship. This person is *another* being—no one is worthy of one's own worship (Smart 1972, pp. 26–7).[3] So even God is not worthy of everyone's worship, for God is not worthy of God's own worship. (God is worthy of God's own love. But not worship.) Nevertheless, we can describe one sort of upper limit on worship-worthiness that is frequently ascribed to God: we might say that x has achieved this upper limit of worship-worthiness if necessarily, if y is an agent (or an agent capable of forming the beliefs, attitudes, etc. relevant to worship) and $x \neq y$, then x is worthy of y's worship.

I also want to say that it is plain that no one is worthy of an *equal's* worship. Even if another being is responsible for one's existence and well-being, what that would call for, perhaps, is gratitude or love, not worship. If the Son is begotten of the Father, then, though both are equally divine, that the Son is begotten of the Father may make it true that various asymmetric responses are fitting between the Father and the Son. But it will not be appropriate for the Son to worship the Father, for they are equal in kind, equally divine.[4]

In my view the key to circumscribing appropriate worship-worthiness relations is this fact of inequality between the parties (Smart 1972, p. 27). There are multiple stricter and looser senses of 'worship,' but I aim here to capture the sense of worship in which it is plain why the beliefs, attitudes, and actions constitutive of worship carried out by us are properly exhibited toward God alone. A being is worthy of worship by some person in this sense only when there is a massive inequality between that being and that person, and the inequality is an inequality of a certain sort of value. Both of these conditions require comment.

him. But that there are reasons to do so is obvious from the fact that there is some point to my worshipping him, that you would not find it unmotivated and unintelligible.) But the presence of these reasons does not contribute to making this threatener worthy of worship.

[3] As I discuss below in this section, worship involves subordination of the worshipper and elevation of the worshipped, and this requires distinct parties.

[4] Objection: Jesus is the Son. Jesus worships the Father appropriately. So the Son worships the Father appropriately. As far as I can tell, this sort of argument is the same as every other puzzle that arises due to the presence of seemingly incompatible properties in Jesus Christ arising from Jesus's having both a fully human and a fully divine nature. So use your favorite account (reduplicative, kenotic Christology, etc.) to deal with the problem.

With respect to the value condition, what is relevant in explaining the appropriateness of one being's worshipping another is not just a difference between these beings, but that the difference is one that is relevant to value. This seems obvious enough: that there is a massive difference between the number of molecules in my body and that in a blue whale's body is not enough to justify a basis for my worshipping the blue whale, as the number of molecules that constitutes one seems on its face not a relevant difference in value.[5] Further, it seems that we will have to say that not just any sort of value matters. One does not worship that which is simply more instrumentally valuable than oneself, or that which counts as being simply a better instance of a kind than oneself (without reference to the kind in question). The sort of value in question has to be inescapable and overriding—it has to be value the practical relevance of which one cannot appropriately escape, and which bears a practical priority over other sorts of value.

With respect to the massive inequality condition, it seems to me that the most plausible view here cannot treat the difference of value between the two beings as being a difference simply in the degree to which some valuable feature is realized. It is not that it is appropriate for us to worship angels because they are so much greater than we are, though we need to tone it down a bit to leave some room to be able to express the superior greatness of God. There has to be a sense in which the worshipped and the worshipper are not even playing the same game, not rightly placed on a common scale.[6] Think of how we think of worship colloquially—one philosopher might worship another philosopher colloquially speaking, but it would be bizarre to do so if the worshipped were simply a much better philosopher; the worshipped would have to be one of those philosophers who is so great that we do not think of him or her as even playing the same game that the rest of us are playing—say, a Plato, or an Aquinas, or a Kant, or an Anscombe. It is true that both Aquinas and Trenton Merricks are better philosophers than I am. It would not be strange to say—colloquially, mind you—that I worship Aquinas. But something has gone wrong, either in me or in your description of me, if you were to characterize me as worshipping Merricks.

The central belief the correctness and appropriateness of holding of which are partially constitutive of the worship-worthiness of God by us is the belief that God is absurdly greater than we are, greater in terms of pure perfection. (As I argued above (4.4), God's goodness is intrinsic goodness and ours merely goodness by participation; it is not simply that God has greater goodness than we do, but that ours is of a meager and reflected type.) The attitudes the appropriateness of which are partially constitutive of the worship-worthiness of God by us are attitudes that are appropriate to display

[5] Unless, I suppose, one being is not composed of any molecules and another is composed of some non-zero number of molecules. It is relevant to God's worship-worthiness that God is not composed of parts.

[6] Thus Otto speaks of the way that in one's encounter with the divine one of the "chiefest" features is "self-depreciation…, the estimation of the self, of the personal 'I', as something not perfectly or essentially real….It starts from a consciousness of the absolute superiority or supremacy of a power other than myself" (Otto 1958 [1923], p. 21).

toward a being who is absurdly greater than we are, greater in terms of pure perfection. And the actions that are appropriately worshipful actions are those that express these beliefs and attitudes: they are actions that express the absolute greatness of this being, that being's being so much greater than we are, and our being so pathetic in comparison to that being. Thus, typical of appropriate worship of God are actions that express glorification of God, praise of God, and our self-abasement in relation to God.

Such an account of the worship-worthiness of God should suffice not only for the worship-worthiness of God in respect to us, but in respect to any created being that has the capacity to recognize and respond to pure perfection through forming appropriate beliefs and attitudes and carrying out actions expressive of those attitudes. For the relevant massive inequality of value will be present in any such created being.

I have elaborated a bit on the character of worship-worthiness in order to make the following point: given this conception of worship-worthiness, there is *no* reason to think that *any* particular conclusion about the Anselmian being's ethics could call into doubt *in any way* the view that the Anselmian being is worthy of worship in the traditional strong sense. By definition, to count as an Anselmian being is to be absolutely perfect. If the arguments of Part I were correct, then what was shown was that the Anselmian being has a different ethics than we might have supposed, not that there is no Anselmian being, or that for some reason we must revise the Anselmian view so that we do not think of the best possible being as absolutely great. And if there is indeed an Anselmian being, then the conditions that make it true that a being is worthy of worship by us are satisfied, and so the Anselmian being is worthy of worship, even though we and the Anselmian being do not by nature share a common ethics.[7]

So the ethics that I have ascribed to the Anselmian being does not threaten that being's worship-worthiness. Early in the book (0.2) I endorsed the view that to be worthy of worship entails being absolutely perfect; I now affirm the other half of the biconditional, that being absolutely perfect entails being worthy of worship. But I want to allow that there is something to the initial disquiet that some may have felt, making them inclined to think that the worship-worthiness of the Anselmian being is threatened by the ethics that I ascribed to that being. In part, I would want to explain that disquiet by distinguishing a variety of attitudes and actions from the attitudes and actions constitutive of worship—thankfulness and actions that express it, for example, are not constitutive of worship, responding not to the nonrelational value of a being but its value to us, by benefiting us in various ways—and allowing that the appropriateness of these attitudes and actions may indeed be threatened by my view of the Anselmian being's ethics (see 7.2). But I think I should also allow that there is a threat more closely connected to worship, a threat to the notion that it is our obligation, or

[7] Cf. Geach 1977: "God is to be loved and admired above all things...The protest that we ought not so to love and admire him if he does not share the moral perfections proper to his creatures is a mere impertinence" (p. 79).

our duty, or in some way all-things-considered a requirement of reason for us to worship the Anselmian being.

It is just true that the Anselmian being is massively greater than us, and those who form that belief based on the reasonable assessment of God's goodness and our own are making no mistake. But the way in which that belief should all-things-considered be manifested in expressive action depends on what other reasons one has. Here is a way to think about it. Whatever the obligation that we have to worship the Anselmian being consists in, it cannot be such that it all-things-considered requires us to be constantly performing expressive actions of worship. What it requires are something like a strong negative requirement against performing actions that express something contrary to our proper ordering with respect to the Anselmian being (for example, requirements against blasphemy and pridefulness), a positive requirement to perform actions that are worshipful when appropriate, and something like a general requirement to order one's life so that there will be plentiful opportunities for appropriate worship. Thus, the positive requirements specifically to engage in expressive actions of worship are shaped by the other reasons for action that a creature has. You are not, for example, failing in the requirement to worship when you are performing some sort of mentally taxing act of justice—say, refereeing a very complex journal submission on which you agreed to submit a report—that precludes your also engaging in worship.

But the ethics of the Anselmian being defended in Part I leaves open the possibility that some group of rational creatures and the Anselmian being may have very different sets of reasons for action, such that the Anselmian being could, without error, treat the good of those rational creatures as of very little account in terms of what the Anselmian being has chosen for creation. In such circumstances, it seems to me to be possible that while God's worthiness to be worshipped by those creatures may be in no way diminished, it may be inappropriate for those rational creatures to perform acts of worship. For it may constitute inadequate solidarity with one's fellow rational creatures for one to devote him- or herself to the worship of the Anselmian being: for, after all, one may owe the concern of familiar welfare-oriented moral goodness to one's fellow creatures, though the Anselmian being may have nothing even in the ballpark of such concern.

Here is a very rough analogy. Suppose that you are being driven out of business by a hard-nosed, but fair, business competitor. You are my friend, to whom I owe the care and concern of a friend; this competitor, though never wronging either of us, owes us no such concern. While it seems to me that I would not be wrong in judging correctly the superiority of this business competitor, it may be that I am wholly excluded from expressing this superiority, honoring it, and so forth. Not because this competitor has done anything wrong; just out of my solidarity with you and my lack of solidarity with this competitor. (For further discussion of this analogy, see Murphy 2011b, pp. 166–7.)

So I grant that there is something unsettling about the views of Part I with respect to worship of the Anselmian being. It would be a mistake to couch this in terms of the

Anselmian being's failing to be worship-worthy because it does not share with us governance by familiar welfare-oriented moral goodness. But it is not a mistake to wonder whether we could be bound to the worship of such a being unless we can see how that worship would be compatible with the solidarity that we owe to our fellow human beings, and that the Anselmian being's not being governed by familiar welfare-oriented moral goodness calls into question whether worship of that being is compatible with the solidarity that we owe to our fellow human beings.

7.2 Allegiance-Worthiness I: Alliance

The point of 7.1 was to deny that we have any basis for thinking that the Anselmian being's worship-worthiness is diminished if we take the Anselmian being's ethics not to be an ethics of familiar welfare-oriented moral goodness. But it seems to me that we should reach a different conclusion with respect to the allegiance-worthiness of the Anselmian being. The power of the argument for the necessary worship-worthiness of the Anselmian being is that worship-worthiness turns entirely on the relative goodness of the beings in question; and so we have reason to think that any created agent will be such that the Anselmian being is worthy of worship by that created agent. But I do not think that allegiance-worthiness can be defended in the same way. When we consider the features that make one party worthy of another's allegiance, different considerations are salient, and given the characterization of the Anselmian being's ethics, it becomes far more difficult to see how the Anselmian being is worthy of the allegiance of created rational beings.[8]

In characterizing worship-worthiness, I appealed to a connection between the worship-worthiness of the Anselmian being in relation to rational creatures and those rational creatures having reasons to worship the Anselmian being. For the Anselmian being to be necessarily supremely worthy of worship, it must be true that, necessarily, any rational creature capable of worshipping the Anselmian being has reasons of the right sort to worship the Anselmian being. I did not claim that this is an analysis of worship-worthiness, though those enamored of the program of giving 'reasons of the right sort' analyses of normative notions generally may take it to be so, as far as I am concerned here. All that I said was that it is a necessary and plausibly sufficient condition for worship-worthiness.

I want to say the same thing about the alleged necessary supreme allegiance-worthiness of the Anselmian being. For the Anselmian being to be necessarily supremely allegiance-worthy, there must necessarily be reasons of the right sort for any rational creature capable of having allegiance to the Anselmian being to have

[8] Recall that in claiming that the Anselmian being is not worthy of the allegiance of created rational beings, the thesis is not that the being who is in fact the Anselmian being is not worthy of the allegiance of the actual created rational beings that are on the scene. The claim is that it is not a necessary truth that any being that counts as an Anselmian being will merit the allegiance of any being that counts as a created rational being. See 1.1.

supreme allegiance to that being. I am going to leave the general idea of 'allegiance' undefined here (though I will discuss some major species of it in some detail just below in this section); we can think of it roughly as *siding with* the Anselmian being in one's attitudes and actions. For the Anselmian being to be fully allegiance-worthy with respect to one would thus require that one have decisive reasons of the right sort to side with the Anselmian being. (Reasons to ϕ are decisive when they are reasons that make ϕ-ing reasonable and not ϕ-ing unreasonable.) So for the Anselmian being to be necessarily fully allegiance-worthy would be for, necessarily, every rational creature to have decisive reasons of the right sort to side with the Anselmian being.

In lieu of attempting a more detailed general account of allegiance, I will focus on what I take to be its two characteristic species, both of which seem to me to be absolutely central to standard understandings of our proper relationship to God: alliance and obedience. The basic worry is this. With respect to both species of allegiance, whether one agent is worthy of another agent's allegiance concerns the agents' ends, goals, purposes, projects, and the like, either descriptively (that is, the ends, goals, etc. that the agents actually have) or normatively (that is, the ends, goals, etc. that the agents ought to have): these ends, goals, etc. must be shared by the parties in question. But the Part I account of the Anselmian being's ethics entails that these ends, goals, etc. are not necessarily shared by the Anselmian being and created rational beings. So the Anselmian being is not necessarily worthy of the allegiance of created rational beings.

Begin with alliance. Our standard case of alliance is describable simply factually: it involves two or more parties who share an end and intend to bring about this end by some sort of coordination (though this coordination may be rather minimal, even dispositional). They are both *for* a common end, and take their distinct efforts to be unified by a common understanding that they are for that common end. So two nations that are otherwise at odds may well be allies in a military conflict, taking themselves to have a common objective in the defeat of a common enemy, and being willing to coordinate for the sake of achieving that goal. This coordinated activity may be rather minimal. But it involves relying in some way on the other's efforts, being willing to engage in common activity if the opportunity presents itself, and so forth.

Given the bare factual notion of alliance we can state some necessary conditions on a normative notion of *alliance-worthiness*. For A to be in some way worthy of B's alliance, A and B must share an end and B must have good reason to coordinate with A in the pursuit of that common end.[9] (I do not take alliance-worthiness to be a symmetric relation: it may be that A is alliance-worthy for B, but B is not alliance-worthy for A.)

[9] I do not take this to state a sufficient condition; as I note above, there is surely a 'wrong sort of reasons' problem with respect to defining alliance-worthiness in terms of reasons, such that B might have reasons to coordinate with A to pursue their common end that are not the sort to make A alliance-worthy for B. If A is totally incompetent and bungling, yet God demands that you make an alliance with A in order to punish you, then you have reasons to ally yourself with A in spite of A's lack of alliance-worthiness.

We can use the notion of alliance-worthiness to distinguish among various sorts of relatively qualified and relatively unqualified forms of alliance-worthiness. We might, for example, distinguish between alliance-worthiness in which the value of the ends shared by A and B is genuine and those in which it is spurious. We might say that given their abhorrent agendas, two racist political parties would be natural allies, or that given their imperialist goals, two nations are understandably allied against a common enemy. But we can speak less qualifiedly of alliance-worthiness in which both parties share an end that is a good and worthwhile end, or not just good and worthwhile, but all-things-considered reasonable to adopt. With these less-qualified forms of alliance-worthiness, we get closer to the view that if one party is worthy of another's alliance, then that other should try to make that alliance, to actually coordinate in the relevant way in pursue of their shared goals. So if there is an aggressive, unjust, and devastating war being waged against the people of A and B, then even though A and B may not have had dealings in the past, it might become immediately clear that A and B both do and should have as an end the defeat of this common enemy, and A and B should be willing to do what is necessary and otherwise reasonable to coordinate their activity to bring about this end.

We can also consider alliance-worthiness at one further step removed, where one or both parties have not yet adopted (or, if they have, abstracting from the fact that they have adopted) the ends to be assessed in terms of worthiness and in terms of which coordination is called for. We can ask about the ends that two or more parties should have, and whether those ends give reason to make the relevant sort of alliance. We can ask, with respect to A's being worthy of B's alliance, whether there is an end that A and B *should* adopt, and in light of that end, whether B has reason to coordinate with A in its pursuit. We can ask this even if neither A nor B has the end in question, for what would be involved is (at least) B's taking on that end and setting B-self to coordinating with A to realize it. (It may be that there could not be such reasons for alliance unless it was supposed that A would come to adopt this end, whether independently, or by B's efforts, or whatever, for otherwise there would arguably be no coordination between them.[10] That will not, however, turn out to be important for the kind of case that I am concerned with.) So, to give an example: imagine that A and B are nations, and are witnessing the brazen military buildup of an outspokenly and historically hostile nation. Neither A nor B has any views yet as to what to think or do about this. It makes perfect sense for a citizen of B to say: A is worth allying ourselves with in order to do something about this hostile nation's military buildup. The justification for this is that there is an end that A and B should have—keeping the hostile nation's ambitions in check—and that coordinated activity between A and B is worth carrying out in light of that objective.

[10] Or maybe there would be. It does not strike me as strange that I could coordinate with someone who does not take him- or herself to be coordinating with me. I do this with small children all the time. Maybe it is strange to call it coordination, but it is organizing one's activity in light of another's in pursuit of a shared end.

So there is a distinction between one's being another's ally and another's being worthy of one's alliance, and there is a distinction between more or less unqualified ways of being worthy of alliance. There is one more distinction to make, between different *scopes* of alliance. Little precision is needed here. There is obviously a difference between alliances that, even though clearly worthy, are very limited in scope, and alliances that are much broader in scope. Two colleagues may ally themselves to write a paper, to write a book, to co-author over a lifetime. Two people may ally themselves for a date, for a vacation, for a marriage. These are obviously different in scope, and we would naturally say that (other things equal) there is fuller alliance in the latter cases than in the former cases.

So the question now at issue, then, is whether it is a necessary truth that for every created rational being, the Anselmian being is fully worthy of that being's alliance.[11] Not all created rational beings are in fact fully allied with the Anselmian being, but that is of course not the topic under discussion. Rather, what is under discussion is whether the Anselmian being is *worthy* of created rational beings' allegiance in the sense I have just described. And I take it that we should not be satisfied with the claim that there is *some* end that the Anselmian being and created rational beings should have in common in order to make the case; that would give us a conclusion that there is *some* sphere in which created rational beings should ally themselves with the Anselmian being, but would not give us the robust conclusion that the Anselmian being is *fully* worthy of allegiance—whether, complete in scope and decisiveness, alliance with the Anselmian being is something we ought to take up.

Given the view of the Anselmian being's ethics defended in Part I, though, it seems obvious that the Anselmian being would not be supremely allegiance-worthy in this sense. For the ends that human beings should have are largely ends set by familiar welfare-oriented moral goodness—the well-being of our fellow sentient creatures. Yet it is plain that the Anselmian being need not share these ends, even given the existence of these creatures; even given the existence of these creatures, their well-being may constitute no more than justifying reasons for the Anselmian being to act, and the Anselmian being need not have taken these as reasons for acting in bringing about a world in which such created rational beings exist. So the strong sharing of ends—at least ends that the parties involved should have—that is part and parcel of supreme alliance-worthiness is just not present in the case of the Anselmian being and created rational beings.

Now, one might retort that I have focused on one sort of alliance—the sort exhibited by comrades in pursuit of common objectives—to the exclusion of other sorts, with the result that I have fixed on the sort of alliance that is least likely to flourish between the Anselmian being and created rational beings. This sort of alliance is reasons-centric,

[11] Recall: this question is not whether the actual Anselmian being, who has acted in certain contingent ways, is one that the actual created rational beings have decisive reasons to ally themselves with. The question is whether it is true *in every possible world* in which there exist created rational beings that the Anselmian being is worthy of those created rational beings' alliance.

and so the lack of shared reasons will undermine the worthiness of such an alliance. But there are other sorts of alliance-worthiness that seem not to be so reasons- and ends-centric. Take the alliance-worthiness that is present between siblings, say, or members of a tribe. Here the explanation for alliance-worthiness does not presuppose that there are such shared reasons; the explanation goes directly to the facts about the relationship between the parties—that *this person is my sister*, or *that person belongs to my tribe*.

In Chapter 8 I will argue that there is something to this point that enables us to see how a being who counts as the Anselmian being could, *contingently*, be someone who is fully worthy of the alliance of a created rational being.[12] But it does not seem to me to answer the central problem we are dealing with. For even in these cases in which the relationship that holds between the parties is what rationalizes one's seeking alliance with the other, it is nevertheless true that the rationalizing character of that relationship presupposes that it is a relationship where mutual concern is appropriate, where one *should* share ends with the other party in the relationship. That I have good reason to look to my sister's well-being just because she is my sister presupposes that siblings are the sort of beings who should take each other's good to be ends to be pursued. This need not be undermined by the fact that my sister might actually hate my guts and not have my well-being as an end at all, and so I might have good reason to seek alliance with her even if she is not inclined to reciprocate. But it is this sort of requirement of mutual concern that I have denied to hold between the Anselmian being and us. Our good does not place any requirements at all on the ends that the Anselmian being promotes, and the only relationship that we have necessarily with the Anselmian being (being creatures of that being) does not bring with it such requirements of concern, either.

Reflection on the conditions of full alliance-worthiness gives us reason to think that that species of allegiance-worthiness, at least in any robust form, is not necessarily exhibited by the Anselmian being with respect to created rational beings. Impressive as the Anselmian being is, it is not necessary that it and we will be *for* the same things, or *should be for* the same things, in such a way as to make the Anselmian being someone with whom we should ally ourselves.

7.3 Allegiance-Worthiness II: Authority and Obedience

Now one might say that we can put to the side, for the sake of argument at any rate, the notion that we and God are necessarily appropriately allied with each other in the way

[12] The idea is that *this person is my Creator* or *this person is my God* is all one needs to explain why this person is supremely alliance-worthy for any created rational being who is capable of forming that thought. I grant the plausibility of the idea that being in a right relationship with the divine is a reason-giving relationship. But I do not think that it is an exception to the point I raise in my text here, that unless one's creator or one's God in some way shares ends with one, being well-related to God is not a good that is available to one. I make the detailed argument for this view in Chapter 8.

that I have characterized in 7.2. One might say that alliance is naturally thought of in terms of something like a condition of equality—that allies are, whatever the natural differences between them, to be thought of as partners in a common endeavor. And that is not the right way to think about the relationship between God and created rational beings. Instead we should emphasize the inequality between God and created rational beings, and appeal to a species of allegiance that is based on inequality rather than equality.

Consider relationships of *authority* and the corresponding stance of *obedience*. When one has genuine and legitimate authority[13] over another, then that other should have allegiance to the authority, at least to the limits of that authority. The authority is, at least within some range, capable of setting ends for one subject to that authority—I will call that person the 'subject,' despite its association with only one sort of authority, political authority—and the subject is bound to pursue those ends. Thus, to be genuinely and legitimately authoritative is to be worthy of allegiance. And we can add that authority seems to entail a sort of derivative alliance-worthiness as well, as the authority sets ends that the subject should take as his or her own and act on as the authority requires, and that seems to meet the conditions of alliance-worthiness described in 7.2.

One might think that, given this connection between genuine, legitimate authority and allegiance-worthiness, we have a direct route to the claim that the Anselmian being must be allegiance-worthy. For God is typically characterized as necessarily authoritative over created rational beings—indeed, typically characterized as having the fullest sort of authority over created rational beings possible. But I think this is a mistake. Even if we do not take into consideration the account of the Anselmian being's ethics offered in Part I, and instead assume that the Anselmian being's ethics is that of familiar welfare-oriented moral goodness, it seems to me that we have no good grounds for holding that the Anselmian being is necessarily authoritative over created rational beings, and we have good grounds for denying it. But once we take into consideration the account of the Anselmian being's ethics defended in Part I, the case becomes clearer still: when we deny that the Anselmian being's ethics are our ethics, we undermine even more dramatically the case that the Anselmian being is necessarily authoritative over created rational beings.

I will here only briefly rehearse the case that can be made against God's being necessarily authoritative over all created rational beings, even assuming that a common moral law necessarily applies to both God and creatures, a case that I made at much greater length in prior work (Murphy 2002a, Murphy 2009). I understand practical

[13] 'Genuine and legitimate' is not redundant. By 'genuine' authority I mean authority rather than de facto authority, where 'de facto authority' is the social condition of being thought of or being treated as or presenting oneself as authoritative. By 'legitimate' authority I mean authority that one holds rightfully. Understanding these terms in this way, it is at least coherent to say that someone has genuine authority, but has it illegitimately. I take it that holding God to be supremely worthy of obedience involves holding God's authority to be both genuine *and* legitimate.

authority in terms of a relation between something's say-so and some party's reasons for action. Say that the coming-to-obtain of some state of affairs 'completes a reason' when that state of affairs is the only non-obtaining part of a state of affairs that counts as a reason, and thus when the state of affairs comes to obtain then that reason is actual. I say that when A has authority over B with respect to some domain D, then A's directing that B ϕ, where B's ϕ-ing is in D, completes a decisive reason for B to ϕ. The idea is that when an authority relationship is in place, the say-so of the authority constitutes, at least in part, a decisive reason for the party under authority to perform the required action (Murphy 2002a, p. 15 and Murphy 2005). Thus, for the Anselmian being necessarily to be supremely authoritative over all created rational beings would be for it to be true that, necessarily, the Anselmian being's say-so completes decisive reasons for action for any rational creature to perform any action, or at least any action within the domain of all actions not otherwise ruled out by the true norms of practical reasonableness.

Given that conception of divine authority, it turns out to be surprisingly difficult to explain why the Anselmian being must have authority over created rational beings. None of the standard divine perfections distinct from authority itself seems to suggest that the Anselmian being must be authoritative in this way. The Anselmian being's omnipotence entails that the Anselmian being stands in a *causal* relationship to creaturely agency, such that the Anselmian being can control the circumstances of creaturely action at will, but it does not suggest that the Anselmian being stands in a certain *normative* relationship to creatures, that is, that the Anselmian being's say-so always completes a reason for action of the relevant content. The Anselmian being's omniscience entails that the Anselmian being will be aware of the stock of creaturely reasons, but not that that being will be able to add to that stock by issuing directives. The Anselmian being's (alleged) perfect moral goodness may tell us something about what the stock of reasons is or how we may act on them, but, again, gives no basis for thinking that the Anselmian being can add to that stock of reasons by that being's say-so (see Murphy 2002a, pp. 46–58, and Murphy 2009, pp. 323–4).

The above arguments attempt to go from some other divine perfection to divine authority of the relevant scope. But one might suggest that authority just is one of the divine perfections, a way it is better to be rather than not be. Note, though, the following serious difficulties for this view. First, given that the existence of rational creatures is contingent, one cannot say that it is constitutive of this perfection that the Anselmian being is actually authoritative over anyone. That itself seems strange, that one could have the perfection of divine authority without having any authority. (Just as it would be strange to say that the Anselmian being has the perfection of knowledge without knowing anything, or the perfection of power without being able to do much.) But suppose we say that this perfection is just to be understood counterfactually: the perfection is being such that if there were any rational creatures, then the Anselmian being would be authoritative over them. This would still be problematic, for it would seem that any such counterfactually characterized feature of the Anselmian being would be grounded in categorical features of that being. But, as I have claimed, there are no good arguments from such categorical perfections to the Anselmian being's bearing authority over whatever rational creatures may exist (see Murphy 2002a, pp. 58–69).

I do not think that we can give an account of necessary divine authority from divine perfection. One might proceed normatively, making an argument that normative principles that must apply to every rational creature entail the relevant divine authority. One might appeal, say, to some of the familiar strategies that have been used to try to show that the state is generally authoritative over subjects—appeals to gratitude, or justice, say—or make special appeal to moral principles that would plausibly apply to the divine case alone—the appeal to the notion that humans are divine property, say. In my view, though, none of these succeeds in providing an argument for necessary divine authority, even granting the correctness (and necessity, for all rational creatures) of the moral principles from which the arguments have been made. (See Murphy 2002a, pp. 93–130, and Murphy 2009, pp. 324–6.)

With respect to only one sort of argument for divine authority do I think that, given the standard understanding of the Anselmian being as bound by familiar welfare-oriented moral goodness, we may have to deny the background view rather than its attempted application to refute the argument that the Anselmian being is necessarily authoritative over all created rational beings. That is the argument based on Raz's "service conception" of authority.

Raz thinks that authority is best understood as a service, a service of enabling agents to act better on the reasons for action that already apply to them.[14] Raz holds that the characteristic way by which a putative authority is established as genuine is given by his "normal justification thesis." On the normal justification thesis, one party is under another's legitimate authority if one "is likely to better comply with reasons which apply to him (other than the alleged authoritative directives) if he accepts the directives of the alleged authority as authoritatively binding, and tries to follow them, than if he tries to follow the reasons which apply to him directly" (Raz 1994a, p. 198). Raz has made clear that the normal justification thesis requires qualification in important ways. For example, the authority may fail to be established in cases in which it is particularly important for one party to deliberate his or her own way to an effective practical conclusion about what he or she is to do, or in cases in which there is some exclusionary reason that prevents one from taking another's say-so as authoritative (Raz 2006, p. 1014).

While there can be deviant cases, the typical way to justify authority under this thesis is to show that a would-be authority is both well-positioned to deliver directives that are backed by reasons in the appropriate way and is well-motivated to deliver such directives. Both of these are of course crucial. My worst enemy may know me and my

[14] Raz does make clear that this is just an account of the typical way that authority is generated, not a universal thesis about all authority relationships. The basic idea is that the role of authority is a *service* role, even if there are cases of legitimate authority that do not fit this pattern.

situation so well that he could issue directives that would enable me to act better on my reasons, but there would be no good reason to suppose that any directives that he gave me would be aiming to be backed by reasons in that way. I may judge that a well-respected elder in my village could serve as an excellent coordinator of common action, but know that she is uninterested in doing that; what she cares about is not the common good, but some more particular (even if worthwhile) ends. So if we are to judge that, say, the state is authoritative over its citizens, we would have to have reasons to judge that the state's combination of reasonableness in practical judgment, information-gathering capacity, coordinating power, and motivation to promote the common good makes the state's directives such that I would do better acting on my reasons by following its directives than by acting on those that I would make for myself. (And, of course, we would have to argue that the disqualifying conditions are absent.)

Given this account of how authority can be established and a conception of the Anselmian being on which we and the Anselmian being share reasons for action, one can offer a relatively straightforward argument for that being's authority over created rational beings in terms of the normal justification thesis. Many, including Raz, doubt the normal justification thesis argument for the state's authority, even in decent states (Raz 1986, pp. 70–80). But one might think that the corresponding argument for divine authority will look much better. The Anselmian being will know better than we what our reasons are, will have all relevant information, and will be able to coordinate agency across space and time in a way that no creature or creatures could. Because we and the Anselmian being ultimately share reasons, the Anselmian being will be motivated to the same ends to which we creatures are rationally motivated, and so we will have a basis for supposing that the Anselmian being is motivated to give us directives, directives superior to what we would come up with on our own. And while one might worry about whether we would lose some goods of autonomy, say, by deferring to divine authority, we can reply that the Anselmian being would have taken those goods properly into account in deciding what directives to issue and in what circumstances to issue them.

I think that, given the normal justification thesis and the conception of the Anselmian being and us created rational beings as fundamentally sharing reasons, this argument for divine authority, and thus for the Anselmian being's supreme allegiance-worthiness, is a plausible argument, or can be elaborated so as to be plausible. The difficulty is with the two givens. First, I take the normal justification thesis to be an implausible thesis. Darwall and others have offered a variety of serious criticisms of it (see, for example, Darwall 2010), but I note here simply that what the normal justification thesis seems to provide is not an account of what reasons for action we have but an account of what reasons for action it would be good for us to have. That we would act better on our existing reasons for action if we were under authority means that we would act better if it were the case that some party's say-so counted for us as reasons for action. That, as far as I can see, gives no basis for thinking that this party's say-so is in fact a reason for acting; what it gives is a basis only for thinking that we have some reason to *make it the case* that this party's say-so is in fact a reason for acting. What the normal justification thesis pretty successfully describes are some typical conditions under which it is desirable for some agent to be under another's authority, but there is of course a gap between some condition's being desirable and that condition's obtaining.

So the considerations invoked in the normal justification thesis argument for divine authority should lead us to say no more than that it would be desirable for us created rational beings to be under divine authority—in effect, that it would be desirable for the Anselmian being to be supremely allegiance-worthy. Suppose, though, that one is unconvinced by these brief criticisms of the normal justification thesis, as well as the more extensive criticism of Raz's account in the literature (see, for a thorough survey of these criticisms, Ehrenberg 2011), and thus takes it to be an adequate foundation on which to build accounts of authority. Should we then go on to say that the Anselmian being is supremely allegiance-worthy, because naturally authoritative over all created rational beings?

No. For the argument from the normal justification thesis to divine authority to be successful, we need some basis not only for taking the Anselmian being to be more knowledgeable about created rational beings' reasons and better able to coordinate their acting on those reasons. We also need two further conditions to be satisfied. First, we need it to be the case that the motivation to issue directives that the Anselmian being has is such that the directives offered will indeed be those that enable us to act better on our reasons than would be directives that we would come up with and attempt to act on were we left to our own devices. Second, we need it to be the case that the Anselmian being has adequately taken into account the goods associated with making decisions for oneself, and has issued directives to us only when all-things-considered we would have decisive reason to forgo those goods of autonomy in order to act on the directives issued by the Anselmian being.

But it seems to me that neither of these further conditions is satisfied, given the argument of Part I. First, the corresponding argument for state authority presupposes that the state is reasonably motivated and that to which it is reasonably motivated is shared by the state and by its subjects. Because the state is motivated by (something like) the common good of the political community, and the common good gives reasons for the subjects to act for its sake, the competent state will not only be able to give directives that subjects would do better to act on, it actually will give such directives. But note that this assumes commonness of reasons between state and subject. The argument of Part I, though, is that we and the Anselmian being do not necessarily share reasons in this sense. There is no basis to suppose that even those objectives given to us humans by reason are objectives that the Anselmian being takes on and by which it regulates what directives to give us and in what circumstances to do so. So we should doubt that the normal justification thesis must be satisfied with respect to the Anselmian being's authority over created rational beings, and thus we should doubt that we can appeal to that thesis as a basis for the Anselmian being's necessary allegiance-worthiness.

There is a second, supplementary reason for doubt. The Anselmian being's say-so satisfying the normal justification thesis can be defeated if the created rational being has sufficiently good reasons to make decisions for him- or herself, not being simply guided by the say-so of the putative authority, however talented at action-guidance that putative authority might be. The basis for rejecting this defeater is that the Anselmian being would place the same sort of value on self-direction as the beings whose action it seeks to guide, and so would regulate its directive activity in light of that value. But, again, the argument of Part I undermines this basis. The Anselmian being might, for example, place much less value on our self-direction, without making any practical error. And thus we would have further reason to think that the normal justification thesis is not satisfied. With respect to this Razian account of divine authority, then, I say that we have two reasons to reject it: first, that the normal justification thesis is false, and second, that even if the normal justification thesis were true, the account of the Anselmian being's ethics defended in Part I precludes its being necessarily true of the Anselmian being's relationship to created rational beings.

In sum, then: it is true that being authoritative over another is a way of being allegiance-worthy, and so if the Anselmian being is necessarily supremely authoritative over created rational beings, then the Anselmian being is necessarily fully allegiance-worthy. But we lack a basis for affirming that the Anselmian being has such authority.

7.4 Contingent Allegiance-Worthiness

While the account of the Anselmian being's ethics defended in Part I (7.1) does not call into question that being's necessary worship-worthiness, that account does indeed undermine the view that the Anselmian being's necessary absolute perfection entails the Anselmian being's being supremely worthy of allegiance (7.2–7.3). Any successful account of the Anselmian being's allegiance-worthiness will be an account of how that being is *possibly* allegiance-worthy—of how it is *compatible* with being a perfect being that it is worthy of complete allegiance—and perhaps also an account of how that contingent allegiance-worthiness is actually realized in our world.

One might object to this enterprise of attempting to account for the Anselmian being's allegiance-worthiness for us rational creatures in terms of some contingent features of the world. One might say that a being who counts as God must necessarily count as God—that God is God is a matter not just of *de dicto*, but also *de re*, necessity—and so if one endorses the conception that to be God is to be supremely allegiance-worthy, then one must reject any account of the Anselmian being's allegiance-worthiness that makes it a contingent matter. Or one might just think that, even if this is not a good analysis of *being God*, nevertheless it is false of the Anselmian being that this being's allegiance-worthiness could be contingent only.

There are some conceptions of God on which it is clear why it would have to be true that to be God would have to be a necessary matter. I think that the Anselmian conception is one, though some have criticized this position.[15] But note that in the case of the Anselmian view the argument for *being God's* entailing *necessarily being God* is internal to the Anselmian picture; it is because necessarily exhibiting these features is better than exhibiting them only contingently that a being that counts as an absolutely perfect being must be so necessarily. Given the close connection between absolute perfection and complete worship-worthiness (7.2), one might also reasonably think this is true of worship-worthiness as well: it is part of the value gap between us and God that not only is God better than us, absurdly so, but God's being so is in no way contingent.

But there seems to be no such internal argument for the necessity of God's being worthy of allegiance, given simply the conception of God as being supremely worthy of allegiance. What supreme worthiness of allegiance requires is that God be worthy of one's devoting oneself entirely to God, in alliance with and in obedience to God, and it is not at all clear why there is any inconsistency or tension between having complete allegiance to God and taking that allegiance to be something that, in some other possible world, would not be called for. There are, of course, some ways of conceiving allegiance-worthiness such that there would be such a tension. If one were conceiving allegiance-worthiness as a divine perfection, for example, or as an implication of a divine perfection, then our thinking of allegiance-worthiness as a contingent feature of some being would commit us to thinking of that being as not absolutely perfect. But, as I have argued, it is an error to think of allegiance-worthiness as a perfection or as an implication of a perfection.

Allegiance-worthiness is not a matter simply of being great; it is a matter of there being the right sort of *fit* between us and God. Unlike the case of worship-worthiness, in which there is necessarily the right sort of fit—massive inequality of value—between God and any creature, in the case of allegiance-worthiness, it is a contingent matter whether the ends we ought to have fit with God's ends in a way that makes complete allegiance the fitting response for us to have to God. To say this is not, I claim, to make a remark about God that demotes God's nonrelational value in any way. To deny that God is necessarily allegiance-worthy disparages God only if necessary allegiance-worthiness is or is entailed by divine perfection. Since it is not entailed by divine perfection, one can say that God is necessarily absolutely perfect while denying that God is necessarily allegiance-worthy. And nothing that one can coherently deny of God while affirming God's necessary absolute perfection can count as a disparagement of God.

I thus abandon any attempt to provide an account of the Anselmian being's necessary allegiance-worthiness. The Anselmian being could have created a world in which there are rational creatures, but for whom the correct relationship for them to have

[15] See, for example, Guleserian 1985, which argues that moral goodness is an Anselmian perfection, that moral goodness requires free choice, and that free choice requires possibility of choosing otherwise. This view entails that Anselmian perfection could not be more than contingent. For some possible responses, see Murphy 2013.

with the Anselmian being is not allegiance, for no allegiance has been invited and none is appropriate. (Though, of course, the attitudes and beliefs characteristic of *worship* are still fitting.) The rational creatures in that possible world might correctly come to the conclusion that the world is created and sustained by a perfect being, but that it is just a mistake to think of themselves as being on the same side as the Anselmian being. (There are certain ways in which it would be foolish to *oppose* that being, of course. But that is different from being on the same side.)

For those (few) who are in the position of being mere Anselmian theists—they accept that the Anselmian being exists, but are committed to no further theistic claims—the inquiry is perhaps finished. Perhaps these few are in the position of those folks described in the previous paragraph for whom the right stance to take, given their other views, is that the Anselmian being is an appropriate object of worship but not of allegiance. But even these folks might want to know whether things might have been different—whether, as a contingent matter, the Anselmian being might have been worthy of our allegiance, and supremely so. And for those who accept the existence of the Anselmian being and also believe that this being is in fact worthy of our complete allegiance—at least, orthodox adherents of Christianity or other Abrahamic traditions—it is crucial to exhibit why the actual Anselmian being is worthy of our allegiance, and fully so.

8

The Good of Religion and Contingent Divine Ethics

8.1 Contingent Divine Ethics and Allegiance-Worthiness

The Anselmian being, though necessarily fully worthy of worship (7.1), is not necessarily fully worthy of allegiance, whether understood in terms of alliance or obedience (7.2–7.3). What precludes the argument from evil from getting purchase against the existence of an Anselmian being—that the Anselmian being's ethics is not necessarily the ethics of rational creatures—also precludes the Anselmian being from being necessarily worthy of the allegiance of created rational beings. But this raises a problem, at least for ordinary orthodox theists, who both believe that God exists and take God to be an absolutely perfect being. According to ordinary orthodox theism, God is supremely worthy of allegiance. Now, the problem is not that there is a contradiction between the claims defended in Chapter 7 and ordinary orthodox theism's view that God is fully worthy of allegiance; there is no such contradiction (7.4). The problem, rather, is to explain how the Anselmian being, who is not necessarily worthy of full allegiance, might nevertheless be actually, albeit contingently, fully worthy of allegiance.

The aim of this chapter is to give an account of how the Anselmian being could be worthy of the full allegiance of us created rational beings. In the main, I will be focusing on the general issue of what are the various ways in which the metaphysical possibility of the Anselmian being's being fully worthy of allegiance could be actualized. But in dealing with this question I am guided by the fact that much of the concern with this question is provoked by whether we can plausibly account for the allegiance-worthiness of the God of orthodox Abrahamic theism, and in my own case it is provoked by whether we can plausibly account for the allegiance-worthiness of the God of Christian theism in particular. So in what follows I will be devoting special attention to the ways in which an Anselmian being could be worthy of full allegiance that seem to fit with the broad outlines at least of Abrahamic theism, especially Christian theism. And since, as we saw in 6.6, some formulations of the problem of evil are directed against Abrahamic theism rather than against generic theism, it will be important to provide an account of how these theisms can affirm that God is wholly worthy of allegiance without re-introducing the vulnerabilities to the problem of evil that I attempted to dispel in Part I; considering whether this aim was accomplished is the topic of Chapter 9.

The problem regarding allegiance to God, I argued in Chapter 7, is that the Anselmian being's ethics is not of the right sort to underwrite the necessary allegiance-worthiness for us of the Anselmian being. The basic outline of my explanation of how the Anselmian being could, contingently, be allegiance-worthy for us is thus predictable: it is that the Anselmian being can have a *contingent* ethics—it can have, contingently, dispositions to treat particular considerations as reasons, and as reasons of certain types (0.1)—of the right sort to do the job. If the Anselmian being's not necessarily having certain ends undermines that being's necessary allegiance-worthiness, perhaps that being's contingently having certain ends underwrites that being's contingent allegiance-worthiness.

Since what makes for allegiance-worthiness of one being by other beings involves a fit between these beings and their ends, the sort of contingent ethics that the Anselmian being would have to exhibit in order to be fully worthy of our allegiance is, in part, fixed by the character of our own ethics, the ethics of human beings. Central to the argument to come is that there is, as some contemporary writers have argued, an important human good to be found in a sort of union with God, a good which they label the good of "religion." This good is, according to these writers, by nature available to us and fully worthy of our pursuit (8.2). They claim that this good's naturally governing role in human practical reason entails that the Anselmian being is necessarily supremely worthy of the allegiance of human beings; the argument of Part I shows, however, that this conception of the good of religion is mistaken (8.3). Rather, the conclusion to draw is that *if* the good of religion is available to us, and the sort of thing that we can reasonably pursue, then we have decisive reason to have allegiance to the Anselmian being; and that good is available to us if the Anselmian being can, contingently, exhibit a certain sort of ethics with respect to us (8.4). Thus, the conditions that make participation in the good of religion a choiceworthy option would also make it true that the Anselmian being will be unqualifiedly alliance- and obedience-worthy (8.5). And the Anselmian being *can* exhibit such a contingent ethics, either by exhibiting a certain sort of contingent fundamental orientation toward the ends to which humans must pursue as a matter of natural practical reasonableness or by contingently subjecting itself to norms that entail the relevant sort of concern with those ends (8.6).

8.2 The Good of 'Religion'

I want to begin by considering 'religion,' a good that has been invoked—though not under that label—in some recent responses to the problem of evil (M. Adams 1999, Dougherty 2014). This good has been most carefully analyzed, though, within the accounts of the human good offered by the 'new natural law theorists'—Grisez, Finnis, Boyle, Tollefsen, and others (see, for example, Finnis 1980, pp. 89–90, 371–410; Grisez 1983, pp. 121–4, 135–6; Grisez, Finnis, and Boyle 1987, pp. 108–9, 141–7; Boyle 1998; Tollefsen 2014, pp. 125–8).[1] I want first to say something about the nature of this good, its plausibility as an aspect of human well-being or perfection, and its centrality to the good life before noting the difficulties that attend their characterization of this good given the Part I account of God's ethics.

The intuitive idea to which these writers are giving voice is that there is something good about being properly related to the divine. Just as there is a proper way to relate to the true, and to the beautiful, and to the right, and to one's fellow rational creatures, there is a proper way to relate to the "more-than-human order" (Grisez, Finnis, and Boyle 1987, p. 108). Boyle suggests that we do not need to think of this more-than-human order as personal in order to recognize religion as a distinct good (Boyle 1998, p. 3), but I think this is wrong; I don't think that we can see the distinct point of being properly situated with respect to the more-than-human order, as opposed to simply responding appropriately to truths about the world or about what it is reasonable to do, unless this more-than-human order is something to which we can ascribe attitudes, at least analogically (Murphy 2001, pp. 131–2). So I will assume that when we are considering the good of religion, we are thinking about a good of being related in a fitting way to the will of a personal being.

Here are the salient features of the good of religion as these writers characterize it. First, the status of religion as a good is *self-evident*: it is immediately knowable by humans who are capable of grasping the relevant concepts that religion is a good worth realizing in one's life (for example, Finnis 1980, pp. 85–6, 89–90).[2] Second, this good has a particular *content*, that of keeping one's will *in harmony with* the divine (Finnis 1980, pp. 89–90; Grisez 1983, p. 124; Boyle 1998, p. 3). Third and fourth, while (third) this good is not of greater basic value as a kind of good than any other human good (life, knowledge, etc.), it (fourth) has a central organizing role in the lives of fully reasonable, well-informed agents. Because the divine being must be conceived—more on this in 8.3—as anticipating human fulfillment and directing all of us toward it, the religious good is well-suited to serve an organizing role in one's practical life; its centrality in the lives of practically reasonable agents is not due to its greater basic value, but its greater value *as a task*, the task of structuring the practical commitments of a reasonable person (Grisez, Finnis, and Boyle 1987, pp. 141–6). This fourth feature of the good of religion presupposes that it is by nature *available* to us, in the following sense: it is a good that we can, at least in normal circumstances, realize robustly in our lives, both in that our circumstances of action[3]

[1] This is true as a matter of philosophical analysis. But the most insightful discussion of the good of religion that I have encountered is Jean-Pierre de Caussade's *Abandonment to Divine Providence*.

[2] I will consider objections to this thesis based on the non-self-evidence of theism at the beginning of 8.3.

[3] I can't make the distinction adequately finely. But the idea is that when we can't realize the good of religion, it is because of a deficiency *in us*—we have become confused about the divine will, or our wills are somehow defective, or our habits are impeding us, etc.

are favorable for the realizing of that good and in that we are not barred from pursuing it by other norms of practical reasonableness.

I want to consider in a bit more detail how we ought to understand the content of the good of religion, because I think that the common idea that these writers appeal to—that it is good for there to be harmony between one's will and the divine will—is in some ways just ambiguous and in some ways very misleading.

One source of ambiguity concerns what are the respective acts of divine and creaturely willing that enter into realizations of the good of religion. On one option, the acts of divine and creaturely willing are of this sort: the divine being wills that p; the creature wills that p. The harmony between divine and creaturely will consists in their willing the obtaining of the same state of affairs, in being unified by having wills with the same content. On another option, the acts of divine and creaturely willing are of this sort: the divine being wills that the creature wills that p; the creature wills that p. The harmony consists in the creaturely will's condition's constituting a fulfillment of the divine will. On the former view, roughly speaking, the good of religion is realized when we will what God wills; on the latter view, roughly speaking, the good of religion is realized when we will what God wills us to will.

I think that the second view has to be at least part of the truth, that one participates in the good of religion by willing as God would have one will, and that one fails in or flouts that good by failing to will as God would have us will. What God wills with respect to our wills is what God is set on our doing, and it is hard to see how one could be well-situated with respect to God if God is set on one's doing something and one is not willing to do that thing. I will thus take this to be unambiguously an aspect of the good of religion.

I deny, though, that the first view gives an essential truth about the good of religion, even though it may be the more familiar way of thinking about unity with God.[4] We should doubt that our wills must, in order to be rightly related to God, share the content of God's will. Aquinas presses this sort of question—whether, generally, we must will that p when God wills that p—and he notes that while there is *some* sense in which we must will what God wills, insofar as both we and God will under the aspect of goodness, it is *not* always true that we are bound to will the object willed by God. So Aquinas says that 'formally' we must will what God wills, willing that, generally and *de dicto*, the good that God wills will come to fruition. But 'materially,' in terms of the content of what we will, it may not in fact be what God wills in particular, *de re*.

Here is a way to look at it. If the religious good necessarily involves willing what God wills, then the religious good must have an element that is the same, materially, for all created persons—an agent-neutral end. Yet there may be aspects of what God wills that some created person could not rightly will. To adapt one of Aquinas's examples, it

[4] It may indeed be required by the good of religion to will what God wills in those cases when God wills that I will what God wills, either generally or in some specific case; that we will not enjoy the good of religion if we fail to will what God wills in this scenario is entailed by the previous conception, on which we must will what God wills that we will to participate in the good of religion.

could be that God wills the punishment of some person, yet it could be wrong for me to will that punishment.

A second source of ambiguity concerns how we are to understand the divine will harmony with which is supposed to constitute the relevant good. There is a sense of 'God wills that p' in which the fact that God wills that p entails that p. If we think of willing here as *intending*, and do not qualify the notion of intending in any way, there is a straightforward argument that if God wills that p, then p. For it is a norm of rational intending that one does not intend that p if one knows that not-p. But given the standard view of divine knowledge, on which for all p God knows that p or God knows that not-p, it follows that God does not intend that p unless it is the case that p.[5]

I take it, though, that the good of religion is not supposed to have a place only with respect to matters about which it is sure to be that if God wills that p, then p. For one thing, this conception would make it impossible for the good of religion to fail to be realized due to one not willing what God wills for one to will. For on this conception of divine will, it follows from God's willing that a rational creature will that p that that rational creature wills that p. As the central case of the good of religion involves willing what God wills one to will, and it also seems possible for the good of religion in this paradigm sense to be violated, be flouted, or otherwise go unrealized, it seems a bad idea to rely on this conception of the divine will in characterizing the good of religion.

Again, Aquinas's treatment of the relevant issue offers helpful guidance toward an alternative. The context of Aquinas' discussion is the seeming incompatibility between God's willing that all humans be saved and some humans not being saved; for, after all, if God wills that all be saved, and necessarily, God's will is fulfilled, then all will be saved. While Aquinas acknowledges that in some sense it must be true that what God wills, God gets, he also recognizes that there must be some sense in which God's will is not always fulfilled. God wills that all be saved, says Paul (1 Timothy 2:3–4); yet not all are saved. So Aquinas finds himself with a task rather similar to that which faces us: specifying a sense of will strong enough genuinely to be God's will and not strong enough that God's willing guarantees that the object of God's willing will obtain.

Drawing on Damascene, Aquinas makes a distinction between God's *antecedent* will and God's *consequent* will. It is worth quoting his discussion of this distinction at length:

> This distinction [between God's antecedent and consequent will] must not be taken as applying to the divine will itself, in which there is nothing antecedent or consequent, but to the things willed.

[5] Of course, it could well be God's intention that explains why it is the case that p; the relation described in the text is only logical, not expressing any sort of metaphysical priority to its being the case that p over God's intending it.

> To understand this we must consider that everything, insofar as it is good, is willed by God.[6] A thing taken in its primary sense, and absolutely considered, may be good or evil, and yet when some additional circumstances are taken into account, by a consequent consideration may be changed into the contrary. That a man should live is good; and that a man should be killed is evil, absolutely considered. But if in a particular case we add that a man is a murderer or dangerous to society, to kill him is a good; that he live is an evil. Hence it may be said of a just judge, that antecedently he wills all men to live; but consequently wills the murderer to be hanged (Aquinas, *Summa Theologiae* Ia 19, 6 ad 1).

What Aquinas calls "consequent" willing is what God simply wills, for "the will is directed to things as they are in themselves, and in themselves they exist under particular qualifications." "Antecedent" willing is, on the other hand, a relative abstraction, for we do not "will simply, what we will antecedently" (Aquinas, *Summa Theologiae* Ia 19, 6 ad 1). While the consequent will is more relevant to thinking about God's efficacious providence—for what God consequently wills, God gets—the various divine antecedent willings are more relevant to the rational reconstruction of what God brings about, for we appeal to what God antecedently intends, abstracting from various circumstances, to make intelligible what God consequently intends. While it is possible, then, that what God antecedently wills does not come to pass, it is impossible that what God wills consequently does not come to pass. Thus, Aquinas holds that antecedently God wills that all humans be saved, but that is compatible with God's not willing such salvation consequently.

The appeal to antecedent intention provides a way for us to say how it is possible for God to will something with respect to our willings such that it is possible for us to fail to will what God wills us to will. Though may God antecedently will that I will that p, it could also be that, given the waywardness of my will, God does not consequently will that I will that p. (This does not mean that God consequently wills that I will that not-p, or even that I do not will that p; God may consequently will only that free, effective creaturely willing take place, while God *allows* or *accepts* that in my case the result will be that I will contrary to God's antecedent will.) The divine will, in the sense of 'divine will' in which sense harmony with which constitutes the good of religion, is God's antecedent will with respect to what we will—God's will for us, abstracting only from what we actually will to do.

So on the conception of the good of religion that I endorse, the relevant act of divine will is the divine being's antecedent will that some rational creature will that p—that all humans worship God, that Abraham take his son to Moriah and make of him there a burnt offering, etc. And the good of religion involves, somehow, rational creatures' willing in accordance with the content of the divine antecedent will, so that the divine antecedent will is satisfied by the relevant act of creaturely willing. How, then, should

[6] That is: whatever exists and is good is willed by God as good. For reasons given above, I doubt that Aquinas should make this claim. For one thing, it seems to involve a denial of his claim that we cannot know by philosophical reasoning what God wills with respect to creatures.

we characterize the *relationship* between the divine will and the creaturely will that makes for the good of religion?

The typical way of characterizing this relationship is that of 'harmony,' but I think this characterization is very misleading. It is misleading because while the notion of a merely accidental harmony is coherent, the notion of merely accidental enjoyment of the good of religion is not. The good in question is, then, more like *harmonizing* than *being in harmony*; just as harmonizing involves *maintaining* a harmony by regulating one's own singing with respect to others', the good of religion involves regulating one's desiring, deciding, choosing with respect to God's.[7] To make this clarification is, I think, not to go beyond what Grisez, Finnis, and Boyle have in mind; I think that they would agree that the good of religion is not fully realized in the alternative possible world in which God wills that Abraham will to sacrifice Isaac, Abraham ignores God's command, and then decides independently to head up Moriah to sacrifice his son. My deeper worry is that this characterization of the good of religion makes it look far too much like just an instance of a good that we might just as much enjoy with respect to one of our fellow rational creatures. Just as it is good to be in harmony with one's fellow humans, it appears, it is good to be in harmony with God. I am not denying that such harmony is good, but I am denying that we can characterize religion adequately in these terms. The idea of 'harmony' does not at all capture the fact that we are dealing with a being far superior to ourselves, and that the good of being properly related to that being should reflect that difference. I suggest, then, that we should think of the good of religion in terms that explicitly capture this deep inequality: the good of religion is the good of *subordinating* one's will to the divine will, so that the direction of fit is creaturely will to divine will. In realizing the good of religion, the will of a created rational being *follows* the will of the divine being. So religion is about how one's will follows the antecedent will of God with respect to one's own willing.

Two further issues regarding the specification of the good of religion remain. We have said that the good of religion involves a relationship in which what the creature wills is subordinated to what the divine being wills the creature to will. But we can still ask about how to characterize the relevant subordination. One interpretation is fundamentally negative: to participate in the good of religion is for one's will to be regulated by the divine will such that what one wills is *compatible* with any of God's willing with respect to one's own willing being satisfied. Another interpretation is fundamentally positive: to participate in the good of religion is for one's will to be regulated by the divine will such that what one wills *satisfies* in some way God's will with respect to one's own willing. The former makes the good of religion consist in not being at odds with the divine will; the latter makes the good of religion consist in realizing some aspect of the divine will.

[7] I am offering no firm view about what is involved in such regulation. Perhaps it need not be conscious. But it must be apprehension-guided, so that the explanation of why one wills that p runs through one's grasp that God wills that one will that p.

The difference in interpretation matters, and I think in a way that favors the latter view. On the former view, one would be realizing the good of religion, though trivially, even if there were no divine being. Even if we add to the former view that the good is realized only if there is a divine being, that interpretation allows that one enjoys the good of religion trivially in any domain in which God does not will anything with respect to one's action. Though I agree that there is some plausibility to the notion—though I will raise questions about this later in this section—that one is not flouting or acting contrary to the good of religion when God does not will one way or another with respect to one's action, I do not think that it is plausible that simply in willing in a way that does not undermine the divine will one is thereby realizing the good of religion. So I adopt the more positive view, that religion is about willing in a way that in part satisfies the will of God with respect to one's own will.

Second, suppose that we adopt this more positive reading, on which to participate in the good of religion is to realize this positive relation between the divine will and one's own will by subordinating one's own will to the divine will. In those cases in which the divine being wills one to will something, it is relatively straightforward to understand how this positive relationship could be realized. If the divine being wills that one preach conversion to the Gentiles, then the good of religion is realized by judging correctly that this is what the divine being wills and thereupon preaching conversion to the Gentiles. But what should we say about the cases—how far these cases are actual is an open question—in which the divine being does not will anything with respect to one's own action?

Here is one thing we could say. We could say that in such cases, the good of religion is just not implicated. Because the good of religion consists in a positive relationship between the divine will and one's own will, and the divine will is absent in this case, the good of religion is just not available, in the sense characterized above: we might, through no defect or failing of our own, be unable to participate in that good. Or we could take a stronger view, and hold that saying that the good of religion simply becomes irrelevant to one's action in contexts in which the divine will is silent does not do full justice to the ideal of subordinating one's will to the divine will. To subordinate one's will wholly to the divine will involves not just willing what God wills one to will; it also involves not willing what God has not willed one to will. To fully participate in the good of religion is for one's will to be awaiting the lead of the divine will, to go where one is bidden to go, and not to go where one is not bidden to go.

Here is one reason to adopt this stronger view. It may seem initially plausible—at least if one is taking theism for granted—that every act of will that one performs should relevantly bear on the good of religion. Every act of will should either relate one properly to God or count as a failure to so relate oneself. But on the weaker version on which religion is participated in only by willing what God wills one to will, there may be parts of one's practical life that make no difference with respect to the good of religion.

Some may take this to be an overly strong conception of the good of religion, ruling out discretionary choice as a failure to relate properly to God, and so a flouting of the good of religion. But we are not forced to this result. We might say that the reason that discretionary choice is a realization of the good of religion is just that God wills that we engage in discretionary choice, so that our discretionary willings are not in the interstices of the divine will but indeed a way of satisfying the divine will. And one might note that if God wills that we do something, then God must will that we carry it out in some way, whether discretionary or not (Murphy 1998, pp. 20–1). So we can be sure that if God aims for us to do something, then God will also aim for us to use some sufficient way to carry it out.

One might worry that this view generates an inconsistency, or at the very least a deeply implausible result, on matters on which the divine will is silent. Suppose that the divine will is silent about my willing that p or my refraining from willing that p. On this conception, then, it seems to follow that the good of religion calls for me to refrain from willing that p (because God does not will that I will that p) and the good of religion calls for me to refrain from refraining from willing that p (because God does not will that I refrain from willing that p). It seems to me that religion should not be a good that calls for incompatible willings from us. But even if we grant that it should not, the argument misunderstands the proposal. The proposal is not that one refrains from willing that p when God does not will that one will that p; it proposes that one not will that p when God does not will that one will that p. This might involve refraining from willing that p, but it may not; it may simply be that one does not will that p, even without having to refrain from willing it. Refraining from willing that p is an action that one performs; not willing that p is not. Thus, in a case in which God is silent about my willing that p or refraining from it, the good of religion could be realized by my neither willing that p nor refraining from willing that p, without any incoherence whatever.

One might object that this is at odds with the view that the good of religion involves *regulation* of one's will so that it is in harmony with the divine will. Not so. It could be that one's not willing except under the apprehension of God's willing that one so will is a condition that one achieves only through education and training, a learned indifference to the prospects of action except in the face of God's taking the lead. By way of comparison, consider a Stoic sage who has achieved an indifference to some goods that the sage nevertheless recognizes as in some way able to be appropriately preferred, so that the sage does not have to refrain from pursuing them but simply fails to be moved by them. Surely we think that this Stoic sage can be responsible for that not-willing, and we would treat the condition of the sage's will as something regulated by that for the sake of which this achieved indifference was pursued—the law of reason, the order of the cosmos, whatever. There seems to be no obstacle to the same sort of moral psychology being realized with respect to the divine will, and that seems enough to dismiss the charge of incoherence.

I find this stronger conception attractive, an expression of the idea that religion is realized not only in doing God's will but in not acting until we are bidden to act by God. Religion is not only in doing, but in awaiting the direction of God. But in the arguments in 8.3 and 8.4 I will not assume this stronger notion, considering difficulties that arise for our understanding of the good of religion whether we take it in a weaker or stronger sense. (I will refer to the 'good of religion in the stronger sense' when I have in mind religion as conceived as consisting both in willing what God wills one to will and in not willing what God does not will one to will; I will refer to the 'good of religion in the weaker sense' when I have in mind religion conceived as consisting solely in willing what God wills one to will.)

8.3 Religion and Familiar Welfare-Oriented Moral Goodness

Now, there have been a number of criticisms of the proposal that religion is a self-evident, basic, authoritative good. One might criticize the notion that the good of religion is self-evident by claiming that there is some tension between the alleged self-evidence of the good of religion and the clear *non*-self-evidence of the existence of the being union with whom is supposed to be constitutive of that good (see, for example, Hittinger 1987, p. 47). But that is a weak objection in itself and no objection at all to the good of religion as I will employ it in the discussion to come. It is a weak objection because it does not seem to be essential to the characterization of something as a good that it be genuinely available for us. Knowledge of the external world is a genuine good for humans, and it would remain so even if it turned out that some skeptical argument undermining the prospects of knowledge of the external world was successful. (Indeed, that knowledge of the external world is good even in such a case is what explains why it would be such a lugubrious discovery to find out that knowledge of the external world is not to be had; see Murphy 2011a, pp. 75–6.) Similarly, even if there were no superior rational being whose existence and will are the appropriate object of the good of religion, that does not undermine its status as a good. As Finnis writes, it is "peculiarly important to have thought reasonably and (where possible) correctly about these questions about the origins of the cosmic order...—whatever the answer to those questions turns out to be, and even if the answers have to be agnostic or negative" (Finnis 1980, p. 89). And this is so not just because it is good to know the truth about the world; it is also so because

> if there is a transcendent origin of the universal order-of-things and of human freedom and reason, then one's life and actions are in fundamental disorder if they are not brought, as best as one can, into some sort of harmony with whatever can be known or surmised about that transcendent other and its lasting order (Finnis 1980, pp. 89–90).

That we can grasp the good of being in union with the will of the divine makes intelligible not just aligning one's will with the divine being whom one takes to exist and whose will one takes oneself to grasp to some extent; it also makes intelligible seeking to find out whether such a being exists and what that being's will for us is.

So it strikes me as false that the grasp of the goodness of religion must be posterior to the grasp of the existence of the being harmony with which is its appropriate object. But even if one rejects this conception of the good of religion as being knowable as good even apart from our knowledge of God's existence, it does not matter particularly for the issues that we are considering here. For it is of no difference to my argument whether the good is self-evidently such, only that it is a good; and we are assuming for the moment the existence of an Anselmian being, absolutely perfect and sovereign over all else, so we do not have to worry that this presupposition of the status of religion as a good is not satisfied.

More promising is a challenge to the goodness of religion in terms of its availability[8] to us, based on skepticism concerning or a flat rejection of our having knowledge of what God wills in sufficient detail. For as the good of religion is not just the good of happening not to be at odds with the divine will but of willing in a way that is positively responsive to the divine will, not being able to grasp the divine will adequately can prevent not only knowing when one is realizing the good of religion but also realizing that good. And of course the absence of such knowledge would preclude the good of religion from serving the organizing role that these writers propose that it serves.

But the defenders of this good and its architectonic role in practical reasoning do not think that this is a great problem, at least in their mature statements of the problem. Grisez, Finnis, and Boyle defend a moral view on which humans are bound by familiar welfare-oriented moral goodness, the norms of which they identify with the *natural law*. And their view is that the fact that we are bound by the natural law shows us something about the availability of religion as a human good. Here are Grisez, Finnis, and Boyle, in one of their few joint writings on the topic:

> Just as the *is* of any contingent reality as such points to its transcendent source, so the *is-to-be* of the directiveness of practical knowledge points to its transcendent source. But since, in this case, the transcendent source is of directiveness, that source can only be thought of as if it were a person anticipating human fulfillment and leading human persons toward it (Grisez, Finnis, and Boyle 1987, p. 142).

Boyle, writing for himself only, frames the view very similarly:

> The divine is the ultimate source of reality and meaning. Therefore, any conception of practical reason and morality which understands them as having a more-than-human source that humans must acknowledge will imply that acting morally is a requirement of harmony with the divine (Boyle 1998, p. 18).

Put to the side any skeptical doubts that one has about their claim that contingent truths about what exists point to a personal, necessary first cause. The idea is that there is a close analogy between contingent truths about what exists and normative truths about what is to be done, and we can employ the fact that God must be taken to be the

[8] Recall what is involved in a good's being available to us: our circumstances of action make it possible to act on it in the absence of some defect in us, and it is reasonable for us to pursue that good.

source of contingent existence to argue that God must be taken to be the source of normativity, about what is to be done by created persons like us. With this conclusion in hand, we can say something detailed about what God's ethics must be: God is disposed to treat human fulfillment as a dominant concern. Because our practical knowledge of what is to be done reveals that human fulfillment is to be pursued, God's character as the source of that to-be-pursuedness makes plain what God is set on with respect to our action.[9] Note that this account does not rely on the claim that the Anselmian being's ethics is necessarily an ethics of familiar welfare-oriented moral goodness, full stop. The claim is weaker; it is that in any world *in which there are beings like us human beings, bound by the natural law that binds us*, it must be true that the creator of those beings favors the ends of that natural law, that is, the joint fulfillment of human beings. Thus, our natural knowledge of how good is to be pursued and evil avoided tells us a good deal of how to act so that the good of religion can be realized: it is to will in accordance with the natural law, understanding that law as the expression of the divine will with respect to our wills. There may, as a contingent matter, be further revelations of the divine will. But there is a clear sense in which the good of religion, on this view, would be naturally available to all those who have a basic grasp of the norms of the natural law and of God's nature as a perfect being, for this grasp exhibits to us what God's ethics must be.

It is also crucial that this account of what God's ethics must be in any world in which there are beings like us is the basis for their claim that the good of religion has a natural priority over other goods of human life. They do not defend this priority on the basis of religion being a fundamentally better kind of good than the other basic forms of human good; indeed, they deny that thesis (Finnis 1980, pp. 92–5; Grisez 1983, p. 124; Grisez, Finnis, and Boyle 1987, p. 137). Rather, they claim that each human is under a practical demand to organize one's pursuit of the good in a reasonable way, and that the Anselmian being's ethics favors the human good in this dramatic way makes religion the reasonable choice for a good, commitment to which can order one's acting for the sake of the other human goods. I am not here evaluating this argument. I am noting only that this argument for a certain account of God's ethics is crucial not just for establishing the knowability of the divine will, but also for establishing its authoritative role in the practical life of reasonable agents. And of course, alternative views of the good of religion, say those that simply claim that religion is a superordinate natural good that should regulate the other goods one pursues, will also presuppose that we can know God's ethics sufficiently to organize our other pursuits by subordinating one's pursuits to the divine will.

Grisez, Finnis, and Boyle hold that the directedness of humans by the natural law and the fact that our being bound by the natural law is somehow the result of God's

[9] The claim is not that God necessarily wills creaturely good. But there is a necessity affirmed here. It is that necessarily, if there are beings like us subject to the sort of norms that we are subject to that favor the fulfillment of humans, then God wills the fulfillment of humans.

creative activity together show that God's ethics entails that God wills our acting in accordance with the natural law's norms. I grant that, given the success of this argument, religion would be a good that is naturally available to us. Given this view, we could regulate our willing such that we will what God wills that we will (because God wills that we do as the natural law calls us) and we refrain from willing what God does not will that we will (because the natural law itself directs us to employ discretionary choice to act in ways that go beyond what the specific norms of the natural law require, at least when there are no better guides—for example, divine or human authority—to direct us). But this account of the availability of the good of religion presupposes, falsely, that we have access to further claims about divine ethics simply in virtue of our knowledge of the natural law.

For the argument of Part I entails that we cannot know, simply from the fact that we humans are directed toward some set of ends by the practical principles that we grasp by nature, that God wills the ends that we are to pursue or that God wills that we will those ends. All that we know about the goods of human fulfillment that are, either in part or in whole, the goods that fix the natural norms of the practical reasonableness is that they provide justifying reasons for the Anselmian being to promote them and requiring reasons for God not to intend their deprivation (4.2, 5.5). The error in the Grisez-Finnis-Boyle argument is that it assumes that because God is somehow the *source* of the correctness of the practical principles that bind us, it must be that God *wills the ends* of those practical principles, or *wills that we adopt the ends* of those principles. But that is a false assumption. It is compatible with the Anselmian being's perfection that the existence of humans who are bound by the practical principles by which humans are bound is an *outcome* of what the Anselmian being wills without being *itself* willed by the Anselmian being. And so the Grisez-Finnis-Boyle argument reveals no further truths about God's ethics, even confined to worlds in which God creates human beings bound by norms of natural practical reasonableness.[10]

The objection that I have raised thus far is framed simply in terms of whether access to the content of the divine will is by nature available to us, at least conditionally (if there is a being that qualifies as God, then this is what God wills), so that the good of religion would be by nature available to us as a real option for human fulfillment if God exists. The worry is formulated epistemologically, in terms of how we apprehend the divine will in such a way that would enable one's will to be regulated by the divine will. But it is pretty plain that the Part I account of the Anselmian being's ethics makes for an even more radical objection to the role of the good of religion. As far as my

[10] By contrast, I would endorse the much more measured remarks by Finnis on this subject from his earlier work: "Those who claim to know what God wills in some human context...are...going beyond what can be affirmed about [God] on the basis of philosophical argumentation" (Finnis 1980, p. 404). Finnis notes Aquinas's endorsement of this more modest account of knowledge of the divine will: "The will of God cannot be investigated by reasoning, except for those items that it is absolutely necessary for God to will. Now, as we have said [*Summa Theologiae* Ia, 19, 3], such items do not include what God wills in regard to creatures" (Aquinas, *Summa Theologiae* Ia, 46, 2). This is, in essentials, the view defended in Chapter 4, on which no creaturely goods can rationally necessitate the divine will (4.3).

objection has been pressed so far, there might be some other way to know the divine will, so that we naturally have sufficient access to what God wills for the good of religion to be available to us. But it is clear that we should hold that the worry is not simply epistemological, given the Part I argument. We should say not only that the Grisez-Finnis-Boyle argument does not succeed in showing that the good of religion is available by nature; we should say that that it is false that the good of religion is by nature available to beings like us.

That the good of religion is not available to us naturally, or available only in a tenuous form, is due to the fact that the Anselmian being does not necessarily will anything with respect to the wills of creatures, even given the existence of creatures with wills. Given the existence of some creatures, even rational creatures, at some level of perfection/well-being, one can conclude that God wills *something* that has brought about the existence of those creatures at that level of perfection/well-being, but there is nothing *in particular* that God must will. The Anselmian being might bring into existence beings just like us while willing nothing with respect to what we will.

Now, one might object that the view that the Anselmian being possibly does not will anything with respect to the actions of created rational beings does not entail that the good of religion as I have characterized it is radically unavailable for those beings. After all, on the stronger account of the good of religion described at the end of 8.2, the good of religion can be realized in not willing what God does not will us to will. And so the absence of divine will on some matter of possible creaturely action does not imply that the good of religion is unavailable, for it might be realized in *not acting*, in simply being in a state of volitional dormancy until and unless summoned by the divine will.

It may be true that the stronger account of the good of religion does entail that one could realize that good through complete inaction if the Anselmian being wills nothing with respect to what we will. One might think this counts against the stronger conception as an interpretation of the good of religion, or that it counts against the very goodness of religion when the divine being is thus indifferent to us. But I need not make any controversial claims on those matters in order to establish that even if this appeal to the stronger interpretation of the good of religion restores one sort of availability to religion, it rules out another. For recall that the availability of a good involves not only whether the circumstances of action make it possible to realize it, but also whether realizing it is compatible with binding norms of practical reasonableness. But binding norms of practical reasonableness do not permit us to remain unmoved until summoned by the divine will, if the Anselmian being wills nothing with respect to the goods of human life. For we know that we are bound to act in certain ways with respect to our own good and the good of other humans. So the good of religion, even if something that it would be possible to realize by being unmoved by other considerations, is not something that one could reasonably pursue, and clearly is not something that could serve as the authoritative regulator of our pursuit of other goods.

8.4 The Conditions of Availability of the Good of Religion

Suppose the Anselmian being exists. Even given this supposition, it does not follow that the good of religion is available to us (8.3). Further conditions would have to be satisfied. It would have to be true that the Anselmian being's will is adequately knowable by us and that we can reasonably will what the Anselmian being wills that we will (and, perhaps, reasonably fail to will what the Anselmian being does not will that we will). It would have to be true that the Anselmian being, though not having the relevant ethics with respect to us and our good *necessarily*, nevertheless has some sort of ethics *contingently* that we could know and which would enable us to reasonably subordinate our wills to the Anselmian being's.

Given that the Anselmian being could exhibit a contingent ethics—I will discuss this assumption in some detail in 8.6—what would such a contingent divine ethics have to be like in order for religion to be available to us? In 8.3 I criticized and rejected the view offered by Grisez, Finnis, and Boyle, on which it is a necessary truth that in any world in which humans exist the Anselmian being wills human fulfillment and humans' acting appropriately for that end. This appeal, had it been successful, would have done double-duty. First, it would have served an epistemological role, telling us what the content of the divine will is so that we can regulate our wills to place them in line with the divine will. But, second, it also would assure us that the content of the divine will is something with which we can *reasonably* align our own wills, both by assuring us that the Anselmian being wills something with respect to our own wills—remember, it is compatible with our and the Anselmian being's existing that the Anselmian being wills *nothing* with respect to what we will—and also by assuring us that what we would need to will in order to align our wills with the Anselmian being's is indeed fitting for us to will, that we are not precluded from willing what the Anselmian being wills or what the Anselmian being wills us to will by the natural requirements of practical reasonableness. Because (on this view) what God wills that we will is, at least, that which is required of us by natural morality, there is no possibility that the goodness of religion might be undermined by the content of what we would have to will to realize it, nor a possibility that the architectonic role of religion with respect to other goods would be challenged by the divine will's guidance of our agency being at odds with natural morality's guidance of our agency.

Here, then, is one way in which the good of religion could become fully available to us, so that we could wholly subordinate our wills to the divine will. The Grisez-Finnis-Boyle view, discussed above, is that God necessarily has something like an ethics of human fulfillment in any world in which God creates humans. Call 'the contingent version of the Grisez-Finnis-Boyle view' an account on which the Anselmian being in fact has the ethics that the Grisez-Finnis-Boyle view ascribes to God, but contingently: it is neither a necessary truth about the Anselmian being that the Anselmian being has an ethics of creaturely fulfillment nor a necessary truth that the Anselmian being has an ethics of creaturely fulfillment in any world in which the Anselmian being creates humans—but, nevertheless, the Anselmian being's ethics is actually an ethics of creaturely fulfillment. The only relevant difference between the Grisez-Finnis-Boyle view and the contingent version is supposed to be the modal status of the divine will's being set on human fulfillment and our adhering to the natural norms of practical reasonableness in pursuit of it.

It does seem to me that the contingent Grisez-Finnis-Boyle view, were it to rest on a cogent account of what the Anselmian being wills, would be sufficient to underwrite the availability of the good of religion and its central role in rightly oriented practical thought. We might, then, turn straightaway to the question of how the Anselmian being can take on a contingent ethics (8.6). But it is important to my argument to ask whether the Anselmian being's having that sort of ethics is indeed *necessary* for the good of religion to be available to us in the relevant sense, and indeed for it to play an authoritative role in our practical lives. Does the Anselmian being have to have adopted the ends that are constitutive of familiar welfare-oriented moral goodness in order for us humans to be able to rightly wholeheartedly pursue and enjoy the good of religion, and to structure our other commitments in terms of it? Or is there something lesser, or different, that would be sufficient for that task?

Here is a way to approach the question. Suppose that we are considering someone who is regulating his or her own deciding and choosing by wholly subordinating his or her decision-making to what the Anselmian being wills for him or her to will. We can grant that there is some *point* to this activity—indeed, that understates things. Of course if there is such a being, one can see why it would be good for one's agency to be unified in the appropriate way with that divine being's agency. But suppose also that we are convinced that the Anselmian being might will nothing at all with respect to our good, or might will in ways that are not governed by our good. So we might ask ourselves: What must be true for someone who subordinates his or her will to the divine will in the good of religion to be doing so reasonably, such that he or she is not subject to rational criticism for allowing the divine will to determine his or her own choices and decisions?

I already allowed that the contingent Grisez-Finnis-Boyle view provides sufficient conditions for reasonable subordination of one's will to the divine will. Subordinating one's will to the divine will is made worthwhile by its realizing the good of religion. That the Anselmian being's ethics is one of realizing human fulfillment and being set on our adhering to the norms of natural practical reason in pursuit of it—and that we can know that this is the ethics of the Anselmian being—ensures that this person would not be subject to criticism on the basis that the divine will might direct one to do something contrary to the norms of practical reasonableness or might fail to direct one to act in accordance with them. And even with respect to those matters that the norms of practical reasonableness leave discretionary, we can be sure that the divine will with respect to this person is not based on factors that would be irrelevant from the point of view of our good practical reasoning—if the divine will with respect to this person is fully governed by the good of human fulfillment, which serves as the basis for the norms of practical reasonableness, then there can be no objection to the reasonableness of acting in accordance with the Anselmian being's will for him or her that this person is being directed on the basis of considerations that he or she would not take to be good reasons for him or her to act.

It looks like what makes the contingent Grisez-Finnis-Boyle view so clearly successful as an account of the reasonableness of subordinating oneself to the divine will is that (a) such subordination is itself a good thing, worth pursuing; (b) such subordination will never direct one in a way that violates the natural norms of practical reasonableness by which all humans are bound; and (c) such subordination will never direct one to act in accordance with a divine will that is based on 'foreign' considerations—that is, considerations that do not count as good reasons for oneself to act. It seems that in this scenario, the good of religion is available—it can be pursued, and it is fully reasonable, and indeed perhaps even required by reason, to do so.

So my question is whether a view like the contingent Grisez-Finnis-Boyle view is not only *sufficient* but also *necessary* for the good of religion to be available to us, and indeed something that it would be unreasonable for us not to pursue, or instead whether a contingent divine ethics that calls for less than that could also be sufficient. It seems right to me that any successful account of what it would take for the good of religion to be available to us would fully share the (a) and (b) conditions that the contingent Grisez-Finnis-Boyle view relies upon. That is, it should (a) affirm that it is indeed good to be unified in will with the Anselmian being. And it should (b) affirm that the Anselmian being does not will that we act contrary to whatever the authoritative norms of practical reasonableness require. For we are bound to will what the authoritative norms of practical reasonableness require, and so we do not have the option of not willing this in order for our wills to be governed by the bidding of the divine will. If we assume the stronger notion of the good of religion, we have to say that our acting in accordance with those norms somehow satisfies the Anselmian being's will for us—either because the Anselmian being wills our adhering to the naturally binding norms of practical reasonableness, or wills something else that our acting on the norms of practical reasonableness can satisfy, while not willing anything that would require us to violate those norms. If, on the other hand, we assume the weaker notion, on which we should just say that our wills must satisfy what God has willed for us to will, then the Anselmian being need not will that we adhere to the norms of the natural law; God must simply not will that we violate those norms, and must will *something* positively so that our wills can satisfy, in some way, the Anselmian being's will for us.

So far, then, I have acknowledged as non-negotiable two of the conditions on the character of the divine will that the contingent Grisez-Finnis-Boyle view relies upon to explain the reasonableness of pursuit of the good of religion. Any view of the reasonableness of setting oneself to that good must incorporate those conditions on what the Anselmian being's ethics is in fact like. But the third condition is open to question. The stance that the Anselmian being takes with respect to human fulfillment in the

Grisez-Finnis-Boyle view is that it is the end that regulates what the Anselmian being wills with respect to what we will. But it does not seem to me to be necessary that human fulfillment have this strictly governing role with respect to what we will in the ethics of the Anselmian being in order for the good of religion to be available to us. To put it vaguely for the moment, what the Anselmian being wills with respect to us does not have to be *dominated* by the end of human fulfillment; what the Anselmian being wills with respect to us need only be *sufficiently* directed toward human fulfillment.[11]

I have endorsed the view, akin to the skeptical theists', that there may well be goods beyond our ken that are reasons for action for the Anselmian being but have no role at all in our own good practical reasoning (6.4). And I endorse the view that there may be other goods that are within our ken, but which may appropriately play a much different role in the agency of the Anselmian being than they appropriately play in our agency (Chapter 3).[12] It may well be that the Anselmian being prefers some of these goods to goods of human fulfillment, even in ways that it would be wrong for us to prefer them to the goods of human fulfillment, and what this being wills with respect to what we will reflects this preference. One might then rightly ask: Why is it reasonable to subordinate one's will to the will of the divine, when the will of the divine is not moved by my well-being or the well-being of my friends, family, and fellow humans in the way that my will, or even the will of a good impartial fellow human, is supposed to be moved by my well-being or the well-being of my friends, family, and fellow humans? It would not be right for me to direct my own action by reasoning that appeals to these alien considerations; why would it be right for me to allow my action to be directed by the divine will, when that will reflects an orientation toward these alien considerations?

I will not attempt to give necessary conditions on when it can be thus reasonable; my claim is that there are sufficient conditions for the reasonableness of subordinating one's will in this way that are less demanding than given by the contingent version of the Grisez-Finnis-Boyle view. Suppose that the Anselmian being takes some positive interest in human fulfillment, and wills that we act in ways that the moral law requires with respect to human fulfillment. Suppose also that the Anselmian being's will with respect to us is not governed entirely or even dominantly by human fulfillment, but rather is also governed by the Anselmian being's commitment to other creaturely goods as well. Nevertheless, I say that the Anselmian being's will is sufficiently set on human fulfillment to make the good of religion available to us if the following were true and known to be true: that we do better with respect to acting for the sake of

[11] I am using human fulfillment, somewhat misleadingly, as a placeholder for all of those creaturely goods that are relevant to the norms of practical reasonableness that apply to us. 'Human fulfillment' suggests a welfarist account of practical reasonableness grounded in the good of human persons (as in Murphy 2001); but so long as (a) we are dealing with creaturely goods that the Anselmian being has at least justifying reasons to promote and (b) the relevant natural norms of practical reasonableness take human welfare to be something that there is requiring reason to promote, using 'human fulfillment' as a placeholder will not affect the structure of the argument to come.

[12] See, for example, van Inwagen's appeal to the value that might be realized by the world's exhibiting certain sorts of regularity (van Inwagen 2006, pp. 115–23).

human fulfillment if we subordinate our wills to the divine will rather than if we regulate our wills in some other way. By 'doing better' I do not assume some consequentialist understanding of human fulfillment and its realization; I mean by 'doing better' that if one is reasonable, then one would prefer acting under the direction of the divine will in light of the goods of human fulfillment than on one's own discretion, or under some other scheme of direction. The similarity between this formulation of the third condition and Raz's service conception of authority is non-accidental. (See 7.3 for a discussion of Raz's view.) Notice, though, that I am not using Raz's view to explain why the Anselmian being is necessarily authoritative, or even as a stand-alone argument for why the Anselmian being, if it has this contingent will, would be authoritative. Raz treats the condition of being subordinated to an authority as no better than neutral. But on the view I am describing, subordinating oneself to the Anselmian being is positively desirable. Thus, Raz's service conception needs to do less work on my view; it need be used only to defeat a certain objection to pursuing what is otherwise very good.

As I said, I do not mean to insist on this being a necessary condition; it may be that the standard *by acting in accordance with the divine will one does no worse than one otherwise would* would suffice, given the importance of the good of religion and the qualification that one is never directed to act contrary to the natural law. But I think that it is sufficient. On the three conditions of this alternative to the Grisez-Finnis-Boyle view, there is a natural worthwhileness in subordination to the divine will, and the two central objections one might have to the reasonableness of such subordination—that it might require action contrary to the natural norms of practical reasonableness, and that it puts the divine will in a role of authority that it is not well-suited to serve—are undermined by the Anselmian being's will being sufficiently oriented to our acting rightly and to human fulfillment generally.

There are multiple ways in which this sufficiency condition might be met, assuming (again, to be discussed in 8.5) that the Anselmian being could have the relevant sort of ethics contingently. The first, and most straightforward, would just be that in which the Anselmian being's ethics involves being set on coordinating and guiding human action in a way that serves human fulfillment. Being vastly superior in knowing our good and in being able to coordinate our action toward the good—not only in giving us a common plan of action, but in offering that plan in light of what sort of failures there would be to act in accordance with it—the Anselmian being's will can satisfy Raz's normal justification thesis (7.3), at least so long as there is an adequate orientation toward our good. Note that in describing this way of the Anselmian being's being adequately oriented to human fulfillment, I did not suppose that the Anselmian being takes human fulfillment as the sole or even regulative interest that the Anselmian being takes in creation. The Anselmian being's interest in human fulfillment could be subordinated to other ends, or incomplete in various ways. But the fact that the Anselmian being is so much better than other beings in effectively coordinating the action of creaturely agents might compensate for its incomplete orientation to human fulfillment, thus making its will the rationally preferable standard for a created agent to employ for the regulation of that creature's conduct.

But there are other ways in which the Anselmian being's contingent ethics could meet these criteria that are structurally different and worth attending to. The most straightforward view, discussed in the previous paragraph, takes the rational preferability of adhering to the scheme of action proposed by the Anselmian being to be independent of one's willingness to subordinate one's will to the divine will. This independence may not present, though, in that the superiority of the Anselmian being's scheme in guiding action toward human fulfillment depends on our willingness to subordinate our wills to the divine will. It could be, for example, that the rational preferability of the scheme for promotion of human fulfillment given by the Anselmian being is *logically posterior* to the fact of one's subordinating one's will to the divine will; perhaps its being preferable depends on one's having made the commitment constitutive of the good of religion. (An analogy: it could be that going along with one's friend's plans is not clearly rationally preferable to doing something else considered in abstraction from the commitment of friendship itself; but given the commitment of friendship, which is itself constitutive of an important human good, going along with one's friend's plans is a no-brainer.) The good of religion, on this possibility, becomes available through one's subordinating oneself to the divine will in the relevant way.

Here is a third possibility. It could be that the Anselmian being's contingent ethics entails that the Anselmian being's directedness to the promotion of any particular rational creature's own good is itself dependent on the creature's subordination of his or her own will to the divine will, so that what makes subordination of oneself to the divine will the right call is that the Anselmian being wills that a fuller realization of each rational creature's good be dependent on that creature's subordination of him- or herself to the divine will. We can imagine the Anselmian being saying to each rational creature, *I assure you that your own good will be better achieved if you subordinate your will to my own.* To some ears this sounds like a threat. But since the baseline of interaction between the Anselmian being and us is the Anselmian being's being indifferent to our good, this is to my ears a quite generous offer, an offer that the Anselmian being will order things so that doing the Anselmian being's will will also be to the good of the rational creature. It is an offer to allow us to cooperate with the Anselmian being in realizing the Anselmian being's ends, with the assurance that one's own good will be looked after. I don't think such an offer would be sufficient to make submitting to the Anselmian being's will open to no objection; one might think that it would display a failure of solidarity with respect to one's fellow human beings to accept an offer like this, even from the Anselmian being, if it involved receiving an assurance of the promotion of one's greater good from the Anselmian being when one's fellows received no such assurance. But if we recall that it would have to be combined with a will that one not violate the moral law in any way with respect to one's fellow human beings, then the offer looks more acceptable, and it looks more acceptable still if a similar offer is—has been, is being, or will be—made to all other human beings, so that one could be assured that if anyone does not receive the benefits of this sort of cooperation with the Anselmian being, it is only because he or she was unwilling to subordinate his or her will to the divine will. (Again: recall I am here only describing what I take to be sufficient conditions for the reasonableness of subordinating one's will to the contingent will of the Anselmian being.)

This 'sufficiency' view, the conditions for which I have been considering distinct ways of realizing, is clearly different from the contingent version of the Grisez-Finnis-Boyle view. The contingent version of the Grisez-Finnis-Boyle view meets the conditions of the sufficiency view; but there are seemingly possible divine ethics distinct from what the Grisez-Finnis-Boyle view ascribes to the Anselmian being that meet the conditions set by the sufficiency view. The view that I am offering takes no stand on the other ends that the Anselmian being has, and how they are prioritized with respect to the goods of human fulfillment that rightly govern the conduct of us human beings. It claims that so long as the Anselmian being's ethics involves the Anselmian being's taking a sufficient interest in our pursuing the good well and in human fulfillment being realized, we can rightly allow our wills to be regulated by the divine will. And if we can in these circumstances rightly allow our wills to be fully regulated by the divine will, then the good of religion is available to us.

I have framed my defense of this sufficiency view in terms of whether there could be any objections to the reasonableness of the agent who subordinated his or her will to the Anselmian being whose will meets these three conditions. I close this defense by asking whether there is an objection from the Anselmian being's ethics' not meeting a fourth condition, a condition met by the Anselmian being's ethics on the contingent Grisez-Finnis-Boyle view but not necessarily on the sufficiency view I propose: that the Anselmian being could not reasonably care more about our well-being than the Anselmian being does. On the Grisez-Finnis-Boyle view, one might claim, the Anselmian being cares about human fulfillment as much as the Anselmian being could; one could thus not sensibly withhold subordination of one's own will to the Anselmian being's on the basis that the Anselmian being could have cared more about us. But the sufficiency view cannot claim that this condition is met; of course it would be possible for the Anselmian being to be more fully set on human fulfillment while still meeting the conditions set by that view.

I of course doubt that there is such a thing as an Anselmian being's not being able reasonably to care more about human fulfillment (2.4). But my digging-in point is not that doubt. Instead, I say that even if it is true that the Grisez-Finnis-Boyle view is a maximal conception of how the Anselmian being wills our good, I do not think that the fact that the Anselmian being cares less about us than it might would count as a basis for objecting to the reasonableness of subordinating oneself to that being's will. Caring about us to any extent is not, I argued above, a requirement of the Anselmian being's perfection, so it is not as if one could appeal to this fact to suggest that this being is less than fully divine, and thus somehow less deserving of the response of religion.

We might reasonably wish that the Anselmian being cared more about us, or cared about us in different ways, and not knowing exactly the shape that this care takes, this wish is perfectly reasonably manifested in requests to the Anselmian being to favor us and our good further. But that does not seem to me to make a difference with respect to the issue of what reasonableness requires in subordinating one's will to the divine being's will. Remember: the Anselmian being might, without error, be *totally indifferent* to us. *Any* concern shown by such a being is to be met with gratitude that the Anselmian being was willing to favor us at all, not with criticisms for not having favored us even more radically.

8.5 Contingent Allegiance-Worthiness, Again

I argued in Chapter 7 (7.2–7.3) that we lack reasons to think that the Anselmian being is necessarily allegiance-worthy, much less necessarily fully allegiance-worthy. I argued in 7.4 that it would be an acceptable result if it turned out that the being who is fully worthy of allegiance is only contingently fully worthy of allegiance. I now want to make explicit the argument that the Anselmian being's having a contingent ethics that makes the good of religion available to us would be sufficient for the Anselmian being to be fully worthy of our allegiance.

Begin with obedience, one of the salient species of allegiance. I say that one being is fully worthy of another's obedience when there are decisive reasons of the right sort for the one to obey the other, and that reasons to perform some action are decisive when there are sufficient reasons to perform that action and sufficient reasons not to do anything incompatible with that action. On this understanding of full worthiness of obedience, we could show that the Anselmian being is fully worthy of obedience in those conditions in which there are sufficient reasons to obey and sufficient reasons not to do anything incompatible with obedience.

Now suppose that the Anselmian being has a contingent ethics such that (a) the Anselmian being does not will that we act in ways that the norms of practical reasonableness forbid of us and (b) whatever further the Anselmian being wills with respect to created rational beings is such that for each creature, subordinating the creaturely will to the Anselmian being's will enables that creature to act in a rationally preferable way with respect to the ends set by those norms of practical reasonableness. In these circumstances, it seems to me that there is an overwhelmingly strong case for the worthiness of the Anselmian being for us to be obedient to that being's will. Not only are we realizing a central human good, religion, in and through subordinating our wills to the Anselmian being's; we are also acting better, generally, on the norms of practical reasonableness by so doing. (Recall the various ways in which this betterness might be realized; see 8.3.) These seem to be reasons of the right sort: the grounds for obedience are the goodness of being well-related to the Anselmian being as well as the relationship of that being's will to the reasons for action that naturally apply to us.

And these reasons seem sufficient to make any course of action incompatible with subordinating one's will to the divine will in these circumstances unreasonable.[13]

One might point out that typically obedience is understood in terms of responsiveness to another's speech-acts, not simply to another's will. One may doubt that this is an important objection, given the centrality in orthodox theistic thought of the idea that one is to obey God's will in all things. But we can also add that when one gives another a command, one implies that one wills that the other perform that action—one presents oneself as willing that the other perform that action. Surely the Anselmian being does not command insincerely (6.4; see also Murphy 2002a, pp. 29–45), and has full self-knowledge. So the Anselmian being, whenever giving a command to ϕ, must will that the party commanded ϕ. We can, then, give a derivative account of the worthiness of the Anselmian being with the relevant contingent ethics to have that being's commands obeyed in terms of the worthiness of the Anselmian being with this contingent will to have that being's will obeyed.

What of the other salient sort of allegiance, alliance? I cannot claim that every end had by the Anselmian being with the relevant contingent ethics is one that the created rational being should adopt and cooperate with the Anselmian being in realizing. This is due to its being false that we must will what the Anselmian being wills in order to be rightly related to the Anselmian being (8.2). But as I argued in Chapter 7 (7.3), worthiness for some sort of alliance is an entailment of authority: as the authority sets ends that the subject should take as his or her own and act on as the authority requires, there is some worthiness to share in and cooperate for the sake of ends built into genuine authority relationships. And on the view I am defending, the Anselmian being sets ends for us by willing that we will certain things. These are ends that are indeed shared by the Anselmian being and the rational creature, and we have decisive reason to cooperate with the divine being by willing what the divine being wills us to will. And so, when we understand the ends to have the proper scope, the Anselmian being is fully worthy of our alliance, as well.

One might object that even if it is true that there are decisive reasons to obey and ally oneself with the Anselmian being in these contingent circumstances, I have not succeeded in showing that the Anselmian being is *supremely* worthy of obedience. For one might deny that supreme worthiness of obedience is adequately captured by there being decisive reasons for obedience, even reasons of the right sort. For one might claim that, at least on my own view, it is possible for the Anselmian being to be fully worthy of obedience even though the Anselmian being could have cared more about us, and could have been set on the furthering of human well-being or perfection more

[13] In an earlier book (Murphy 2002a) I argued against the view that God is universally authoritative, even given the contingent stance that God has taken with respect to us humans. Am I taking back what I said there? No. The worthiness for obedience means that one has decisive reasons to take a stance of obedience. But the thesis that God is worthy of obedience does not entail that one who does not take that stance is under authority. It just entails that if one is not under divine authority, that is due to creaturely agents' failure.

than the Anselmian being in fact is. But surely, one might say, one exhibits a greater failure of reasonableness, all other things being equal, if one fails to subordinate oneself to the Anselmian being if the Anselmian being is more set on our good than if one fails to subordinate oneself to the Anselmian being if the Anselmian being is less set on our good. So how could the Anselmian being be supremely worthy of obedience if there is a condition the Anselmian being could be in such that failure to obey would be a greater failure?

If this is a problem, everyone has it. Or at least everyone who thinks that God could have done something more for one that would have engendered, say, an additional debt of gratitude, or everyone who thinks that one could take a further vow of obedience to God that would make one's disobedience even more unreasonable. But I don't think that it is a problem. I concede that it may just be part of our condition with respect to the Anselmian being that there could always be further reasons to obey the Anselmian being, and thus further ways to fall short of reasonableness with respect to obedience to that being. There is no such thing as 'supreme worthiness for obedience,' if we construe 'supreme worthiness' as its being impossible for the unreasonableness of disobedience to be greater. And we should not be bothered by that result. For, first, it is not as if worthiness for obedience is a divine perfection, so that must have an intrinsic maximum (1.4, 7.4). And, second, the sense of full worthiness of obedience that is characterized in terms of decisive reasons is a sufficiently well-worked-out sense that captures what is indeed non-negotiable for theistic practice: one who fails to obey the Anselmian being, if the Anselmian being exhibits the relevant sort of contingent ethics, is making a grave error.

8.6 How the Anselmian Being Can Have a Contingent Ethics

In the Introduction I characterized an 'ethics' as a disposition to treat considerations of various kinds as reasons, and as reasons of distinct types (0.1). In the first Part of this book, I argued that we have a reason to ascribe a certain necessary but very limited ethics to the Anselmian being. The Anselmian being necessarily has justifying reasons to promote the existence and well-being/perfection of creatures (Chapter 4) and necessarily has decisive requiring reasons not to intend creaturely evil (Chapter 5). The Anselmian being, an absolutely perfect agent, acts on its reasons in whatever way those reasons merit being acted upon by the Anselmian being. And so we know that the Anselmian being is disposed to take these considerations as the reasons that they are, and thus that the Anselmian being may or must act in various ways.

There is obviously nothing to the very idea of an 'ethics' that it must be *necessarily* exhibited by the agent who exhibits it, though. One way that an ethics need not be necessary is not relevant to the possibility of a contingent ethics for a divine being: that there is nothing to the idea of an ethics that a being must have the ethics that it is admirable for it to have, or that is appropriate for the being to whom it belongs. When we humans have dispositions to act that are admirable and appropriate, that is a contingent matter, at least in part due to its being contingent that we have the dispositions that we are supposed to have. But that is not the sort of contingency at stake for the Anselmian being, who necessarily exhibits any disposition that that being would be better for having.

Rather, the sort of contingency with which we are concerned is the contingency of the *applicability* of some possible set of norms to some agent, that is, whether the norms that are appropriately invoked by an agent to guide that agent's conduct have that appropriateness as a contingent matter. This seems familiar enough in the mundane human context. One might think that Teresa of Calcutta's particular ethics is not required of all human beings, but that it is indeed appropriate for her, and that she appropriately guides her own conduct by it, and if she fails to live up to it, then she is at least correct to self-criticize for those failures. This is due, many think, to Mother Teresa's vocation, her being called to a particular way of living to which not all human beings are called. Or one might think that an ethics' appropriateness for some human might be the result simply of being born into a certain family, or a certain community. (I am not endorsing this view; I am just describing it, and noting that I am not ruling it out.) A family might take its members to have a distinctive set of norms applying to them, definitely not required of all persons, such that to be a member of that family makes it the case that those standards are appropriately applied by one to oneself, and by fellow family members to each other. (In my house we do occasionally invoke how Murphys are to act, and we do not hold non-Murphys to the same standards generally.) This is a very familiar phenomenon, though how central it is to the practical life, and how such contingent standards can come to appropriately apply to one, are of course disputed questions.

But I think that some of these disputed questions are less disputable in the context of the Anselmian being. For example: one might think that there are contingent norms, norms that apply only contingently to human beings, or some subset of human beings, that do so willy-nilly—that in virtue of being born or adopted into some family, or being a member of some society, some contingent norms are appropriately applied to one. And we might think that one can be called by a superior being to a particular form of life that is at least partially constituted by having a certain ethics. But even if this sort of requirement might bind some of us human beings irrespective of what we would have willed for ourselves, we should deny that such contingent binding could hold in the case of the Anselmian being. It would be an imposition on the divine discretion, and thus on divine sovereignty itself (4.3), to hold that there are any norms that apply contingently to the Anselmian being the application of which is not due to the exercise of the Anselmian being's own discretion. Even if it is part of the human condition to find oneself subject to contingent norms not of one's own doing, that is not part of the divine condition. So if the Anselmian being is under a contingent ethics, it is by the Anselmian being's own agency that it is under that ethics.

How, though, is it possible for the Anselmian being to come under a contingent ethics as the result of that being's own discretion? I will defend two ways, both of which are variations on a theme. I should note that in defending these ways I am going to speak of the divine being as performing multiple acts of willing, though I think that a more metaphysically serious account would characterize the constraints that I am going to describe as constraints on what a divine being could coherently will in its single act of willing rather than constraints imposed by some acts of divine will on other acts of divine will. But I do not think that this simplification in the presentation will affect the overall argument.

Here is the template for the Anselmian being to take on a contingent ethics by the exercise of its discretion. The way for the Anselmian being to have a contingent ethics is for the Anselmian being to perform some discretionary act of will A that is sufficient to render some other act of will B a defective exercise of agency, where B would not, in the absence of A (or some other such discretionary act of will), count as a defective action.[14] For divine action is necessarily *never* defective; any defective divine action would entail that the divine being counts as a less than absolutely perfect agent, for there would be some way in which its agency is flawed. All action has standards of defectiveness internal to it: those standards are given by the reasons for action that bear on the action, its alternatives, and its circumstances. For reasons that govern the Anselmian being's action necessarily, these reasons determine that there are certain actions that would make the Anselmian being's action defective if, counterpossibly, the Anselmian being were ever to perform them. (For example, the Anselmian being's lying to creatures would necessarily be defective divine action, for lying is an act by which evil to creatures is intended, and the Anselmian being has decisive requiring reason not to intend evils (5.5).) But some standards of defectiveness for action are not necessary but contingent, indeed chosen by the agent, set by the agent for him- or herself. My action is not defective simply because I take a bunch of materials that could be made into a shoe and instead turn them into something that looks like a shoe at a distance but would be terrible for wearing on one's foot; such a description of the case does not say enough to support a charge that I performed a defective act of shoemaking. For it could be that I am not *trying* to make a shoe but to make a prop for a play; and thus my action may well have been an adequate exercise in propmaking and not at all a defective exercise in shoemaking. Had I been *trying* to make a shoe, though, identical behaviors may have been partially constitutive of defective rather than nondefective action.

One might find it incredible that the divine being necessarily never performs a defective action. After all, I have allowed that the Anselmian being might act in ways that result in our being *much* worse off than we could have been if the Anselmian being had

[14] Indeed, often we can't even characterize what it would be to perform that action B without the agent's having subordinated him- or herself to further standards of nondefectiveness. For example: *striking out* in a game of baseball.

acted differently, and indeed the Anselmian being might act in these ways even without a reason not to promote our good more than the Anselmian being does. Surely, one might protest, we can call this defective action. But, no, we cannot: for something to be defective is not for it to be regrettable, unfortunate, or any of these other negative things. A shark's devouring a swimmer is extremely regrettable, but that does not make the shark's activity defective. (Though a domesticated dog's nipping the hand of its owner might well be defective doggy activity.) A defect in something is its lacking a feature that it is supposed to have, a feature that belongs in a thing of that kind. So unless we can identify some *applicable* standard of agency that the Anselmian being is failing to meet in creating this world, though we may regret or find unfortunate various aspects of it, that is not enough to support even a prima facie charge that the Anselmian being's creative act is defective; and nothing in the necessary ethics of an Anselmian being supports that charge (6.2–6.4).

I have so far argued that the very idea of the Anselmian being's having a contingent ethics is a coherent one, so long as we take that contingent ethics to be self-imposed by the Anselmian being; and I have so far argued that the way that a contingent ethics can be self-imposed by the Anselmian being is for the Anselmian being to perform some act of will that subjects the Anselmian being to standards of nondefectiveness in action that go beyond those that hold necessarily of the Anselmian being. I am going to consider a few ways in which this general mechanism can be realized in divine willing: first, in ways that are explained most perspicuously by norms of rational intending, and, second, in ways that are explained most perspicuously by speech-act norms, most prominently, those of promising. I will also consider and reject the claim that by willing to create, the Anselmian being thereby subjects itself to further norms of nondefectiveness beyond that given by the Anselmian being's necessary ethics.

One way that the Anselmian being can take on a contingent ethics is through willing itself. Recall that to have an ethics is, crudely, to have a disposition to treat certain considerations as reasons, and as reasons of certain types (0.1). To treat a consideration as a reason is to have it play a certain role in one's decision-making, to allow it to weigh in favor of some options over others, and to treat it as a reason of a certain kind is to have it play a specific sort of role in that decision-making. Now, one sort of psychological state that I have been ascribing to the Anselmian being, and about which I have affirmed various other claims, is *intention*. Intentions are, for the Anselmian being, always going to be for something good (5.3). There is a massive discretion that the Anselmian being has in what intentions the Anselmian being forms with respect to creatures (4.3). And there is a distinction that has some explanatory importance in understanding the action of the Anselmian being, that between intentions that are more or less antecedent of the actual, consequent divine will (8.2).

On the basis of such claims, we can construct a case that the Anselmian being can take on a contingent ethics through having discretionary, broad high-level intentions to promote various ends in certain sorts of circumstances (where the limiting case is: always). For example, it is open to the Anselmian being to have a general, unqualified intention to promote the well-being of rational creatures. This is not an intention the presence of which is entailed by the Anselmian being's perfection, since the well-being of creatures gives justifying reasons only. But it falls within the Anselmian being's discretion to form this intention.

Given the presence of this intention, though, it could be correct to ascribe to the Anselmian being a certain ethics: for the Anselmian being's intention to promote the well-being of creatures entails that the Anselmian being will be disposed to treat certain considerations—considerations involving human flourishing and languishing—as reasons for action. That the Anselmian being will treat such considerations in this way is given by the fact that the Anselmian being is rational, and principles of rational intending require that one's further, more particular intentions will cohere with one's broader intentions. And this contingent ethics will be stable. For if an agent forms the intention, then a rational agent does not retract that intention unless it was the result of some sort of shortcoming in deliberation or new information has arisen (Murphy 2001, pp. 210–12). The Anselmian being's intentions are subject to no deliberative shortcoming and God does not receive new information that could make possible rational changes in intention. So the Anselmian being's intentions could not change.

This way for the Anselmian being to take on a contingent ethics is an instance of the general pattern I described above. If the Anselmian being, with discretion, wills to treat some consideration as relevant to what is brought about in the world, then that act of will makes defective a variety of other sorts of willings that would not otherwise be defective: withdrawing that intention, or failing to will in a variety of more particular ways that reflects that broader intention. The phenomenon most familiar to this one in the human case is commitment: one can take on a contingent ethics, at least within certain bounds, by committing oneself to living a certain way; aside from the causal effects that such a commitment has, by making a rational commitment one seals off a number of the routes by which one can lack that commitment or fail to act in accordance with it while remaining a nondefectively rational agent.

If the Anselmian being's contingent ethics were to some extent fixed by the Anselmian being's high-level willings with respect to creaturely goods, how can this ethics be known by us? (For unless this ethics is something that we can reasonably believe to belong to the Anselmian being, then there is still an obstacle to the availability of the good of subordinating one's will to the Anselmian being's; see 8.3–8.4.) There is some limited knowledge that we can gain through observation of the world that the Anselmian being has created, but it is mostly negative: we can know that if some fact obtains, the Anselmian being did not intend that the fact not obtain, at least not consequently. But that is itself of little use, as this sort of contingent ethics concerns the Anselmian being's antecedent, not consequent, will. One can also rule out the possibility that there are certain antecedent intentions the Anselmian being has; if some states of affairs fail to obtain, then we may be able to rule out or take to be far less likely that the Anselmian being has antecedent intentions of broad scope that aim for the realization of those facts. (This is one way to try to revive the problem of evil, as we will see in Chapter 9.) But the most straightforward way to get positive knowledge of the Anselmian being's intentions, at the right level of abstraction for this to be informative of the Anselmian being's ethics, would be for the Anselmian being simply to tell us, for the Anselmian being never lies (6.4), and thus would never lie about the Anselmian being's aims, plans, purposes.

The other major way for the Anselmian being to take on an ethics contingently is by the Anselmian being's willingly entering into a social practice that is norm-constituted, thus constituting new ways by which divine action can be defective. Consider the social practices by which agents are capable of performing illocutionary acts of various sorts. For each sort of illocutionary act there are success conditions that constitute the performance of an act of that sort and there are nondefectiveness conditions that constitute the nondefective performance of an act of that sort. So the success conditions for making an assertion involve what makes it the case that one has indeed asserted something (rather than merely vocalizing, or making a mere joke) and the nondefectiveness conditions for making an assertion involve what makes it the case that the assertion successfully made does not fall short in some way specifically as an assertion—that the proposition asserted is not taken by the speaker to be true, there are no grounds for the speaker's believing it, and so forth (Searle and Vanderveken 1985, pp. 54–5).

So while there is in general no requirement on the Anselmian being to reveal any truths to any created person, if the Anselmian being chooses to enter into our practices of communication—rather than to, say, just miraculously mess with our neurons to get us to believe what the Anselmian being wants us to believe—through the Anselmian being's willingly making an assertion with a certain content, then the Anselmian being's assertion must be of a truth, or else the Anselmian being is acting defectively, which is incompatible with the Anselmian being's perfect agency.

Particularly important with respect to a contingent ethics for a divine being is, on my view, the illocutionary act of promising. For nondefectiveness conditions on promising include that the promisor believes possible what the promisor promises to do and indeed intends to bring about what the promisor has promised to do (Searle 1969, p. 60 and Searle and Vanderveken 1985, pp. 55, 192). But the Anselmian being will not be in error about whether it is possible to do what the Anselmian being promises to do, nor will the Anselmian being fail to bring about what the Anselmian being intends through some other sort of irrationality. The Anselmian being's failing to do what the Anselmian being promises would entail that the Anselmian being's agency is defective in some way.

Because this is so, the Anselmian being's promises are extremely important with respect to the shape of the Anselmian being's ethics. For we can ask whether, at a sufficiently high level of generality, the Anselmian being has made promises about how the Anselmian being will choose and act with respect to various considerations, most saliently, human flourishing and languishing. We can know that if the Anselmian being has made these discretionary promises to us, then they exhibit the Anselmian being's intentions with respect to us, and show us more of what the Anselmian being's ethics is like.

Now, one might claim that by making an argument of this sort, I am taking back what I have claimed earlier about the Anselmian being being under no moral requirements with respect to the promotion of creaturely good (4.3). It turns out, the objector might claim, that the Anselmian being *is* under familiar moral requirements to tell the truth, to keep promises, and so forth, so all of these moral requirements concern acting in accordance with the nondefectiveness norms that are defining of various sorts of illocutionary act. But I deny this. Put to the side whether such requirements are aptly characterized in terms of the *promotion* of the good of those to whom these illocutionary acts are directed. What is relevant is that the general moral requirements that we are under with respect to truth-telling, promise-keeping, etc. are not explained in the way that God's telling the truth and keeping promises are explained. The correct explanations for us appeal *somehow* to creatures' good; the correct explanation for God appeals simply to the impossibility of God engaging in any sort of defective agency. When we are explaining why we must speak the truth, keep promises, not command insincerely, and so forth, the explanation appeals to the wrong done to those to whom one speaks; it does not stop with the point that the action in question would be a defective instance of its kind. But that is where I am stopping the argument in the case of the Anselmian being; the Anselmian being does not engage in defective action, and that is why we can say that the ethics of the Anselmian being is self-imposed by the Anselmian being's subjecting itself to the norms that constitute some social practice.

By performing speech-acts in the family of commissives—that is, illocutionary acts in which the point is the taking on of a commitment by the speaker—the Anselmian being can place itself under a contingent ethics. But we should note that other sorts of speech-act, even if they do not *place* the Anselmian being under a further contingent ethics, can *reveal* the further contingent ethics of the Anselmian being. As we noted above, specific assertions by the Anselmian being about the Anselmian being's intentions regarding our action are the clearest case. But there are other cases, more interesting. Consider, for example, commands. Suppose that the Anselmian being commands some created person to perform some action. It is among the sincerity conditions of commanding that if one commands another to perform some action, then the commander intends for the commanded to perform that action (Murphy 2002a, pp. 29–45). That does not tell us anything yet about the Anselmian being's own intentions with respect to the Anselmian being's own action. But it can reveal, via further principles of rational intending, how the Anselmian being intends to act, or does not intend to act, with respect to us. If the Anselmian being commands us to follow some set of moral norms, for example, then the Anselmian being (being sincere) intends for us to follow those norms, and thus does not intend to preclude our acting in accordance with those norms.

There are other ways for the Anselmian being to give itself a contingent ethics. Incarnation is one dramatic example: I think that the Anselmian being's becoming a human being involves the Anselmian being's taking on a contingent ethic, though it raises some special casuistical questions that I will not deal with here.[15] There may be others; I do not claim to give an exhaustive treatment. But I want to make clear a denial, and an argument for it. Some may think that by *creating* the Anselmian being imposes new norms on itself, taking on new responsibilities and new ways of acting defectively. If all that is meant by that is, say, that the Anselmian being has requiring decisive reasons not to intend creaturely evil (5.4) and now, given creation, here are some creatures to whom the Anselmian being should not intend evil, I have no objection. But some want to say that there are new ways of the Anselmian being's acting defectively that are logically posterior to creation, so that, for example, logically prior to creation there is no more than justifying reason to create, logically posterior to creation, there are requiring reasons to promote the good of the beings thus created. That I have denied.

I deny this because we do not have any good arguments for thinking that by creation the Anselmian being makes it the case that new ways of acting will count as defective. The contrast between cases like that of rational willing and entering into a social practice on one hand and that of creation on the other is pretty dramatic. There is an obvious rational relationship that one bears to further actions by intending something, or by participating in a norm-governed social practice. But the only thing that happens in creation is causal. There are no constitutive norms of creation, like constitutive norms of promise-making or shoemaking, that the Anselmian being subjects itself to by deciding, with discretion, to create. There is nothing to be said about what counts as creating well except that the Anselmian being creates in a way appropriately shaped by the relevant reasons for action. But those are just the reasons for divine action characterized in Part I.

I mentioned at the beginning of the book that there are reasonable rival conceptions of God, of what a being must be like in order to count as God. There is the conception of God as absolutely perfect being; there is the conception of God as that being that is supremely worthy of worship; and there is the conception of God as that being who is fully worthy of our allegiance (0.2). From this point forward I will use the title 'God,' semi-stipulatively, to refer to a being who satisfies all three conceptions. So far as I have argued, only an Anselmian being who has taken on one of the sorts of contingent ethics described in 8.4 qualifies as God in this semi-stipulative sense.[16] The topic of the

[15] I believe that God became incarnate in Jesus Christ, and I accept the formulation that Jesus Christ is fully human and fully divine. Humans are bound by familiar welfare-oriented moral goodness. God is not. So we have the standard incompatible properties problem for the Christian doctrine of the incarnation. I do think, though, that this will end up being solvable in the way that more familiar versions of the incompatible properties problem are solved.

[16] As being an Anselmian being entails being supremely worthy of worship (7.1), we do not need a further qualification to meet the 'supremely worthy of worship' criterion, but we do need the contingent ethics qualification to ensure that the Anselmian being is fully worthy of allegiance.

final chapter of this book is whether the argument from evil can be revived, not as an argument against the Anselmian being's existence, but against *God's* existence. Do the facts about this world's evil give us reason to believe that there is no Anselmian being who has taken on such a contingent ethics? And do the facts of evil give us reason to believe that there is no Abrahamic and specifically Christian God, one whose particular contingent ethics is that which is suggested by Abrahamic and specifically Christian theism?

9

The Argument from Evil and God's Contingent Ethics

9.1 Two Revived Formulations of the Argument from Evil

In response to my argument that a proper understanding of the Anselmian being's ethics undermines the argument from evil against the existence of an absolutely perfect being, I considered two criticisms, criticisms that could be offered even by those who are otherwise friendly to the argument of Part I (6.5). One of these criticisms is that even if the existence of the evils of our world is not in tension with the existence of an absolutely perfect being, the existence of these evils is in tension with the existence of such a being with whom we ought to side, to whom we ought to have allegiance. The other is that even if the existence of the evils of our world is not in tension with the existence of an absolutely perfect being, the existence of these evils is in tension with the existence of a *certain* Anselmian being, the God of orthodox Abrahamic monotheism, and in particular of Christian theism.

This final chapter responds to these two objections: in 9.2 I argue that the facts of evil are not in significant tension with the existence of God, where by 'God' I mean an absolutely perfect being who is fully worthy of our worship and allegiance (8.6); in 9.3 I argue that the facts of evil are not in significant tension with the existence of the Christian God. I cannot hope for the argument of 9.3 to be anywhere near as potent as the argument of 9.2: without selecting some set of authoritative affirmations of what features are essential to God as characterized by Christianity, I cannot offer a characterization of the Christian God precise enough to make a fully rigorous argument that this conception of God has safe harbor against the problem of evil; by selecting some set of authoritative affirmations, I would thereby leave to the side those Christians who do not accept the conception of authoritative Christianity that I select. But I will try to make some headway toward showing that the conception I have offered coheres with the main lines of the ecumenical Christianity.

The final section of the chapter, and of the book, considers an objection to my overall argument that is commonly expressed against responses to problem of evil: that it constitutes a 'rearguard' action, merely a delaying maneuver against advancing and strengthening formulations of the argument from evil. Aside from re-emphasizing the point that the account of divine ethics that I have offered has been defended entirely independently of its specific application to the problem of evil, I draw out in this section the resources that my view offers to make room for a central claim of various theistic views: that God loves us, though God does not have to.

9.2 Contingent Divine Ethics and the Argument from Evil

Recall the dialectic concerning evil, absolute perfection, and full allegiance-worthiness. What guarantees the failure of the argument from evil against the existence of an absolutely perfect being is the thinness of the necessary ethics of such a being (6.2–6.3). But the thinness of the ethics of the Anselmian being provides a key premise for an argument that a being with such an ethics would not be, as such, necessarily worthy of allegiance (6.6, 7.2–7.3). In the face of this argument I conceded that the allegiance-worthiness of the absolutely perfect being could be no more than contingent (7.4), but argued that the absolutely perfect being could take on a contingent ethics that would make that being fully worthy of our allegiance (8.4–8.6). But the outcome of this dialectic, it might well be thought, revives a form of the argument from evil. For if the Anselmian being takes on a contingent ethics sufficient to make that being worthy of our full allegiance, then the Anselmian being's having that ethics would entail the Anselmian being's being motivated to rid the world of the evils that we find in it—that is, the Anselmian being will prevent every evil that is in that being's power to prevent, so long as there are not adequate reasons to the contrary. And so the existence of the evils of this world is incompatible with, or at the very least gives strong reasons against belief in, the existence of *God*, for to be God is to be a being who is not only perfect but fully worthy of our allegiance.

Thus, the critic offers a dilemma based on the evils of this world. The evils of this world give strong evidence either that there is no Anselmian being or that the Anselmian being is not worthy of our allegiance. Since we have identified 'God' with the perfect being who is fully worthy of our allegiance (8.6), the evils of the world give strong evidence that there is no God. At this point, the critic might say, we must return to more standard theodicy, having exhausted any resources offered by a re-examination of divine ethics.

The obvious premise to press in the critic's attempt to revive the argument from evil is the conditional *If the Anselmian being takes on a contingent ethics sufficient to make that being worthy of our full allegiance, then the Anselmian being's having that ethics would entail the Anselmian being's being motivated to rid the world of the evils that we find in it.* I conceded in 8.4 that one way for the Anselmian being to take on a contingent ethics that would make that being worthy of full allegiance is the contingent version of the Grisez-Finnis-Boyle view, on which God wills that each of us act in the way that the natural law requires of us and wills for each of us the totality of human fulfillment. And we might well then suppose that having this complete ethics of human fulfillment entails that God will prevent any setbacks to human well-being, at least in the absence of adequate considerations to the contrary. But to be so motivated is to be motivated in accordance with the norms of familiar welfare-oriented moral goodness. Since my response to the problem of evil in Chapter 6 depends on the Anselmian being's not being bound by familiar welfare-oriented moral goodness, it would follow that I have not offered any resources to respond to the problem of evil as pressed against the existence of a God who has taken on this sort of contingent ethics.

But the objector cannot take for granted that a contingent ethics sufficient to account for the full allegiance-worthiness of the Anselmian being would also be sufficient to motivate the Anselmian being in such a way that would revive the argument from evil. The contingent version of the Grisez-Finnis-Boyle view is, I claimed (8.4), only one of a number of contingent ethics that the Anselmian being could adopt by which the Anselmian being would be fully worthy of allegiance. To show that the problem of evil cannot be raised simply against the existence of God, where God is conceived as *an absolutely perfect being, fully worthy of allegiance*, we can exploit the gap between the ethics that is necessary for the Anselmian being to be fully worthy of allegiance and the ethics that is necessary for the Anselmian being to be motivated along the lines of familiar welfare-oriented moral goodness. And it seems very clear from the criteria for such an ethics and the types of realizations of such ethics described in Chapter 8 that this gap can be exploited.

There is a great good in being in union with God through subordinating our own wills to what the Anselmian being wills for us (8.2–8.3). What is needed in order for us to pursue this good is not a guarantee that God thinks of the human good in the way that we do, as a regulative objective of willing, but rather simply an assurance that subordinating our wills to the divine will does not involve us in first- or second-order unreasonableness: either the first-order unreasonableness of performing an action that the norms of practical reasonableness forbid, or the second-order unreasonableness of employing a too-unreliable proximate standard for guiding our action in light of the ends set by the norms of practical reasonableness (8.4). Thus, what is required for compliance with the will of the Anselmian being to not send us astray with respect to the natural norms of practical reasonableness is (1) that that will does not direct us to violate these norms and (2) that using that will as a guide is rationally preferable for securing reasonable ends to using our own judgment and discretion, or some other standard, for securing those ends. It does not appear, on the face of it, that the Anselmian being's having a contingent ethics that meets these conditions entails that the Anselmian being will be motivated to prevent each setback to human well-being, such that that being will prevent it if metaphysically and rationally possible.

Let us consider several models for such contingent ethics, fashioned after the sketches developed in Chapter 8 of how the Anselmian being's possible allegiance-worthiness could be realized. What these models have in common is that in them the Anselmian being does not will that we violate the norms of practical reasonableness that apply to us.[1] This could be on account of the Anselmian being's willing that we adhere to those norms. Or it could be simply on account of (on that issue) the Anselmian being's will being silent: perhaps, while the Anselmian being wills definite things with respect to us and what we should do, the content of what the Anselmian being wills with respect to us is entirely compatible with our doing what the natural norms of practical reasonableness require.

Taking this first condition to be common to all of the models to follow, there are multiple ways of filling out a divine being's contingent ethics that would not entail that an Anselmian being that took on such an ethics would be motivated generally to prevent setbacks to human well-being. Here are three representative models.

For the first, I begin with an analogy. Suppose that one lives in a political community in which the de facto authority—the party who is actually listened to by the populace, who is actually likely to be obeyed, and with respect to whom there is no viable competition for the role—lays down rules in a way that exhibits the following pattern. None of the rules that the authority lays down for the community members to follow requires them to do anything that constitutes a violation of the norms of morality. They are not required to lie, cheat, steal, or defraud their fellow political community members. The de facto authority has, however, very strange views on the goods worth pursuing by members of the political community, and even announces such: there are ends that enter into its deliberations concerning what to command the community members to do which are not judged to be worthwhile by the members of that community, and they are indeed correct about this—they themselves lack reason to pursue those ends. Nevertheless, because what the de facto authority commands tracks the ends set by the norms of practical reasonableness to a not insignificant extent, the rationally preferable mode of acting by members of that community includes subjecting themselves to the norms laid down by the de facto authority. This because of two factors: first, that they are never called upon to do what is in itself wrong; and second, that the ends set by the norms of practical reasonableness will be furthered significantly by adhering to the de facto authority's rules, given the significant tracking of those ends by the de facto authority's rules and the salience of the de facto authority as a coordinator of community members' action. (Another way of getting at the point is that it can be far more reasonable to subject yourself to an imperfectly practically rational, but effective, would-be authority rather than a more practically rational, but ineffective, would-be authority; this is an implication of the rather obvious point that while the worthiness of a would-be authority does indeed depend on whether it guides based on the guided party's reasons, departures from that can be compensated by the effectiveness of the guiding that is done.) But in such a community, if there were certain aspects of the good of subjects that the de facto authority were in a position to do something about,

[1] That is: it is never true that what is necessary for acting in accordance with the divine will constitutes a violation of the natural law. It is compatible with this that in the absence of a divine willing to perform the action, or if the agent performs the action except under the description "acting in accordance with the divine will," the action is a violation of the natural law.

but did not, this might not be in the least a surprising fact; it could be that these aspects of the good of subjects were just not among those matters in which the de facto political authority takes an interest. So we can see how, given a certain pattern of concern, it could be true both that a de facto political authority is worthy of being treated as authoritative and that it is entirely unsurprising that the political authority is unmotivated to anything about some of the evils that are taking place on its watch.

The setup for the case involves a de facto political authority who is imperfectly practically rational, and of course, God is not in any way imperfect. But what is relevant in the analogy is not the imperfection as such but the fact that God, like the imagined de facto authority, may have a plan for us that is based on reasons not entirely shared between the would-be subjects and the would-be authority, while nevertheless subordination of the would-be subject to that plan laid down by the would-be authority is perfectly reasonable. Suppose, for example, that the Anselmian being's fundamental concern is with the created world as a whole, its exhibiting a certain sort of orderliness, perhaps some of which is identifiable by us as an important sort of good, perhaps some of which is beyond our grasp. And suppose that the realization of some human goods is part of this ordering, and perhaps even the Anselmian being wills *some* human good for its own sake, though in a way that is wholly regulated by the goods of orderliness that dominate the Anselmian being's concern for the created world. Even though it is plainly possible for the Anselmian being to be more fully set on human good than is the case in this model, it still may be that the goods of human fulfillment are in fact better realized through subordinating one's own will to the will of the Anselmian being for humanity rather than by acting in accordance with one's own discretion, or some other such norm. For given the Anselmian being's aim to pursue certain ends that constitute human fulfillment, it may be rationally preferable to subordinate one's own willing to the Anselmian being's, given the greater success that one will have in pursuing those worthwhile ends in cooperation with the Anselmian being. On this view, one could point to some evils that are setbacks for human well-being, and ask why they are present, and the answer would simply be that God is not interested in preventing those evils; their presence is a foreseen, but not intended, outcome of some wholly worthwhile end that God is set upon.

Here is a second model, which again I introduce with a political analog. Suppose that there is some de facto authority who does not treat all of the matters of human well-being as relevant to political action. Instead of viewing matters of the comfort and enjoyment of the citizenry as reasons for political action and for regulating the rules laid down for the citizenry, the de facto authority judges only a certain category of those reasons—say, those that concern the bare safety and security of the citizenry—as reasons. This is not some policy that the de facto authority has taken on in the face of the scarcity of resources, or anything to that effect. Rather, the de facto authority simply rejects the view that anything above and beyond the bare safety and security of the members of the political community counts in favor of a law or policy. The authority never, however, requires subjects to act in a way contrary to what the norms of practical reasonableness in their fullness in fact demand; perhaps with respect to some of these norms, the authority directs subjects to act in accordance with them, and perhaps with respect to the remainder, the authority has left sufficient discretion for the subjects to honor the de facto authority's rules so that they can comply both with those rules and with the norms of practical reasonableness. Again, it seems plain that such a de facto authority could be someone whose law, though perhaps based on defective judgments about the human good and the role it should play in justifying political action, might nevertheless be worthy of obedience. And again we would not be surprised if there were a variety of ways of making subjects' lives better that this de facto authority could do something about, but simply does not, for that de facto authority does not treat these aspects of subjects' well-being as reasons for political action.

Correspondingly, it could be that the Anselmian being has a sort of general interest in human well-being among its other ends. But this general interest does not involve treating every instance of human good as something to be promoted, as a requiring reason for promoting it, and every instance of human evil as something to be prevented, as a requiring reason to prevent it; rather, it involves treating only certain types of human goods and evils as requiring reasons, say, those that are absolutely essential to the ultimate flourishing of a human. Consider, for example, Adams's category of "horrendous evils": evils that prima facie preclude the possibility that one's life on the whole could be good for one (M. Adams 1999, pp. 26–9). An Anselmian being might take on a contingent ethics with respect to humans that treats only horrendous evils as requiring reasons for action. Again, though, given what the Anselmian being otherwise wills for humans to will, it could be true that subordinating one's will to this being would enable one to act better on the ends given by the natural norms of practical reasonableness than acting on some other proximate guide for action. But we would not be surprised to find many of the evils of this world—even terrific evils, so long as non-horrendous—present, even in a world known to be providentially ordered by an Anselmian being with this sort of contingent ethics.

Here is a third model. Again, suppose that there is an abnormally powerful person on the scene in a situation that is otherwise the state of nature—no one naturally bears authority over any other. (So we are imagining, for a moment, that we are dealing with mature adults, say, who are not under the authority of parents.) This person seems to have motivations that are not wholly in line with the requirements of familiar welfare-oriented moral goodness, and this person does not claim to be a follower of familiar welfare-oriented moral goodness. Thus, one is justifiably a bit afraid of such a powerful person, and what her plans are, and whether they will serve one ill or well. But, interestingly, this abnormally powerful person makes each person whose well-being she is in a position to affect an offer: "If you place yourself under my authority," she says, "I will see to it that all will, eventually, go well for you. You will do better for yourself and your projects than you could ever do for yourself and your projects by your own lights." You are concerned. "You realize I am unwilling to violate the norms of morality." The abnormally powerful person gives an assurance that she will not command you to do what, upon her command, would be contrary to the norms of morality. "But there are others," you note. "What about them?" "They too will receive this offer," you are assured. And you ponder: this being is incredibly powerful, and able to influence one's own life prospects, and those of others, in dramatic ways. This being's track record for giving commands that do not require those who follow them to violate the moral law is a strong one. And those who have accepted the offer testify that it has been for the good, that whatever this being's strangeness with respect to their motivations and concerns, this being seems to have been faithful to her promise.

What reason do you have to turn down this offer? There are reasons, I am sure—expressive reasons concerned with subjecting oneself to a moral equal in this thoroughgoing way, or reasons concerned with whether those who receive this offer will respond to it appropriately, and so forth. You might wonder about whether this being really does have the power to fulfill the conditions of the conditional promise, or whether this being is really trustworthy. But my thought is not to offer a decisive account of this case. It is to note that there are clearly very strong reasons to place yourself under the authority of even this morally imperfect person, even if there are some reasons to the contrary. But these reasons to the contrary are not those that would be exhibited in an analogous scenario when the party making the promise is the Anselmian being. An Anselmian being is not our equal, is not a failure by not acting in accordance with familiar welfare-oriented moral goodness, has the power to bring about the good promised, and is indeed worthy of complete trust with respect to the fulfillment of promises. So the third model is: the Anselmian being's ethics might involve conditionally willing with respect to every created agent: *for each created agent who (freely) subordinates its will to my own, that created agent's ultimate good—that is, the created agent's well-being in his or her life as a whole—will be better realized for him or her.*[2] And this will might be knowable by all, such that each person knows that every person knows that this is what the Anselmian being wills.

One might think that this model is one in which the commitment to fulfill the created agent's good on the whole entails the motivations of familiar welfare-oriented moral goodness. But I say that such a conditional will does not guarantee that the Anselmian being who has this contingent ethics will be motivated to prevent each setback to human well-being, and in two ways. First, more straightforwardly, it does not guarantee that the Anselmian being will see to it that *every* human's ultimate good will be realized; what is treated as a consideration in favor of divine action is not each person's ultimate good, but each person who subordinates his or her will to the divine will. And second, it does not guarantee that the Anselmian being is at all motivated to prevent particular evils within persons' lives, even those who have subordinated

[2] Here is the test I have in mind for assessing the betterness of an agent's well-being in his or her life as a whole: if, from a merely self-interested perspective, an agent should prefer one complete possible life-history to another possible complete life-history, then the more preferred possible-life history better realizes the agent's well-being in his or her life as a whole than the less-preferred. This test is compatible with a number of different views on what makes for well-being and its assessment.

themselves to the divine will. The only commitment made in this case is to the subject's *life being better on the whole*; this does not involve a commitment to the prevention of any particular evils or the bringing about of any particular goods in the subject's life. (This point is discussed in further detail in 9.3.)

I have offered multiple models of how a contingent ethics taken on by the Anselmian being might be sufficient to meet the conditions by which the Anselmian being is fully worthy of allegiance yet not sufficient to guarantee that the Anselmian being would be motivated to prevent evils in the mode of familiar welfare-oriented moral goodness. It is thus unclear why we would think that the problem of evil arises again for God, even where God is understood not simply as a being absolutely perfect but also as a being fully worthy of allegiance. If the evils of this world make trouble for the existence of God, it must be that one or another thesis from Chapter 8 is false, because the account of the contingent allegiance-worthiness of the Anselmian being offered there does nothing to revive the argument from evil.

9.3 Christian Theism and the Argument from Evil

Even if the argument in 9.2 is correct—even if this world's evils do not call into question the existence of an absolutely perfect being who is fully allegiance-worthy—one might nevertheless claim that this is not the true target of the argument from evil. The argument from evil is best framed, it might be claimed, against the existence of an absolutely perfect being who is fully worthy of allegiance, *given a certain understanding of what that full allegiance-worthiness amounts to.* Fine, one might say, suppose that there is no particular tension between the existence of an absolutely perfect being fully worthy of our allegiance and the existence of the evils of this world. But what is presented in the actual monotheistic traditions is not God in this generic sense, as if what the Torah, or the Old and New Testaments, or the Koran offers is just a God who has *some* ethics such that that God is worthy of full allegiance. Rather, what we are presented with is a God with a *very specific* ethics. We are presented with some aspects of this ethics from revelation, and by knowing these aspects of God's ethics we can see why this ethics satisfies the conditions for being fully worthy of our allegiance. And this very specific ethics is enough, the critic might claim, to raise the problem of evil against the standard Abrahamic monotheisms, or against one of these monotheisms in particular.

One might, then, put this argument from evil in the following way. We can concede, at least for the sake of argument, that there is no good argument from evil against the existence of an absolutely perfect being who is fully worthy of allegiance. But the context in which the argument from evil has been, for the most part, developed and wielded is that in which it is the existence of the God of Abrahamic theism that is at issue. The God of Abrahamic theism is a being whose ethics is given to us in putative revelation, but the ethics given to us in this putative revelation entails that God is motivated to prevent setbacks to human well-being, unless there are reasons to the contrary.

Again, the argument can be framed as a dilemma. The evil of this world gives evidence that there is no God or God is not the God of Abrahamic theism. The idea is that as the God the existence of which is 'live' for the audience to whom the argument from evil is addressed is that of Abrahamic theism, this argument should be sufficient to make a good deal of trouble for the prospects of theism.

I am going to focus on Christian theism, and as I also noted above (9.1), I cannot hope to convince Christians generally that the ethics that I am going to ascribe to the Christian God is compatible with authoritative Christian teaching. There is disagreement among Christians about what the authoritative sources of such teaching are, and about their authoritative interpretation. So my claims are more limited. I will now simply describe one view, thinly set out, of God's ethics and its content, a view that I take to be consistent with affirmation of the existence of the Christian God.

I take it that it is consistent with ecumenical Christianity to hold that God is not necessitated by the prospect of any creaturely good to promote that creaturely good. This lack of necessitation is manifested most plainly in creation's being a matter of divine discretionary choice. Matters are not altered when we assume the existence of the creatures and ask whether there is some level of well-being that God must provide for them in the absence of considerations to the contrary. For there is no further agent-neutral goodness brought into the world by creating rather than not nor by seeing to it that creaturely well-being/perfection is realized to a further level rather than to a lesser. God undoubtedly has reasons for creating, and creating in a certain way, but these are justifying rather than requiring. Whatever the ends, ultimate or subordinate, to which God's creation is directed, God creates perfectly. But it is God who sets the ends of creation, by discretion, from the vast range of options given by the justifying reasons to create.

This, so far, tells us something about the possibilities for divine action. What we may add to the story is that in setting the range of ends to be furthered by creating and ordering that creation, God chooses, contingently, to act in a way that is fully justified but entirely discretionary: to include as part of God's plan for creation, antecedently intended, that rational creatures act in a certain way that fits into the plan of the unfolding of that created world, and that rational creatures' goods be realized in a certain way that fits into that plan. In particular—and, again, I emphasize that these are matters of divine discretion: (1) What God wills for us to do may well include actions that go beyond what the natural norms of practical reasonableness would require of us in the absence of further divine particular intentions for us. Indeed, they may involve furthering ends that we do not recognize, maybe even could not recognize, as ends that we could pursue, or pursue in that particular way, without some sort of practical error, in the absence of our acting in conformity with the divine will. Nevertheless, the divine will for us comes with an assurance—the divine assurance that if one seeks to do the divine will, if one subordinates oneself to the divine plan for one, then all will be well for one. (2) What God intends for us to do in part includes acting in accordance with what the norms of practical reasonableness require of us. That we act in accordance with the norms of practical reasonableness is a creaturely good, and thus something that God has justifying reasons to intend, but need not intend; in some worlds the Anselmian being might fail to intend that we act contrary to those norms without intending that we act in accordance with them. But God does intend that we act in accordance with them. We need not settle why. It could be just that God takes among God's plans to be that rational creatures act well. It could also be that the way in which God aims to see to it that all will be well involves a personal relationship with God, and a personal relationship between God and a rational creature is made possible, or made better, through the rational creature's being a morally good rational creature.

The contingent ethics that I am ascribing to the Christian God thus involves God's willing our acting in accordance with the norms of practical reasonableness that apply to us and willing that, should we subordinate our wills to the divine will for our action, then all will be well for us. Like any ethic, this commits God to further willings. God's willing our acting in accordance with the norms of practical reasonableness entails God's willing that we have adequate understanding of these norms, at least in the standard case, helping us to carry out action in accordance with those norms, and so forth. (Recall, these will be antecedent intentions of God's, and thus God may fail to will in particular cases someone's understanding the natural law or receiving divine assistance on some occasion given the presence of certain circumstances.) God's willing that all will be well for those who subordinate themselves to the divine will commits God to carrying through with this intention, to making all well for those who subordinate their practical lives to the divine will.

I think that this is the primary message of the expressions of divine will and the expressions of divine commitment through promise, covenant, and command that are found in authoritative Christian Scripture. The primary message is not that God is a being who is bound by the norms of familiar welfare-oriented moral goodness, and thus will make sure to honor those norms by acting for the sake of our well-being in the appropriate ways. The primary message is that God has made covenants with us, and that God is faithful to those covenants.[3] What these covenants make clear, on our side, is that God has an interest in our acting well, manifested both in God's reaffirming moral truths through the direction of divine positive law and in Scripture's affirming that God has made knowable through natural processes, or general revelation, what those norms are. It is also expressed in the calls for repentance, for turning back to the proper path of upright conduct, and treating one's past corrupt life as something to

[3] Note: I am neither endorsing nor rejecting an account of the notion of covenant as the central concept through which our understanding of Scripture should be mediated. This view, associated with 'covenant theology,' is much stronger than what I am claiming here, which is not an interpretive thesis but a first-order claim about the source of the norms of divine action with respect to us.

be deplored and for which forgiveness should be sought and atonement done. But there is no suggestion that what God might will for one is going to be restricted to the recapitulation of this moral law. Rather, it may well go beyond it, in ways that are either temporarily or permanently—in this life, anyway—beyond our ken. But coupled with God's willing for us our adherence to the moral law and action that may go beyond that moral law in strange and incomprehensible ways, there is an assurance given. It is an assurance given both in God's declarations of God's own purposes—and since God would never lie, these can be wholly trusted—and in God's promises—and since God would never break faith, these can be wholly trusted as well.[4]

I claim that God never gives us an assurance the upshot of which is a commitment to follow something like a familiar welfare-oriented moral goodness with respect to us, where God treats each earthly setback to a human's well-being as something that God will prevent unless God has good reasons to the contrary. The thought is that what God gives is assurances of great goods—some very particular (that this battle will be won, that this land will be gained), some very general (that all will be well for you)—that structure and give content to a particular contingent divine ethics.

The Old Testament assurances are to the Jewish people, for important goods that are beyond what they could hope to achieve through their own efforts, but more basically, an assurance that they will be His people—that he will see to it that, should they remain faithful, then they will ultimately flourish as a people. The New Testament assurance is more widely extended, to all people, and it is expressed in the assurance that those who will recognize Christ as Messiah—who acknowledge and subordinate themselves to Him—will have life, and have it abundantly. Thus, the model of divine ethics that I am ascribing to the God of Christian Scriptures is that of the third model set out in 9.2, in which one's fuller achievement of one's good is conditional on one's subordinating one's own will to the divine will.

There are conflicts for Christians to have over the adequacy of this view of the fundamental image of God's relationship to humanity. (I will say something about a potential rival fundamental image, one that I have discussed already at numerous points in the text—that of God's being loving, in a very specific way—in 9.4.) But I want not to enter into those further disputes here. I want rather to consider two objections to this account: one that claims that this account does yield the conclusion that divine action is governed by a familiar welfare-oriented ethics, and one that claims that any account that avoids the conclusion that God is bound by the familiar welfare-oriented ethics will thereby fall into an objectionable 'pie in the sky when you die' response to the problem of evil.

Here is the first objection. The assurance that the Christian God gives, I have claimed, is that all will be well (Julian of Norwich, *Showings*, chs. 13–16; see also M. Adams 2011)—that if one surrenders oneself to the divine will, then one's life will

[4] For a Christian theist's response to the problem of evil that focuses on God's promises to humans rather than God's alleged moral goodness, see Geach 1977.

go well for one. But at least *one* way, the objection goes, for one's life to go well for one is for the particular goods that might go unrealized were God to act otherwise to be realized through God acting for the sake of them and for the particular evils that might be realized were God to act otherwise to go unrealized through God's acting in order to prevent them. So God *does* have requiring reason to promote all aspects of a faithful creature's good and to prevent setbacks to that good: for God has decisive requiring reason to keep God's commitment to see to it that a faithful creature has a richly good life, and one way to do so is to act in a welfare-oriented way with respect to each faithful creature. So, at least where the faithful are concerned, we should expect that some more standard theodicy or defense would be available.

I deny that this is a good argument from God's commitment to good lives for the faithful to God's being bound by something like a familiar welfare-oriented ethics, even with respect to those who have subordinated themselves to the divine will. I am committed to the view that God takes on a requiring reason, even a decisive one, to see to it that the lives of those who subordinate themselves to the divine will will go well for them overall. And I do not deny that one way that one's life could go well for one could include one's earthly life going smoothly, without the dramatic setbacks to well-being with which humans are all-too-familiar. But I reject the validity of the argument. The argument form upon which the objection relies is: there is a requiring reason to bring about A; bringing about B is one way to bring about A; therefore, there is requiring reason to bring about B. This argument accepts the correctness of the following reason-transfer principle:[5]

> *Instantiation.* If Xing is *a way of* Ying, and one has a requiring reason to Y, then one has a requiring reason to X.

I think Instantiation is an incorrect principle. When one has a requiring reason to do something, then one is rationally required to do it in the absence of considerations to the contrary. But the fact that some action is simply one way of doing what one has requiring reason to do is not sufficient to make it true that, in the absence of considerations to the contrary, one is rationally required to perform that action. What is rationally required is (in the absence of considerations to the contrary) to take one of the ways to accomplish what one has reason to accomplish; it is not rationally required to take any particular one of those ways.

Here is another basis for rejecting Instantiation. Consider two much more obviously correct principles governing the ascription of reasons. The first is another reason-transfer principle:

> *Necessary Means.* If Xing is a *necessary means to* Ying, and one has a requiring reason to Y, then one has a requiring reason to X.

[5] By 'reason-transfer principle' I mean a principle that holds of two distinct act-types that if there is a reason to perform an act of one type, then there is a reason to perform an act of the other type.

The other is a constraint on the correctness of reason-transfer principles:

> *Relevance.* From the positing of a reason to perform some action and the application of correct reason-transfer principles, one should not be able to derive the existence of a reason that obviously has *nothing* to do with the original posited reason.

Of course one will need wisdom to apply this Relevance constraint and to wield it against alleged reason-transfer principles. But such is philosophy. And I will not appeal to an application of the constraint that should be very controversial.

The argument is that Instantiation and Necessary Means together yield implications that Relevance condemns.[6] Assume Instantiation and Necessary Means. Now, I have a reason to help anyone who is severely injured.[7] But I could help someone either silently, or while talking to myself, or while singing show tunes. So *helping a severely injured person while singing show tunes* is a way of *helping a severely injured person*. By Instantiation, then, I have a reason to help, while singing show tunes, anyone who is severely injured. But I know no show tunes, and will have to learn some if I am to perform this action. So by Necessary Means I have a reason to learn show tunes. But this is foolishness. My learning show tunes has nothing to do with the helping of severely injured people, and so Relevance condemns the reason-transfer principles that generated this implication. It is pretty obvious that the irrelevance gets introduced by Instantiation. So the culprit is Instantiation.

Any intuitive notion of 'a way of doing something' will allow the possibility that something that has nothing to do with the posited reason is included as a component of an action one has reason to do. That does not make Instantiation all by itself have trouble with Relevance, because so long as it is a way of acting on the posited reason, it will obviously satisfy Relevance, even if the action has some features that are of themselves irrelevant to the posited reason. But an action can fulfill Necessary Means just by doing something that is necessary for some, *any*, component of an action to be carried out. Thus, a reason can be generated by focusing on the bit of the action, a reason to perform which is entailed by Instantiation, that is nevertheless irrelevant to the posited reason. So a reason to help while singing show tunes, implied by Instantiation, satisfies Relevance because it is a helping, even though it has an irrelevant bit, the show-tune-singing. But Necessary Means implies that an action that is a necessary means to carrying out only the irrelevant bit is something that I have reason to do. And that ensures that Instantiation and Necessary Means will violate Relevance.

Now, one might say that even if the argument as formulated relies on a false reason-transfer principle, the basic idea of the argument has not been addressed. Perhaps we need to accept some sort of relevance-limited Instantiation principle to make the argument—say, one has reason to X if one has reason to Y and Y-ing is a relevant way of X-ing, where *relevance* is defined in a way to avoid the unfortunate implications that

[6] This is a further-elaborated version of an argument I sketched in Murphy 2011a, p. 54.

[7] If you think this reason needs qualification, do whatever qualifying you think matters.

the unrestricted Instantiation principle has. We could get to work on giving the definition of relevance, or just affirm that relevance must be satisfied in the case of the relationship between *God's seeing to the realization of some rational creature's complete good* and *God's preventing some setback to that rational creature's well-being*. But I don't think we can make this move. However we define 'relevance,' with respect to promoting ends by action, the relevance relation surely must somehow involve improving likelihoods, making it more likely that the end in question will be brought about (Schroeder 2007a, p. 113). But the application of this sort of relevance criterion is massively complicated when the party who has the reasons in question is absolutely perfect, all-powerful, all-knowing. Is it true that God's failing to prevent some significant setback in my life makes it any less likely that my good on the whole will be achieved?[8] Only if God is not set on my good on the whole being achieved. This cannot count as evidence against the existence of a God who is set on my good on the whole being achieved.

This reply provides ammunition to those who would press an alternative worry. It is as suspected; what is being offered here is *pie in the sky when you die*. We know that the divine promise to the faithful is not realized in this life, at least in many cases. So what this view has to appeal to is the life to come, an extended life either post-bodily or post-resurrection, in which the divine promise will be fulfilled. But this is the classic 'pie in the sky when you die' account. We should not be willing to think, the objector presses, that God's having us undergo all sorts of awfulness in this life can be adequately compensated by a wondrous postmortem existence. Dougherty remarks that theodicies that appeal to such greater goods involve the unsavory image of God "buying off" creatures who have been subjected to suffering for no further point (Dougherty 2014, p. 98).[9]

My response to this objection is to be unembarrassed by what I am supposed to be embarrassed by. I concede that there is a way of understanding the 'pie in the sky' objection that would make perfect sense out of it as an objection. I concede, that is, that there is something untoward about holding that God could compensate us for God's failures to bring about adequate promotion of our well-being or adequate protection to setbacks to it by providing some heavenly good. As Dougherty remarks, it is not okay for a rich person to come into my house and break my arms, even if this rich person is known to be reliable about compensating people for the mayhem that he does to them. For the typical scenario in which compensation is called for is this: One party has some

[8] In M. Adams 1999, Marilyn McCord Adams considers *horrendous* evils, which she defines as those evils which give prima facie reason to believe that one's life could not be a great good to one on the whole. Is it true that the presence of these evils in one's life makes it less likely that one's life will be on the whole a great good for one? Only if there is no life after death or no God who aims to make it true that in spite of these horrors, one's life will turn out well for one. This is the thrust of Adams's argument: that there are goods available within the world theistically conceived that can make it true that even a life containing horrendous evils is good for the person who lives it. The most salient of such goods are those to be realized in the life to come.

[9] When Dougherty tries to make this criticism of greater good accounts rigorous, he appeals to God's being perfectly morally good and a certain understanding of God's being perfectly loving (Dougherty 2014, p. 98)—conceptions of divine agency that I rejected in Part I.

sort of duty of care with respect to some other party; there is a failure in the fulfillment of that duty of care, and as a result that other party is made worse off; it is then incumbent on the duty-holder to try to make things right, to make the injured party whole. The idea is to make matters as if, at least with respect to the failure to take care, the wrong had not occurred (Murphy 2006b, pp. 170–1). But compensation is a second-best scenario; we are not to think of violation-of-the-duty-of-care-plus-compensation as equivalent to honoring the duty of care. So intentionally breaking someone's arm, even with the easily realizable intention to offer compensation for it later, is not an acceptable alternative, at the point of choice, to not breaking that person's arm.

But note that this model does not apply here. When I speak of God's promise to the faithful that all will be well for them, and that this promise might well be fulfilled in the life to come, I do not at all suggest that the fulfillment of this promise is *compensation* for our earthly troubles. *God does not owe us any compensation for our earthly troubles, for God has no duties of care with respect to us.* That is part of the point of Part I. So if the absurdity of the view that I am offering is based on the absurdity of God's compensating us by pie in the sky, my reply is that the absurdity is not in the pie in the sky but in the notion that what God is doing in serving our good in this way is compensation for earlier divine failures, or even what would, in the absence of such compensation, count as divine failures. There have been no such failures.

Is there, then, *any* force to the pie-in-the-sky objection? It is, I think, to be found in the idea that the Christian God is not *really* loving in the way that Christian sources testify that God is loving if God is motivated only to secure our good on the whole—which might be realized by assuring a sort of life postmortem—rather than through being motivated to realize the particular goods to be found in our antemortem existence. Even if God's love is not a maximal notion, the Christian God is supposed to love us, and God does not really love us unless God is motivated to prevent setbacks to our earthly goods in the absence of considerations to the contrary. I take up this objection in the final section.

9.4 Is This Book a Rearguard Action against the Argument from Evil?

When an army must retreat, it is sometimes worthwhile for some of the soldiers to fight at the back, to prevent the retreating army from being overwhelmed and scattered. This is a 'rearguard' action. A success in a rearguard action is not a victory in battle, but a prevention, at least for a time, of obvious and final defeat.

It is often suspected that those writers who are themselves theists and who are responding to the argument from evil are fighting a rearguard action. The idea is even if particular responses to the argument from evil have had some success, they have been successful only in the manner of rearguard actions. We can see that responses to the problem of evil have required theists to modify their views on God's power, or on

God's knowledge, and in ways that seem unflattering to the absolute perfection of the divine being. We can see that responses to the problem of evil have led theists to take on ad-hoc hypotheses, which theists would never have taken seriously were it not for the threat posed by the argument from evil.

It might, then, be further suspected that my views on God's moral goodness and God's lovingness constitute part of this rearguard response to the argument from evil. By my own admission, contemporary philosophers responding to the argument from evil overwhelmingly commit themselves to God's being morally perfect and maximally loving. When one departs from this sort of consensus and attempts to make use of this departure to answer a forceful objection, it may look very much as if one is making an ad-hoc emendation to a view in order to rescue it from a serious difficulty. And so I may appear to be simply fighting a rearguard action.

I do not want to give too much credit to this objection. Sometimes theses that are marked as ad-hoc dodges to deal with an objection are in fact important truths, even entailments of a view, that are brought out only by the pressure that considering objections from all comers can generate. (I think this is true of skeptical theism, which in its main lines—forget for a moment whether it is a good response to the problem of evil—is a rather obvious implication of truths about the divine nature together with some relatively uncontroversial claims about the sorts of goodness that might be relevant to divine action.) And I could defend my view, in part, along these lines. But I think even this would be too much of a concession. The conception of God as morally perfect in the sense of being governed by familiar welfare-oriented moral goodness and being maximally loving of creatures, even if popular among Christian philosophers who have been at the center of the discussion of the problem of evil, is not one that is required or even suggested by canonical Christian sources. And it was denied by prominent Christian philosophers, especially those in the medieval period (see, for example, Davies's (2011) discussion of Aquinas's views, or Adams' discussion of Scotus's (M. Adams 1987)). So it seems to me that what I am doing is not some sort of dodgily inventive recasting of what God's perfect agency consists in; rather, I am indicating that the argument from evil as typically posed assumes a contentious and theologically no-more-than-optional characterization of the divine nature.

Here is the second part of my response. It is not merely that this is not an ad-hoc emendation of our characterization of the divine nature; it is that the characterization of God's ethics advocated here has been defended in terms of what is necessary to satisfy the requirements of absolute perfection. This is not a chopping down of the divine perfection in order to meet what are allegedly independent limits on what God's greatness could consist in.[10] The point is to see what sort of ethics we should ascribe to God in order to *magnify* that greatness.

[10] Compare to Plantinga's denial that an omnipotent being can even weakly actualize any logically possible state of affairs (1974, pp. 180–4), or van Inwagen's denial that an omniscient being knows propositions regarding future creaturely free action (2006, pp. 80–3). Regardless of whether these are true and defensible, they look like attempts to rein in what these authors take to be overly extravagant claims about divine

So I am unimpressed by the 'rearguard' action objection to responses to the problem of evil generally, and I am especially unimpressed in the case of my own view, which I have defended entirely independently of its virtues as the basis for a response to the argument from evil. The argument for an account of the Anselmian being's ethics has proceeded largely from considerations of the demands of perfect being theology on the ascription of perfections to the Anselmian being. I want to conclude, though, with one further comment about a thesis about God that my view accommodates, which I think is poorly accommodated by other views of God's ethics.

The thesis is *God loves us, though God did not have to*. Here is how my view accommodates this thesis. God does indeed love us. God cares about our well-being, in the following way: God invites all human beings into a cooperative relationship with God, and ensures that those who accept this invitation will have lives that are good beyond all telling, and our lives being good beyond our telling involves our coming to be in a particularly intimate sort of relationship with God. It is clear from this that God invites us into a relationship of unity with God and also wills our good on the whole, and indeed our good on the whole, on this view, is constituted by the good of this sort of intimate union with God. It is also quite clear the sense I would give to *though God did not have to*. God does not necessarily create; even if God creates, God need not create us or beings like us; even if God creates us, God need not provide for us any particular level of perfection or well-being. God's not having to love us is simply its being contingent that God loves us: though God does in fact aim for our good and for unity between us and God, there is a possible world in which the Anselmian being creates humans but does not love them.

But how would these views I oppose, these standard views on which the Anselmian being is necessarily motivated by the prospects of our well-being/perfection, offer a gloss on *God loves us, though God does not have to*? It is clear about the first part of the conjunction; God loves us, and the sense in which God loves us is at least that in which God is motivated by each of the opportunities to promote our well-being/perfection. But how the second part is to be glossed on this view is less apparent. In what sense is it true that God does not have to love us?

What is plain is that, whatever gloss is offered, it has to be one that makes it possible to say that God does not have to love us even though God *necessarily* does just that. There are, though, possibilities for maneuver. One might say, as some recent writers have, that the way that we distinguish obligation from practical necessity, or even moral necessity, is that when one is under obligation, there is not just moral necessity, but the presence of some party who has the standing to enforce, demand, or otherwise hold one to compliance (see, for example, R. Adams 1999, pp. 233–48; Darwall 2006, pp. 11–15). And we often do use the language of 'have to' to indicate the presence of obligation. So perhaps they might offer the following gloss: even if it is true that God is

perfection. My theses, by contrast, aim to be an enlargement, a making more extravagant, of what we should say about the divine nature, in particular, divine sovereignty.

under a moral necessity to love us, we nevertheless lack standing to enforce, demand, or otherwise hold God to compliance. The point is not just that we lack the power to get God into line. The standing to hold another to compliance need not be contingent on having sufficient power to be effective at changing behavior; I have standing to tell off a bully who has the power to beat up my middle-aged self and who would be impervious to my demands to leave me alone.

I have two objections to this gloss. First: While I do find plausible the notion that we make this distinction between what is obligatory and what is simply morally necessary, and that the distinction turns on whether others have standing to hold one to compliance, I do not see why those who would offer this gloss are entitled to the claim that we would thereby lack standing to hold God to compliance. I mean: the background view is one in which we not only know that our value is such that we should treat each other a certain way; it is also such that we know God must treat us in these ways as well. It is not clear why, given such a background view, we would not have standing to complain were God to fail with respect to God's requirements with respect to us. Of course, God is not going to fail. But having standing to hold another to compliance is not explained simply in terms of the *need* of such holdings to keep each other in line; it is about our *status* as being equally subject to an equal moral law. And that is just the background view assumed here, one on which we and God are both subject to a common set of moral norms that directs both God and us to treat our welfare/perfection as reasons for action.

Second, the fact that such motivation is not a matter of obligation on God's part would not be sufficient, in my view, to disarm the objection. The force of the point that God does not have to love us is that there is nothing about us and our value that would make it necessary for God to promote our good in the relevant ways. Put to the side what I can hold God to; it simply seems false that I am the sort of being the value of which could make it necessary for God to respond to me and my good in these ways. The notion that it is amazing that God would take such a positive interest in beings that are as relatively trivial as we are is a central idea in these theistic traditions, and that we lack status to hold God to a requirement to treat us in these ways seems insufficient to respect that idea.

Perhaps this second objection points the way to a second gloss. Another possible gloss is that the relevant contrast is between two ways of thinking of the *source* of this divine necessitation: even though God necessarily loves us, the necessity has its source in God and not in anything about us. I find puzzling how the source of the necessity makes a difference to whether it is true that God has to love us. But one might just say that to 'have to' do something suggests that one is being *made* to do it, and to be made to do something requires that there be some distinct cause that is making one do it. Now, no one in this debate is claiming that anything distinct from God *efficiently* causes God to do anything. The idea is, rather, that we do not appeal to creaturely goods as final causes that necessitate God into promoting them. On this view, even though God necessarily is motivated by the goods of us rational creatures, so that necessarily they are final causes of divine action, the explanation of their being final causes of divine action is not to be found in the goodness of those creatures but in the divine nature.

But how God is motivated with respect to creatures, on this view, is supposed to be a divine perfection. It is a divine perfection because God is *acting well* with respect to creatures. But if there is nothing in the creature that accounts for why God is acting well with respect to the creature by promoting that creature's good—and would fail to be acting well by not being motivated to promote that creature's good—then it is unclear why acting in these ways with respect to these creatures constitutes a divine perfection. If there were something about the value of the creature that called for a response by all beings capable of grasping and acting on that value, then it would indeed be explicable. But the point of this gloss is just to deny that there is any value in the creature that makes it necessary for God to promote that creature's good in order for God to be acting well. So I do not think that this gloss succeeds either.

I do not know other plausible glosses for the view that God loves us, though God does not have to. I have no impossibility proof that every more standard account of God's ethics cannot accommodate this thought adequately. But I do put it forward as a mark in favor of my view that it can clearly and easily accommodate it.

Without offering an alternative gloss, one might claim that we are all equally in the dark about how to accommodate this idea, because however well my view handles the idea that God's love for us is no more than contingent, it does not handle the claim that God loves us. "Even if the standard view does not make much sense of the idea that God doesn't have to love us," the objector might say, "it at least makes sense of the more important part of the conjunction: that God loves us. On our view, God's love includes God's taking each aspect of our well-being to be a good worth promoting, to be something that God will promote unless God is dealing with considerations to the contrary, to be something setbacks to which God will prevent unless God is dealing with considerations to the contrary. But the view defended in this book does not make sense of the idea that God loves us in this sense. On this view, God could fail to prevent setbacks to our well-being, without having any reason to. And that is a view of God's stance with respect to us that is incompatible with God's loving us."

Well, I allow that it is incompatible with God's loving us a certain way. But not all loves take the same form, as Stump (2010, pp. 97–100) and Pruss (2012a, pp. 44–6) have emphasized in recent work. There is the love of parents for children, of spouses for each other, of pet owners for their pets, and so forth. Even if each of these loves involves willing good to another and willing unity with that other, they treat different sorts of unity as appropriate and different aspects of the others' good as relevant to that love. So we might ask: What is the appropriate form of *divine* love for rational creatures? And my answer is plain from the foregoing: the appropriate form of divine love is largely a matter of divine discretion; God settles by God's free choice, by divine will and commitment, what the standards of divine love are to be. It seems absurd to claim that there is no love at all in the stance toward us that I ascribe to God. God invites us to cooperate with God in the unfolding of creation and to thereby enjoy eternal communion with God. This is an invitation toward unity and an assurance of the ultimate good of all those who accept that invitation, freely given, gratuitously bestowed. God deserves no *praise* for that special offer, for that would be as if to commend God for getting our value right by offering us a chance to be cooperators with God in this life and in union with God forever in the next. But we should indeed *thank* God for this generosity. For though there is nothing about us humans such that God must keep us in mind, nevertheless God has enabled us to be little less than angels.

Works Cited

Any dates in brackets refer to year of original composition or publication. Citations in my text are by author and date, except in the case of classic texts, which I cite by abbreviated title.

Adams, Marilyn McCord. 1987. "Duns Scotus on the Goodness of God." *Faith and Philosophy* 4, pp. 486–505.

Adams, Marilyn McCord. 1999. *Horrendous Evils and the Goodness of God*. Cornell University Press.

Adams, Marilyn McCord. 2011. "Julian of Norwich: Problems of Evil and the Seriousness of Sin." *Philosophia* 39, pp. 433–47.

Adams, Marilyn McCord. 2014. "What's Wrong with the Ontotheological Error?" *Journal of Analytic Theology* 2 (http://journalofanalytictheology.com/jat/index.php/jat/article/view/jat.2014-1.120013000318a/222).

Adams, Marilyn McCord and Robert Merrihew Adams, eds. 1990. *The Problem of Evil*. Oxford University Press.

Adams, Robert Merrihew. 1999. *Finite and Infinite Goods: A Framework for Ethics*. Oxford University Press.

Adams, Robert Merrihew. 2006. *A Theory of Virtue: Excellence in Being for the Good*. Oxford University Press.

Almeida, Michael J. and Graham Oppy. 2003. "Sceptical Theism and Evidential Arguments from Evil." *Australasian Journal of Philosophy* 81, pp. 496–516.

Altham, J. E. J. and Ross Harrison, eds. 1995. *World, Mind, and Ethics: Essays on the Ethical Philosophy of Bernard Williams*. Cambridge University Press.

Anderson, Elizabeth. 1995. *Value in Ethics and Economics*. Harvard University Press.

Anscombe, G. E. M. 1957. *Intention*. Blackwell.

Anselm. 1996 [*c.*1075–1076 and 1077–1078, respectively]. *Monologion and Proslogion*. Ed. and trans. Thomas Williams. Hackett.

Aquinas, Thomas. 1975 [*c.*1261–1264]. *Summa Contra Gentiles*. Trans. Anton Pegis. University of Notre Dame Press.

Aquinas, Thomas. 1981 [*c.*1265–1274]. *Summa Theologiae*. Trans. Fathers of the English Dominican Province. Christian Classics.

Aquinas, Thomas. 2001 [*c.*1270–1275]. The De Malo *of Thomas Aquinas*. Trans. Richard Regan. Oxford University Press.

Aristotle. 1999 [*c.*350–340 BC]. *Nicomachean Ethics*. Trans. Terence Irwin. Hackett.

Audi, Robert and William Wainwright, eds. 1986. *Rationality, Religious Belief, and Commitment*. Cornell University Press.

Aulisio, Mark P. 1995. "In Defense of the Intention / Foresight Distinction." *American Philosophical Quarterly* 32, pp. 341–54.

Bayne, Timothy and Yujin Nagasawa. 2006. "The Grounds of Worship." *Religious Studies* 42, pp. 299–313.

Bergmann, Michael. 2009. "Skeptical Theism and the Problem of Evil." In Flint and Rea 2009, pp. 374–99.

Bergmann, Michael and Patrick Kain, eds. 2014. *Challenges to Religious and Moral Belief.* Oxford University Press.

Bergmann, Michael, Michael J. Murray, and Michael C. Rea, eds. 2011. *Divine Evil? The Moral Character of the God of Abraham.* Oxford University Press.

Boyle, Joseph. 1998. "The Place of Religion in the Practical Reasoning of Individuals and Groups." *American Journal of Jurisprudence* 43, pp. 1–24.

Boyle, Joseph and Thomas Sullivan. 1977. "The Diffusiveness of Intention Principle: A Counter-Example." *Philosophical Studies* 31, pp. 357–60.

Caussade, Jean-Pierre de. 1975. *Abandonment to Divine Providence.* Trans. John Beevers. Doubleday.

Chalmers, David, David Manley, and Ryan Wasserman. 2009. *Metametaphysics.* Oxford University Press.

Chisholm, Roderick. 1970. "The Structure of Intention." *Journal of Philosophy* 67, pp. 633–47.

Dancy, Jonathan. 2004. *Ethics Without Principles.* Oxford University Press.

Darwall, Stephen L. 2006. *The Second-Person Standpoint: Morality, Respect, and Accountability.* Harvard University Press.

Darwall, Stephen L. 2010. "Authority and Reasons: Exclusionary and Second-Personal." *Ethics* 120, pp. 257–78.

Davies, Brian. 2011. *Thomas Aquinas on God and Evil.* Oxford University Press.

Davison, Scott. 2011. *On the Intrinsic Value of Everything.* Continuum.

DeGrazia, David. 2012. *Creation Ethics: Reproduction, Genetics, and Quality of Life.* Oxford University Press.

DeRose, Keith. 1991. "Plantinga, Presumption, Possibility, and the Problem of Evil." *Canadian Journal of Philosophy* 21, pp. 497–512.

Diller, Jeanine. 1999. "A Proposal to Change the Tradition of Perfect Being Theology." *Southwest Philosophy Review* 15, pp. 233–40.

Donagan, Alan. 1980. *The Theory of Morality.* University of Chicago Press.

Dougherty, Trent. 2014. *The Problem of Animal Pain: A Theodicy for All Creatures Great and Small.* Palgrave.

Draper, Paul. 1996 [1989]. "Pain and Pleasure: An Evidential Problem for Theists." In Howard-Snyder 1996a, pp. 12–29.

Draper, Paul. 2009. "The Problem of Evil." In Flint and Rea 2009, pp. 332–51.

Draper, Paul. 2013. "Explanation and the Problem of Evil." In McBrayer and Howard-Snyder 2013, pp. 71–87.

Duns Scotus, John. 1962. *Philosophical Writings.* Trans. Allan Wolter. Nelson.

Ehrenberg, Kenneth. 2011. "Critical Reception of Raz's Theory of Authority." *Philosophy Compass* 6, pp. 777–85.

Enoch, David. 2011. "On Mark Schroeder's Hypotheticalism: A Critical Notice of *Slaves of the Passions.*" *Philosophical Review* 120, pp. 423–46.

Finnis, John. 1980. *Natural Law and Natural Rights.* Oxford University Press.

Flint, Thomas and Michael Rea, eds. 2009. *The Oxford Handbook to Philosophical Theology.* Oxford University Press.

Foot, Philippa. 2001. *Natural Goodness.* Oxford University Press.

Freddoso, Alfred. 1986. "The Necessity of Nature." *Midwest Studies in Philosophy* 11, pp. 215–42.

Freddoso, Alfred. 1987. "Medieval Aristotelianism and the Case against Secondary Causation in Nature." In Morris 1987b, pp. 74–118.

Freddoso, Alfred. 1991. "God's General Concurrence with Secondary Causes: Why Conservation is Not Enough." *Philosophical Perspectives* 5, pp. 553–85.

Freddoso, Alfred. 1994. "God's General Concurrence with Secondary Causes: Pitfalls and Prospects." *American Catholic Philosophical Quarterly* 67, pp. 131–56.

Gale, Richard. 1999. "Some Difficulties in Theistic Treatments of Evil." In Howard-Snyder 1996a, pp. 206–18.

Garcia, J. L. A. 1998. "Lies and the Vices of Deception." *Faith and Philosophy* 15, pp. 514–37.

Gauthier, David. 1986. *Morals by Agreement*. Oxford University Press.

Geach, Peter. 1977. *Providence and Evil*. Cambridge University Press.

Gert, Joshua. 2004. *Brute Rationality*. Cambridge University Press.

Gert, Joshua. 2008. "Michael Smith and the Rationality of Immoral Action." *Journal of Ethics* 12, pp. 1–23.

Grisez, Germain. 1983. *The Way of the Lord Jesus, Volume 1: Christian Moral Principles*. Franciscan Herald Press.

Grisez, Germain, John Finnis, and Joseph Boyle. 1987. "Practical Principles, Moral Truth, and Ultimate Ends." *American Journal of Jurisprudence* 32, pp. 99–151.

Guleserian, Ted. 1985. "Can Moral Perfection Be an Essential Attribute?" *Philosophy and Phenomenological Research* 46, pp. 219–41.

Hampton, Jean. 1998. *The Authority of Reason*. Cambridge University Press.

Hartshorne, Charles. 1966. *Anselm's Discovery*. Open Court.

Hill, Thomas E. 1973. "The Hypothetical Imperative." *Philosophical Review* 82, pp. 429–50.

Hittinger, Russell. 1987. *A Critique of the New Natural Law Theory*. University of Notre Dame Press.

Hoffman, Joshua and Gary Rosenkrantz. 2002. *The Divine Attributes*. Blackwell.

Howard-Snyder, Daniel, ed. 1996a. *The Evidential Argument from Evil*. Indiana University Press.

Howard-Snyder, Daniel. 1996b. "Introduction." In Howard-Snyder 1996a, pp. xi–xx.

Howard-Snyder, Daniel and Frances Howard-Snyder. 1994. "How an Unsurpassable Being Can Create a Surpassable World." *Faith and Philosophy* 11, pp. 260–8.

Howard-Snyder, Daniel and John O'Leary-Hawthorne. 1998. "Transworld Sanctity and Plantinga's Free Will Defense." *International Journal for Philosophy of Religion* 44, pp. 1–21.

Hudson, Hud. 2014. "The Father of Lies?" *Oxford Studies in Philosophy of Religion* 5, pp. 147–66.

Jacobs, Jonathan. 2015. "The Ineffable, Inconceivable, and Incomprehensible God: Fundamentality and Apophatic Theology." *Oxford Studies in Philosophy of Religion* 6, pp. 158–76.

Jordan, Jeff. 2006. "Does Skeptical Theism Lead to Moral Skepticism?" *Philosophy and Phenomenological Research* 72, pp. 403–17.

Julian of Norwich. 1978 [1670]. *Showings*. Trans. Edmund Colledge, O.S.A. and James Walsh, S.J. Paulist Press.

Kagan, Shelly. 1989. *The Limits of Morality*. Oxford University Press.

Kamm, F. M. 2007a. *Intricate Ethics: Rights, Responsibilities, and Permissible Harms*. Oxford University Press.

Kamm, F. M. 2007b. "The Doctrines of Double and Triple Effect, and Why a Rational Agent Need Not Intend the Means to His End." In Kamm 2007a, pp. 91–129.

Kolodny, Niko. 2003. "Love as Valuing a Relationship." *Philosophical Review* 112, pp. 135–89.

Korsgaard, Christine. 1983. "Two Distinctions in Goodness." *Philosophical Review* 92, pp. 169–95.

Kraut, Richard. 2007. *What is Good and Why: The Ethics of Well-Being*. Harvard University Press.

Kretzmann, Norman. 1991. "A General Problem of Creation: Why Would God Create Anything at All?" In MacDonald 1991, pp. 208–28.

Langtry, Bruce. 2008. *God, The Best, and Evil*. Oxford University Press.

Leftow, Brian. 2011. "Why Perfect Being Theology?" *International Journal for Philosophy of Religion* 69, pp. 103–18.

Leftow, Brian. 2012. *God and Necessity*. Oxford University Press.

Leibniz, Gottfried Wilhelm. 1996 [1710]. "Essays on the Justice of God and the Freedom of Man." In *Theodicy*, ed. Austin Farrer and trans. E. M. Huggard. Open Court.

McBrayer, Justin. 2010. "Skeptical Theism." *Philosophical Compass* 5/7, pp. 611–23.

McBrayer, Justin and Daniel Howard-Snyder, eds. 2013. *Blackwell Companion to the Problem of Evil*. Blackwell.

McBrayer, Justin and Philip Swenson. 2012. "Scepticism about the Argument from Divine Hiddenness." *Religious Studies* 48, pp. 129–50.

McDaniel, Kris. 2009. "Ways of Being." In Chalmers, Manley, and Wasserman 2009, pp. 290–319.

MacDonald, Scott, ed. 1991. *Being and Goodness*. Cornell University Press.

MacIntyre, Alasdair. 1999. *Dependent Rational Animals: Why Human Beings Need the Virtues*. Open Court.

Mackie, J. L. 1990 [1955]. "Evil and Omnipotence." In Adams and Adams 1990, pp. 25–37.

Maitzen, Stephen. 2009. "Skeptical Theism and Moral Obligation." *International Journal for Philosophy of Religion* 65, pp. 93–103.

Mann, William. 1975. "The Divine Attributes." *American Philosophical Quarterly* 12, pp. 151–9.

Markovits, Julia. 2014. *Moral Reason*. Oxford University Press.

Merricks, Trenton. 2009. "Truth and Freedom." *Philosophical Review* 118, pp. 29–58.

Mill, John Stuart. 1964 [1865]. "Mr. Mansel on the Limits of Religious Thought." In Pike 1964, pp. 37–45.

Milo, Ronald. 1995. "Contractarian Constructivism." *Journal of Philosophy* 92, pp. 181–204.

Morris, Thomas V. 1987a. *Anselmian Explorations*. University of Notre Dame Press.

Morris, Thomas V., ed. 1987b. *Divine and Human Action*. Cornell University Press.

Murphy, Mark C. 1998. "Divine Command, Divine Will, and Moral Obligation." *Faith and Philosophy* 15, pp. 3–27.

Murphy, Mark C. 2000. "Hobbes on the Evil of Death." *Archiv für Geschichte der Philosophie* 82, pp. 36–61.

Murphy, Mark C. 2001. *Natural Law and Practical Rationality*. Cambridge University Press.

Murphy, Mark C. 2002a. *An Essay on Divine Authority*. Cornell University Press.

Murphy, Mark C. 2002b. "The Natural Law Tradition in Ethics." In *Stanford Encyclopedia of Philosophy*, ed. Ed Zalta (http://plato.stanford.edu/entries/natural-law-ethics/).

Murphy, Mark C. 2004. "Intention, Foresight, and Success." In Oderberg and Chappell 2004, pp. 252–68.
Murphy, Mark C. 2005. "Authority." In *Encyclopedia of Philosophy*, 2nd edition, ed. Donald Borchert. Macmillan.
Murphy, Mark C. 2006a. *Natural Law in Jurisprudence and Politics*. Cambridge University Press.
Murphy, Mark C. 2006b. *Philosophy of Law: The Fundamentals*. Wiley-Blackwell.
Murphy, Mark C. 2009. "Morality and Divine Authority." In Flint and Rea 2009, pp. 306–31.
Murphy, Mark C. 2011a. *God and Moral Law: On the Theistic Explanation of Morality*. Oxford University Press.
Murphy, Mark C. 2011b. "God Beyond Justice." In Bergmann, Murray, and Rea 2011, pp. 150–67.
Murphy, Mark C. 2013. "Perfect Goodness." In *Stanford Encyclopedia of Philosophy*, ed. Ed Zalta (http://plato.stanford.edu/entries/perfect-goodness/).
Nagasawa, Yujin. 2008. "A New Defence of Anselmian Theism." *Philosophical Quarterly* 58, pp. 577–96.
Nagel, Thomas. 1970. *The Possibility of Altruism*. Princeton University Press.
Nagel, Thomas. 1986. *The View from Nowhere*. Oxford University Press.
Nussbaum, Martha. 1995. "Aristotle on Human Nature and the Foundations of Ethics." In Altham and Harrison 1995, pp. 86–131.
Nygren, Anders. 1969 [1938]. *Agape and Eros*. Trans. Philip S. Watson. Harper and Row.
Oderberg, David S. and Timothy Chappell, eds. 2004. *Human Values: New Essays on Ethics and Natural Law*. Palgrave Macmillan.
Otto, Rudolf. 1958 [1923]. *The Idea of the Holy*. Trans. John W. Harvey. Oxford University Press.
Parfit, Derek. 1984. *Reasons and Persons*. Oxford University Press.
Pearce, Kenneth and Alexander Pruss. 2012. "Understanding Omnipotence." *Religious Studies* 48, pp. 403–14.
Pike, Nelson, ed. 1964. *God and Evil*. Prentice-Hall.
Pike, Nelson. 1970. *God and Timelessness*. Schocken.
Plantinga, Alvin. 1974. *The Nature of Necessity*. Oxford University Press.
Pruss, Alexander. 2012a. *One Body: An Essay in Christian Sexual Ethics*. University of Notre Dame Press.
Pruss, Alexander R. 2012b. "A Counterexample to Plantinga's Free Will Defense." *Faith and Philosophy* 29, pp. 400–15.
Quinn, Warren. 1993a. *Morality and Action*. Cambridge University Press.
Quinn, Warren. 1993b. "Putting Rationality in its Place." In Quinn 1993a, pp. 228–55.
Rachels, James. 1971. "God and Human Attitudes." *Religious Studies* 7, pp. 325–37.
Rawls, John. 1971. *A Theory of Justice*. Harvard University Press.
Raz, Joseph. 1986. *The Morality of Freedom*. Oxford University Press.
Raz, Joseph. 1990. *Practical Reason and Norms*, revised edition. Oxford University Press.
Raz, Joseph. 1994a. "Authority, Law, and Morality." In Raz 1994b, pp. 194–221.
Raz, Joseph. 1994b. *Ethics in the Public Domain*. Oxford University Press.
Raz, Joseph. 1999 [1975]. *Practical Reason and Norms*. Oxford University Press.
Raz, Joseph. 2006. "The Problem of Authority: Revisiting the Service Conception." *Minnesota Law Review* 90, pp. 1003–44.

Rieder, Travis. 2016. "Why I'm Still a Proportionalist." *Philosophical Studies* 173, pp. 251–70.
Rogers, Katherin. 2000. *Perfect Being Theology*. University of Edinburgh Press.
Rowe, William. 1990 [1979]. "The Problem of Evil and Some Varieties of Atheism." In Adams and Adams 1990, pp. 126–37.
Rowe, William. 1993. "The Problem of Divine Perfection and Freedom." In Stump 1993, pp. 223–33.
Rowe, William. 2005. *Can God Be Free?* Oxford University Press.
Scanlon, Thomas. 1998. *What We Owe to Each Other.* Harvard University Press.
Schroeder, Mark. 2005. "The Hypothetical Imperative?" In Schroeder 2014, pp. 201–15.
Schroeder, Mark. 2007a. *Slaves of the Passions*. Oxford: Oxford University Press.
Schroeder, Mark. 2007b. "Reasons and Agent-Neutrality." In Schroeder 2014, pp. 42–59.
Schroeder, Mark. 2014. *Explaining the Reasons We Share: Explanation and Expression in Ethics, Volume 1*. Oxford University Press.
Searle, John. 1969. *Speech Acts: An Essay in the Philosophy of Language*. Cambridge University Press.
Searle, John and Daniel Vanderveken. 1985. *Foundations of Illocutionary Logic*. Cambridge University Press.
Sidgwick, Henry. 1981. *The Methods of Ethics*, 7th edition. Hackett.
Smart, Ninian. 1972. *The Concept of Worship*. Macmillan.
Smith, Michael. 1994. *The Moral Problem*. Blackwell.
Sobel, David. 2007. "Subjectivism and Blame." *Canadian Journal of Philosophy* 37, pp. 149–70.
Speaks, Jeff. Forthcoming. "Permissible Tinkering with the Concept of God." *Topoi.*
Stump, Eleonore, ed. 1993. *Reasoned Faith*. Cornell University Press.
Stump, Eleonore. 2010. *Wandering in Darkness: Narrative and the Problem of Suffering*. Oxford University Press.
Suárez, Francisco. 2002 [1597]. *Disputationes Metaphysicae,* disputations 20–22 trans. Alfred Freddoso as *On Creation, Conservation, and Concurrence*. St. Augustine's Press.
Sumner, L. W. 1996. *Welfare, Happiness, and Ethics*. Oxford University Press.
Swanton, Christine. 2003. *Virtue Ethics: A Pluralistic View*. Oxford University Press.
Swinburne, Richard. 1993. *The Coherence of Theism*, revised edition. Oxford University Press.
Swinburne, Richard. 2004. *The Existence of God*, 2nd edition. Oxford University Press.
Swinburne, Richard. 2011. "What Does the Old Testament Mean?" In Bergmann, Murray, and Rea 2011, pp. 209–25.
Thompson, Michael. 2004a. "Apprehending Human Form." *Philosophy* 54, pp. 47–74.
Thompson, Michael. 2004b. "What is it to Wrong Someone?: A Puzzle about Justice." In Wallace et al. 2004, pp. 333–84.
Thompson, Michael. 2007. *Life and Action*. Harvard University Press.
Timpe, Kevin, ed. 2009. *Metaphysics and God: Essays in Honor of Eleonore Stump*. Routledge.
Tollefsen, Christopher. 2013. "Does God Intend Death?" *Diametros* 38, pp. 191–200.
Tollefsen, Christopher. 2014. *Lying and Christian Ethics*. Cambridge University Press.
Trakakis, Nick and Yujin Nagasawa. 2004. "Skeptical Theism and Moral Skepticism: A Reply to Almeida and Oppy." *Ars Disputandi* 4, pp. 222–8.
Ullman-Margalit, Edna and Sidney Morgenbesser. 1977. "Picking and Choosing." *Social Research* 44, pp. 757–85.
van Inwagen, Peter. 2006. *The Problem of Evil*. Oxford University Press.
van Inwagen, Peter. 2009. "God and Other Uncreated Things." In Timpe 2009, pp. 3–20.

van Inwagen, Peter. 2014a. *Existence: Essays in Ontology*. Cambridge University Press.
van Inwagen, Peter. 2014b. "Introduction: Inside and Outside the Ontology Room." In van Inwagen 2014a, pp. 1–14.
Velleman, J. David. 1999. "Love as a Moral Emotion." *Ethics* 109, pp. 338–74.
Wallace, R. Jay, Phillip Pettit, Samuel Scheffler, and Michael Smith. 2004. *Reason and Value: Themes from the Moral Philosophy of Joseph Raz*. Clarendon Press.
Wielenberg, Erik. 2004. "A Morally Unsurpassable God Must Create the Best." *Religious Studies* 40, pp. 43–62.
Wielenberg, Erik. 2010. "Sceptical Theism and Divine Lies." *Religious Studies* 46, pp. 509–23.
Williams, Bernard. 1995a. *Making Sense of Humanity*. Cambridge University Press.
Williams, Bernard. 1995b. "Internal Reasons and the Obscurity of Blame." In Williams 1995a, pp. 35–45.
Wolterstorff, Nicholas. 2008. *Justice: Rights and Wrongs*. Princeton University Press.
Wolterstorff, Nicholas. 2011. "Reading Joshua." In Bergmann, Murray, and Rea 2011, pp. 236–56.

Index